DogLife 🐾 Lifelong Care for Your Dog™

BULLDOG

tfh

Tracy Libby

BULLDOG

Project Team
Editor: Stephanie Fornino, Mary E. Grangeia
Indexer: Dianne L. Schneider
Design: Mary Ann Kahn
Series Design: Mary Ann Kahn, Angela Stanford

T.F.H. Publications
President/CEO: Glen S. Axelrod
Executive Vice President: Mark E. Johnson
Publisher: Christopher T. Reggio
Production Manager: Kathy Bontz

T.F.H. Publications, Inc.
One TFH Plaza
Third and Union Avenues
Neptune City, NJ 07753

Printed and bound in China

10 11 12 13 14   1 3 5 7 9 8 6 4 2

Library of Congress Cataloging-in-Publication Data
Libby, Tracy, 1958-
  Bulldog / Tracy Libby.
     p. cm. -- (Doglife. Lifelong care for your dog)
  Includes bibliographical references and index.
  ISBN 978-0-7938-3603-1 (alk. paper)
  1. Bulldog. I. Title.
SF429.B85L53 2010
  636.72--dc22
                    2010001872

This book has been published with the intent to provide accurate and authoritative information in regard to the subject matter within. While every reasonable precaution has been taken in preparation of this book, the author and publisher expressly disclaim responsibility for any errors, omissions, or adverse effects arising from the use or application of the information contained herein. The techniques and suggestions are used at the reader's discretion and are not to be considered a substitute for veterinary care.
If you suspect a medical problem consult your veterinarian.

Note: In the interest of concise writing, "he" is used when referring to puppies and dogs unless the text is specifically referring to females or males. "She" is used when referring to people. However, the information contained herein is equally applicable to both sexes.

The Leader In Responsible Animal Care for Over 50 Years!®
www.tfh.com

CONTENTS

INTRODUCTION

INTRODUCING THE BULLDOG

Visualizing the modern-day Bulldog's life several hundred years ago as a tenacious and supreme bullbaiting dog may be difficult. Yet this noble breed's history is inextricably intertwined with the sport. Many of the Bulldog's characteristics still reflect the purpose for which he was originally bred—especially his stoical manner and tough-guy persona, which give him the look of a formidable opponent. His short muzzle and undershot jaw were necessary to enable a vise-like grip. His nose, placed well back into his head, enabled him to breathe freely while gripping the bull and pinning him down. Yet the Bulldog of today and his ancestors from years ago differ in appearance, with today's Bulldog being a much more exaggerated version of the original. His courage, determination, and fortitude compare favorably, but today's Bulldog is no longer an aggressive or "savage" dog, which is a good thing. No longer bred for the rough and tumble world of bullbaiting, he is a companion par excellence, with a steadfast and devoted, if not obsessive, following.

Through the years, various theories and a great deal of speculation have been put forth regarding the Bulldog's ancestors and his precise origin. These speculations have, naturally, sparked heated and spirited debates among past- and present-day breed enthusiasts. It is safe to say that the history of the Bulldog is not a documented record. Much of what is known about the breed, as with most old breeds, is shrouded in mystery. What historians must rely on has been passed down throughout history—through historical writings and documents, nineteenth century legends, and by word of mouth—from those who had the opportunity to know the breed long before our time.

FIGHTING DOGS IN HISTORY

Bulldogs ceased to be "sporting" or "fighting" dogs in the mid-1830s, when the sport of bullbaiting was outlawed by the British parliament. Yet to understand the essence of the breed, one must look back in time—even beyond its bullbaiting heritage—because we can only understand our dogs from their history, from the purpose for which they were originally bred. Writing about the annals of dogs would require someone to first write about the history of man because dogs appear to be associated with man in some form or

The Bulldog's ancestors were originally bred to be guardians and fighting dogs.

fashion throughout time. Doing so would, understandably, fill an entire book, so fast-forwarding a few centuries is necessary here.

Dogs have been used for thousands of years as hunters, herders, guardians, and trackers. For the most part, these dogs were known as "fighting dogs" or "ancient fighting dogs"—a broad term generally used to describe dogs that were bred and selected for exceptional qualities suitable for military campaigns, protecting humans and livestock, and for hunting dangerous game and fighting wild animals. Typically, the physical or foundational structure of such a dog was described as "a large, low-slung, heavy breed, with a very powerful build, strongly developed head, and tremendously threatening voice." While his outward appearance alone needed to instill fear in his enemies, his weight, for the most part, prevented him from quick movements other than his initial powerful charge. His strength and powerful jaws allowed him to protect himself or his flock against strong enemies, as well as to "overpower and pull down large animals on the hunt, and to control large unmanageable domestic animals." He also needed to be intelligent, strong-willed, tenacious, courageous, and tireless. These qualities were important because centuries ago a dog's working tasks were much more dangerous and harsh than they are today. His job as a war dog in countless military campaigns was precarious and brutal. Hunting wild boar and bear was perilous, often taking place in inaccessible swamps, forests, or mountains. Cattle driven to market were much more dangerous and difficult to handle than today. Fifteen hundred years ago, life was harder, riskier, and more perilous, and guard dogs needed to protect their owners and their owners' families, as well as protect their flocks against wild animals, intruders, and marauders.

In the years leading up to the 1900s, many dog breeds were not as clearly defined as they are today; and much interbreeding of the various strains of fighting dogs would have been inevitable. Many modern dog breeds, including the Bulldog, descended from these breeds, but only years later were they bred true to a physical type.

EARLY DEVELOPMENT OF THE BULLDOG BREED

The further one delves back into history, the more evidence is found that the Bulldog, or more specifically his ancestors, existed in the earliest parts of history. While not distinguished from the mastiff or bandog until the 16th and 17th centuries, the English Bulldog's roots are firmly intertwined throughout most of England's history.

Pugnaces of Britain

When the British Chieftain Caractacus was defeated by the Roman Emperor Claudius in the year 50 CE, there were "pugnaces," or war dogs, in Britain. During the period of Roman domination, these fighting dogs of Britain were known as "the broad-mouthed dogs of Britain." Primarily used in battle, and later for contests in the amphitheater, these dogs proved far superior to the Romans' own dogs, and a considerable number of them were exported to Rome. The Romans greatly admired the British war dogs because in fierceness and aggressiveness they far exceeded any dogs they had previously come across. Prior to encountering the British war dogs, the strongest and most proficient dogs in battle known to the Romans were the Molossian

dogs of Epirus. Although trained in their native Greece specifically for battle, the Molossians were no match for the British war dogs. Breed historians contend there is very little doubt that the pugnaces of Britain were the original and remote ancestors of the Bulldog.

Mastiffs, Bandogs, and Alaunts

During the Middle Ages, "breeders" weren't concerned about pedigrees and most likely a scientifically selective breeding program still did not exist. Dogs were bred based on the individual dog's traits. At this time, and throughout most of the early centuries, the terms mastiff, alaunt, and bandogge were ambiguously and randomly applied to not one specific breed but rather to most large or massive dogs. "Bandogge" (or "Band dog") is a term that William Harrison in his *Description of England* of 1586 attributes to the fact that many dogs of this breed were "tied up in chains and strong bonds in the daytime..." A 1632 dictionary defines the alaunt as being a mastiff-like dog who served butchers by corralling fierce oxen and keeping them in their stalls.

Along with their duties as guard dogs, these massive fighters were wanted for the baiting of bulls and bears, a popular sport as early as Henry II's time. Many competitions were held at Bordeaux in France, which Henry Plantagenet, later Henry II, gained upon his marriage to Eleanor of Aquitaine in 1152, and which remained in England's possession for three centuries. While England still held Bordeaux, French writer Gaston Phoebus, Comte de Foix, described the French Alaunt in his writings. Around the same time, about 1390, Geoffrey Chaucer, the father of English poetry, wrote "The Knight's Tale" and extolled the English Alaunt as a dog of great size, strength, and courage, used in the chase of the lion and the bear. Breed historians believe

Most historians agree that the Bulldog's name is derived from the fact that these dogs were once used to guard, control, and bait bulls.

there is little doubt that the French Alaunt described by Comte de Foix and the English Alaunt described by Chaucer were one and the same animal. Most likely, the Alaunt of England was exported to Bordeaux from 1151 to 1411, where he was crossed with some remote descendants of the British war dogs who hundreds of years previously had traveled to France via Rome. The French Alaunt is the descendant of the English Alaunt exported to Bordeaux, and in turn the ancestor of the Dogue de Bordeaux, the huge fighting dog of the South of France. (The Dogue de Bordeaux of today is possibly the nearest breed in type and conformation to the historic Alaunt.)

In 1576, Dr. Johannes Caius of Cambridge (Queen Elizabeth I's personal physician) described the "mastive" or "bandogge," which is believed to be a descendant of the Alaunt, as a "vast, huge stubborn, ugly, and eager dog, of a heavy and burdenous body, serviceable to bait and take the bull by the ear." Caius does not specifically mention a bulldog, suggesting that the bulldog is not yet a breed of its own at this point in time.

The bandog is also mentioned in Shakespeare's Henry VI: "The time when Screech-owls cry, and Bandogs howle, and spirits walke, and Ghosts break up their graves." Possibly one of the earliest references to the breed appears in *The Silent Woman*, written by Shakespeare's friend Ben Jonson and first acted in 1609 by the Blackfriars children: "By that light, I'll have you chain'd up, with your bull-dogs, and bear-dogs, if you be not civil sooner."

In 1631, during the reign of Charles I, the name "bulldog" is clearly distinguished from the "mastiff," and historians believe it to be definitive proof that they were becoming separate breeds. In a letter written by an Englishman called Prestwich Eaton from St. Sebastian, Spain, to his friend George Wellingham in St. Swithin's Lane, London, a request was made for a good "mastive" dog and two "bulldoggs" to be sent to him there. Obviously, one cannot know with absolute certainty what the writer meant by "bulldoggs"—whether it be a smaller "mastive" or "bandogg."

There has been dispute between admirers of both the Bulldog and Mastiff as to which originated first, and from which stock the other is derived. In his book *British Dogs: Their Varieties, History, Characteristics, Breeding, Management, and Exhibition* (1897), Hugh Datziel writes: "All I can gather on the subject points to the conclusion that the ancestor of both breeds was the dog called the alaunt, mastive, or bandogg."

Defined by Their Job

Most historians agree that the Bulldog's name is derived from the fact that these dogs were once used to guard, control, and bait bulls. Originally the primary purpose of the mastiff- or bull-type breeds was to assist butchers in controlling the savage bulls that would eventually find their way to the supper table. The baiting of bulls prior to slaughtering them was based on the belief that a baited bull would be more tender and nutritious. It was thought that the bull's blood boiled because of excitement and exertion, which made the meat all the more tasty. As incredible as it seems, laws were put in place in various parts of England that prohibited a butcher from slaughtering a bull that had not been set upon by dogs.

As previously mentioned, we know that bullbaiting was taking place in England as early as the 12th century. However, the first historical account appears to come from Survey of Stamford: "William, Earl Warren, Lord of the town in the reign of King John (1199-1216), standing upon the walls of his castle at Stamford, saw two bulls fighting for a cow in the castle, till all the butchers' dogs pursued one of the bulls, which was maddened by the noise and multitude, through the town. This so pleased the Earl that he gave the castle meadow where the bulls' combat began, for a common to the butchers of the town after the first grass was mowed, on condition they should find a mad bull on a day six weeks before Christmas for the continuance of that sport forever."

In the reign of King John, a few accounts are noted where bullbaiting was held in large arenas where the bull ran free. The dogs, large and sufficient in size, were capable of pinning the attacking bull by the nose and pulling it down through their own strength, agility, and fierce determination alone. An apparent shortage of secure arenas led to the practice of tethering the bull.

In time, through judicious outcrosses, the Bulldog breed transformed and was bred specifically for bullbaiting. This was because the dog had to keep his body low when attacking a bull, thereby exposing as little area as possible to the bull's horns, which was known as *"to play low."* Larger dogs needed to crawl on their belly to avoid the bull's horns, so as a result a smaller dog was selected for breeding.

During the reigns of Mary I, Elizabeth I, James I, and Charles I, which covered the period late 1553 to early 1649, the baiting of bulls and bears became a popular sport with noblemen and royalty, and it eventually trickled down to the common folk. In 1802, a bill to ban animal fighting was introduced but defeated. In 1829, a second bill was introduced in the House of Commons, but despite public outcry regarding the cruel sport, the bill was defeated. Many worried that the "valuable ancient breed of the English Bulldog—the symbol of the English national character—could die out." The practice of bullbaiting continued until 1835, when an Act of Parliament finally prohibited the sport of animal fighting.

MODERN-DAY BULLDOGS IN ENGLAND

Bullbaiting was a deplorable practice, yet few can deny that many of the characteristics so admired in the Bulldog breed emerged and were shaped by breeders trying to produce a dog suitable for the bullbaiting ring. Once bullbaiting was banned, many breeds, including the Bulldog, had a hard time surviving. The Bulldog had lost its peculiar job

After the sport of bullbaiting was banned in England in 1835, the Bulldog became fashionable as a show dog and companion.

and purpose, and the demand for the breed began to diminish, although some dogs were preserved from extinction in the families of some of their admirers.

Since the mid-to-late 1800s, the Bulldog has become fashionable as a show dog and companion. In 1864, the first Bulldog club was formed, with the motto "Hold Fast." Founded by R.S. Rockstro, the club only lasted three years, but that was long enough to see the first breed standard drafted in 1864 and adopted in 1865; it was known as the "Philo-Kuon" standard. Ten years later, The Bulldog Club, Inc., was founded to promote the "breeding of pure Bulldogs of the true type, and to urge the adoption of such type upon breeders, judges, committees, and promoters of canine exhibitions." An improved standard was written to "tidy up" the Bulldog while still preserving all of the essential features of the old English Bulldog. Through the years there have been minor revisions, which have resulted in slight departures from the original. In 1986, the Kennel Club revised the standard in order to explain things in plainer English.

The first show for the Bulldog breed was held in Birmingham, England, in 1860. The best of the first show was a dog named King Dick.

Many Bulldogs and their collective gene pools influenced the modern-day Bulldog. However, the Bulldog considered by many to be the one nearest to perfection was Crib. Also, the outline of Rosa in the 1817 painting *Crib and Rosa* is considered to represent perfection

Bulldogs appear to have been present in America as early as 1774.

in the shape, make, and size of the ideal type of Bulldog. One criticism is the lack of wrinkles about the head and neck and also of substance of bone in the limbs. Other prominent dogs who influenced the foundation of today's Bulldogs include Sir Anthony, Byron, Tiger (full brother to Sir Anthony), Sancho Panza, Duke, Smasher, Sepoy, Slenderman, and Lord Nelson, to name a few.

BULLDOGS IN AMERICA

When the English began immigrating to America, many brought their Bulldogs with them, with some stories indicating that the breed has been present in America as early as 1774. The Bulldog was accepted into the newly formed American Kennel Club in 1886. One of the first to be shown was a male named Donald, a brindle and white exhibited in 1880 by Sir William Verner in New York. The first Bulldog to become an American Kennel Club champion was a dog named Robinson Crusoe, who achieved the title in 1888.

The Bulldog Club of America (BCA) was formed in 1890 utilizing the English standard. In 1896, a standard was adopted by the BCA and revised in 1914 to declare the Dudley nose a disqualification. In 1976, the Dudley nose disqualification was redefined as a "brown or liver colored nose." The standard was reformatted in 1990 with no changes in wording.

The BCA remains the parent club of today's Bulldog. Originally a small club in the northeastern United States, membership grew across the country, and in 1950 the BCA was reshaped into a national organization. The club's purposes remain the same:

- to maintain a standard of excellence for the guidance of breeders, owners, and judges
- to improve the breed through encouragement of effort directed toward approach to, or attainment of, the degree of excellence set forth in the standard of the Bulldog breed
- to stimulate interest in competitive public showings of Bulldogs
- to further the interests of the breed
- to work for the general good of breeders, owners, and exhibitors of Bulldogs

FAMOUS BULLDOG MASCOTS

Some of the more famous Bulldog mascots in the United States include:

Sergeant Chesty XI: The official mascot of the Marine Barracks, Washington, DC, Sergeant Chesty XI is affectionately referred to as "Molly," which comes from the term "Molly Marines," the name given to the first women to serve in the United States Marine Corps.

Handsome Dan: Handsome Dan was a mascot of Yale University's athletic teams. Legend has it that in 1889 Andrew B. Graves saw a Bulldog sitting in front of a New Haven blacksmith shop. Graves, an Englishman in the Yale class of 1892, offered $50 for the dog.

The blacksmith countered with $75. Graves purchased the dog for $65. (Some reports indicate the price was $5.) Graves cleaned up the dog and named him "Handsome Dan." While he was once described in physical appearance as a "cross between an alligator and a horned frog," he was considered one of the finest specimens of the Bulldog breed in America. Handsome Dan died in 1898. To date, 17 different Bulldog's have served as "Handsome Dan," the university's mascot.

UGA: The University of Georgia's mascot's name, UGA, was derived from his alma mater's name. Since 1956, UGA mascots have come from a line of Bulldogs owned by the Frank W. Siler family of Savannah, GA.

Jack: Jack has been the Georgetown University mascot since 1962. While the school's sports team is the Hoyas, the official mascot is a Bulldog because Georgetown athletes are as "tenacious as Bulldogs." Purchased as a two-year-old, Jack stubbornly refused to respond to anything but his given name, even though students had hoped to rename him Hoya. The dog won out, and the students continued calling him Jack—a tradition that continues today.

Mack Truck: In 1917, a British company referred to Mack trucks as Bull Dog Macks because of their sturdiness. In 1921, the first usage of a Bulldog as a symbol was riveted to each side of the cab. In 1922, the Bulldog became the corporate symbol of Mack trucks, and it has adorned them ever since.

PART I

PUPPYHOOD

CHAPTER 1

IS THE BULLDOG RIGHT FOR YOU?

Bulldogs are one of the most popular breeds in America, as well as in England, which isn't surprising considering the breed was favored by Winston Churchill and is a true English emblem. Currently the breed ranks in the top 10 for American Kennel Club registrations. Despite its popularity and characteristically charming, albeit unusual, looks, the Bulldog is not a dog for everyone. Bulldogs are like no other breed. They are distinctive and special dogs, but the unique qualities that set them apart from other breeds can also be problematic for first-time dog owners, as well as for a few experienced ones.

Bulldogs are charismatic and appealing, but adding one to your family is not a decision to be taken lightly. Puppies need more supervision than adult dogs, and because the breed is known for its independence, Bulldogs require a good deal of patience and can take longer to train than other breeds. Tough, stalwart, and famously stubborn, the breed also has health issues that require special care and consideration.

STANDARDS OF EXCELLENCE

Every breed has a blueprint for success. This blueprint is called the breed standard, and it describes the perfect or ideal dog to which dedicated breeders aspire. In the game of conformation (showing), there are no "perfect" dogs. All dogs have faults; some are just more objectionable or noticeable than others. The best breeders, however, strive to remain true to the original function and purpose of the breed as outlined in the standard. Judges also use the standard to evaluate the dogs exhibited before them at a show. Every breed is judged based on how closely it conforms to its standard.

To the newcomer, a breed standard may seem nothing more than a cluster of strange-sounding words strung together on a piece of paper. However, it is really an outline of the perfect specimen, describing everything from size, weight, color and coat, to angulation of limbs, the size, color, and shape of the eyes, and what a dog should look like when he's moving. The Bulldog, like most other breeds of

The Bulldog is one of the most popular breeds in America.

dog, was developed for a particular task, and each breed characteristic listed in the standard is there for a purpose.

Why does all this matter to you? Taking the time to learn and understand the breed standard will help you to better understand your Bulldog: Why he does what he does, what makes him tick, and why and how each component of your dog should work together harmoniously.

The Bulldog Club of America's breed standard does a good job describing in detail the breed's features. To help you better understand the Bulldog, some unique and notable features of the AKC-approved standard are provided in this section.

Breed Type

When you see a Bulldog, you know he is a Bulldog without consciously stopping to think about it. But how? How do you know he is a Bulldog and not, say, a Bull Terrier? What separates one breed from another are the breeds' individual attributes and characteristics. Those attributes and characteristics are called breed type—or, in canine terminology, the *essence* of the breed, the breed's complete package, i.e., the mental and physical characteristics that define what he is, how he looks, and how he moves.

Breed type is rooted in a breed's origin, the original purpose and function for which it was bred. The Bulldog has identifiable characteristics, such as size, shape, temperament, and personality, which were selected, developed, and bred specifically for the purpose of bullbaiting. Obviously, his aggression and savagery have through the years been bred out. However, his physical traits have been bred into the breed long enough so that they have become stable, recognizable, reproduced with some uniformity, and unique to the Bulldog breed. They are the distinguishing features that help you to recognize a Bulldog as being a Bulldog.

Character and Temperament
The Bulldog's disposition should be equable and kind, resolute and courageous (not vicious or aggressive), and his demeanor should be pacific and dignified. These attributes should reveal themselves in his expression and behavior. Equable, as defined by the *American Heritage Dictionary*, means unwavering; steady; even tempered; not easily disturbed. Pacific is defined as tending to diminish conflict; of a peaceful nature; tranquil. The framers of the original breed standard chose those words for a reason—they define the essence of the breed's character.

Theoretically, the breed standard describes the ideal temperament of the Bulldog. In the real world, Bulldogs can run the gamut in temperament, and the genetic lottery can produce dogs who are happy-go-lucky, shy, fearful, or dog-to-dog aggressive. The best indicator of a puppy's temperament is the disposition of his sire (father) and dam (mother). That said, human and environmental influences and conditions under which a puppy is whelped, reared,

Clarifying the Bulldog Name
While some still call the breed the English Bulldog, the American Kennel Club (AKC) dropped the "English" part of the name some 80 years ago. However, the Bulldog is customarily and affectionately referred to as a "Bully." The United Kennel Club (UKC), which recognized the breed in 1935, still refers to the breed as the English Bulldog. As far as the English are concerned, *English* Bulldog is redundant and superfluous. They consider them Bulldogs. Just Bulldogs.

The breed, as well as its name, is occasionally confused with its distant cousins— the Bull Terrier and Boston Terrier. However, both are distinct and separate breeds. The Bull Terrier evolved in England from crossing the Bulldog and the now-extinct English White Terrier. The Boston Terrier, or erroneously named Boston Bull Terrier, developed in America, specifically Boston, out of the Bulldog and a white English Terrier. Also separate and distinct breeds are the French Bulldog and the American Bulldog. The French Bulldog looks like a miniature Bulldog with bat ears. While its ancestors most likely included the Bulldog, the breed did not become popular until after it traveled with English lace workers to France during the Industrial Revolution, where it was crossed with other breeds. The American Bulldog, which is not recognized by the American Kennel Club, is a more athletic and less exaggerated version of the Bulldog, and in many instances is still used as a working and/or guard dog.

and socialized also play an important part in defining temperament.

When acquired from a reputable breeder, a Bulldog usually possesses the classic Bulldog temperament, which embodies all that is courageous and noble, the epitome of "Britishness." His general character is a combination of kindness and courageousness, as well as cautious combativeness. While his forbidding appearance is frequently sufficient to discourage intrusion, once provoked he is determined in attack and defense, and if necessary will guard and defend his family to the end. By no means, however, is a Bulldog a full-time guard dog. Nor is he the first dog to come to mind when considering a protection-type companion. This self-assured tough guy is actually quite the charmer. He's observant, devoted to his loved ones, and sensitive to their moods. The Bulldog is solid, sensible, and patient, and his tolerance with children and elderly people is legendary. Walter E. Simmonds recounts a story in his book *The Complete Bulldog—A Complete Book of Guidance and Authoritative Information Regarding Bulldogs* (1926), about a mother who returned after a short absence and was horrified to find her baby's face covered in blood. Upon washing the child's face, she was amazed to find not one scratch. On examining the dog, however, she found that the child had bitten the tip of the family Bulldog's ear clean off.

The Bulldog's favorite pastime has been described as lying at the feet of his owner—or, more likely, on the couch next to his owner. Granted, Bulldogs are happiest when they live indoors with their families, but despite the breed's lazy or couch potato reputation, they can and do compete in a number of competitive canine sports, including agility and obedience. That said, the Bulldog is not capable of scaling mountain peaks or jogging for hours on end. He is neither high drive nor high energy. He's not a push-button breed, either. A Bulldog ranks low on every trainability scale known to man and is famously stubborn, always weighing your commands against his own priorities. He will never possess the speed and workaholic attitude of popular turbo-charged breeds such as the Border Collie or Australian Shepherd. Nor should he. After all,

The Bulldog has a kind, even-tempered, and courageous disposition.

By the Numbers

Generally speaking, the Bulldog is considered a puppy until about 12 months of age. Dogs are considered to be adults around one year and older. However, Bulldogs are slow to mature. Many do not reach mental maturity until 24 or 36 months of age or older. It has been said that some Bulldogs never mature, instead remaining perpetual puppies—playful, puppy-like, and unpredictable.

he is a Bulldog. Traits that are suitable for some breeds are not the ideal by which we measure all breeds. Most Bulldogs are likely to enjoy a stroll around the block or a game of tug, tag, or hide-and-seek. This is understandable due to the breed's predisposition to respiratory problems and its unique structural assembly, which are not conducive to intense or prolonged activity.

The Bulldog's Unique Structure

In 1905, H. St. John Cooper wrote about the immense difference in appearance between the Bulldog of that time and the breed's ancestors of a hundred years prior. He described the Bulldog's ancestors as being an "extremely powerful and active animal, far more active than it would be possible for the present-day low-to-the-ground specimen to be." While the breed still retains its centuries-old courage, determination, and fortitude, the present-day Bulldog is physically different from the "modern-day dog" H. St. John Cooper described more than 100 years ago. When bullbaiting was

outlawed, the Bulldog eventually developed into the shorter, squatter version of its ancestors popular in today's show ring. The breed standard of today varies only slightly from the original standard adopted about 100 years ago. Yet breeders can—and often do—interpret the standard differently, and while differences in appearance between the generational Bulldogs exist, many of the breed's unique and ancestral characteristics remain.

Body, Size, and Gait

There's no denying that the Bulldog has a unique physical appearance, and it cannot be overstressed that a Bulldog must look like a Bulldog and nothing else. The Bulldog standard, unlike many other breed standards, does not mention specific minimum or maximum sizes but only proportions because the Bulldog must be well proportioned. Some call it balance or harmonious balance, or even symmetry. Regardless of the terminology, it means that the proportion of each part of the dog, and all parts to the whole, should be well distributed and no feature so much in excess or lacking in quality as to destroy the dog's general symmetry or make him appear deformed or ill-proportioned. In order for the dog to be structurally correct, the parts that create the whole must themselves be pretty close to correct.

Today's Bulldog is a medium-sized dog with a heavy, thickset, low-swung body, massive short-faced head, wide shoulders, sturdy limbs, weighing in at about 50 pounds (23 kg) for mature males and 40 pounds (18 kg) for mature females. Like everything else about the Bulldog, his size served a purpose. Nearly two hundred years ago, his physical structure allowed him to perform his duties with amazing efficiency. His low-to-the-ground forefront challenged the bull's frontal attacks,

The Bulldog's large and compact short-faced head is perhaps his most unique physical trait.

While females and males should have equal qualities, a clear distinction between the sexes (known as sexual dimorphism) should be evident. Simply put, males should look like males, and females should possess femininity. Sex-specific differences include size, weight, and grandeur, and females should be less imposing and less well developed than males.

Gait describes a dog's movement, such as walk, canter, trot, or gallop. The Bulldog's gait is a bit peculiar and differs from that of nearly all other dogs. It is described as a loose-jointed, shuffling, sidewise motion, with a characteristic roll. The action must be unrestrained, free, and vigorous. The breed's structural assembly is what gives him the characteristic and unique Bulldog shuffle. He gaits with his front legs going straight forward from his wide shoulders, while the rear legs swing in and out, hitting the ground closer together than the front legs.

Movement is an important element of breed type, but it must be correct for the dog and the job he was bred to do. Granted, Bulldogs are no longer sporting or fighting dogs, but a dedicated and responsible breeder strives to preserve the intent of the founders of the breed. Nothing in the Bulldog standard requires or describes an anatomy built for speed or a ground-covering action. A Bulldog does not have nor does he need the same structure and gait as, say, a German Shepherd Dog. He is not and never will be a German Shepherd Dog. He is and always will be a Bulldog and should therefore move in the proper manner for his breed.

Head and Facial Features

The Bulldog's head is perhaps his most unique physical trait. Massive in size, it houses his brain, eyes, ears, nose, and teeth and is one of the most defining characteristics and an essential Bulldog feature. However, many

while the shortness of his hocks provided excellent stamina. "His sound sturdy limbs and the suggestion of great stability, vigor and strength are as important to the present day Bulldog as they were to its ancestors." Again, it all comes down to the purpose for which he was bred. Remember, years ago the dogs originally used by butchers and eventually for bullbaiting were much larger, and it was through selective breeding that the Bulldog emerged as the perfect size and proportion necessary for the sport. Can you imagine a small, fine-boned dog, say the size of a Chihuahua, going head to head with a 1500-pound (680-kg) bull? I think not.

breeders contend that the large head size required by the standard is the cause of so much trouble and mortality during whelping. When measured, the circumference in front of the ears should measure at least the height of the dog at the shoulders. Every aspect of his large head defines the purpose for which he was originally bred. His undershot jaw, for example, is a distinct and essential attribute of the breed, allowing him to perform his bullbaiting job with efficiency. ("Undershot" means that the lower jaw should project out a considerable distance from the upper jaw.) The well-laid-back nose with its wide, large nostrils facilitated his breathing while retaining a prolonged grip on the bull. His facial wrinkles directed the bull's blood away from his nose and eyes. The widely set eyes and the deep furrow between them channeled the bull's blood and fluids away from the dog's eyes. The breed's well-pronounced "stop" (the depression or step down situated almost centrally between the eyes) is said to have diverted the fluids away from the dog's nostrils and into the creases formed by the facial wrinkles. The flews (the fleshy upper lips of the Bulldog) and chops (jowls, or pendulous flesh of the lips and jaws) directed the blood and fluids away from the dog's extremities.

The size, placement, and carriage of his ears and eyes also evolved to facilitate the purpose for which he was bred. When viewed from the front, the Bulldog's eyes should be round, moderate in size, neither sunken nor bulging, very dark in color, and situated "low down in the skull, as far from the ears as possible." They should be set in front of the head and as wide apart as possible. When the dog is looking forward, the eyelids should cover the white of the eye, and no haw should be visible (haw being a "drooping, pouching, or sagging of the lower eyelid or lids due to looseness, resulting in the exposure of an abnormally large amount of conjunctival lining," as you might see in the Bloodhound or Saint Bernard.) The physical appearance of the ears is important and contributes greatly to the overall appearance of the head. The ears should be small and thin

Multi-Dog Tip

Dogs of the opposite sex usually are less likely to squabble or fight. Long before dogs were domesticated, they lived in packs, and survival was based on a hierarchical system. Males fought other males mainly to establish their position in the group. Rather than fight to the death, the loser survived because that was in the best interest of maintaining the species. Even today, fighting males will growl, snap, bite, make a lot of noise, wreak havoc, and cause a lot of damage until a human intervenes or the subordinate dog cries "Uncle." On the other hand, a female's aggression stems from the instinct to protect her babies. Survival of the enemy was of no particular interest to her. For this reason, fights between females generally have more severe consequences than encounters between males. Therefore, if you are thinking about adding another dog to your household, consider choosing one of the opposite sex.

◎ Training Tidbit

At dog shows, Bulldogs are evaluated against the breed standard and how close—in the judge's opinion—each dog measures up to the ideal Bulldog as outlined in the standard. If you are interested in showing your Bulldog, you will want to start teaching him early on to "stack." Free stacking involves positioning your Bulldog by walking him into a show pose or stance. Hand stacking involves manually positioning his feet and legs. You'll also want to teach your puppy to enjoy being handled and touched, including putting your hand in his collar.

and set "high in the head." The most desirable ear shape is the "rose ear"—an ear that folds over and back so as to expose the bur. Erect prick or button ears are not desirable, and the ears should never be cropped. The Bulldogs neck should be "short, very thick, deep and strong and well arched at the back." However, too short a neck gives an overall unbalanced appearance. During the breed's bullbaiting days, dogs with short thick necks and short backs stood the best chance of surviving when they landed on the ground after being tossed in the air by the bull. While a Bulldog's head can be reduced to measurements, and the standard does an excellent job of defining the particulars

of each component, what is equally important is the dog's expression. It projects the very essence of his nature. The correct size and placement of each individual feature—properly balanced—is critical in defining the correct Bulldog expression. As H. St. John Cooper writes, "He is not a true Bulldog if he has a soft and benign expression of countenance; he is not a true Bulldog if he betrays any weakness of character."

Coat and Color

A Bulldog's coat, according to the AKC breed standard, should be "straight, short, flat, close, of fine texture, smooth, and glossy (no fringe,

feather, or curl)." The color should be uniform, pure of its kind, and brilliant, with the following colors listed in order of preference: 1) red brindle; 2) all other brindles; 3) solid white; 4) solid red, fawn, or fallow; 5) piebald; 6) inferior qualities of all the foregoing. However, a perfect piebald—piebald being adapted from horse terminology and applied to "dogs with irregular black body patches superimposed upon a white background"—is preferable to a muddy brindle or defective solid color. Solid black is not desirable, although it is less objectionable if it occurs to a moderate degree in piebald patches. Perfect brindles have a fine, even, equal distribution of the composite colors. In brindles and solid colors, a small white patch on the chest is not considered detrimental. In piebalds, the color patches should be well defined, pure of color, and symmetrically distributed.

Skin and Wrinkles

The Bulldog's skin should be soft and loose, especially at the head, neck, and shoulders. The looseness of his skin, according to historians, often served as a deterrent to penetration of the bull's horns. His head and face should be covered with heavy wrinkles, and at the throat, from jaw to chest, there should be two loose pendulous folds, forming the dewlap. The dewlap is the loose, pendulous skin, usually arranged in folds, on the chin, throat, and neck regions of some breeds.

BULLDOGS IN DAY-TO-DAY LIFE

Bulldogs are companions par excellence, provided, of course, you are not looking for a jogging, hiking, or cycling companion. While their favorite pastime is spending time curled up next to their owners, they do have a few quirks, idiosyncrasies, and health

Want to Know More?

For more detailed information on activities you can enjoy with your Bulldog, see Chapter 11: Bulldog Sports and Activities.

issues that must be carefully considered and monitored.

The Bulldog's shortened muzzle is part of the breed's complete package, just like his formidable looks and tough-guy persona. However, nearly all short-nosed, or brachycephalic, dogs have some degree of increased work associated with breathing, resulting in a compromised ability to cool themselves. Subsequently, Bulldogs are predisposed to heat-induced illnesses and are more likely to be subjected to a moderate or life-threatening case of heatstroke in a shorter period of time than nonbrachycephalic breeds. (See Chapter 8 for more information on brachycephalic airway syndrome and heatstroke.) Temperatures higher than 80°F (27°C) can be dangerous to them. If you live where the weather is hot or humid, you need to provide appropriate areas, such as an air-conditioned room, where your dog can breathe more comfortably and stay cool.

Bulldogs do well in suburban, rural, or city environments, provided the smog doesn't get too bad. They are not big barkers, so condo and apartment living works well for them. Ideally, buildings without stairs are preferable, unless they also have an elevator. A few stairs won't deter most Bulldogs, but structurally they are not built to ascend and descend multiple flights of stairs on a regular basis. Besides, their compromised airway is not designed for strenuous exercise.

Sociability: Kids and Other Pets

If you have navigated adolescence with a Bulldog—or any other dog for that matter—you were surely loved. No doubt you passed the days playing together. Your dog probably tracked mud in the house, licked your face, shared your lunch, protected you, and at the end of the day collapsed on your bed in a heap of sleep. In retrospect, one might question how either of you (or your parents) survived the chaos and craziness, not to mention the germs. Bulldogs can be the most delightful and patient childhood companions, but they require guidance.

A sturdy breed, Bulldogs can take some rough play, but interactions between children and other dogs should always be supervised. Although they may be tough enough to take down a bull, even the most accepting Bulldog may not tolerate the rough-and-tumble behavior of young kids who try to smother him with affection, tug on his ears or tail, bang pots on his head, or poke little fingers in his eyes. These types of behavior can startle, frighten, and even injure any dog.

When well socialized, Bulldogs are remarkably accepting of other household pets. Lacking adequate socialization, however, they can be quarrelsome with other dogs, especially those of the same sex. Male dogs may not always get along with each other, especially once they reach maturity, and some females, despite your best efforts, simply will not live together harmoniously.

Introduce your Bulldog to other pets in a safe, positive, and controlled environment—

Bulldogs can be wonderful companions for children, but they require guidance and supervision.

Known for their independence, Bulldogs can take longer to train than other breeds.

one in which you are supervising the situation. Puppy kindergarten classes provide ideal opportunities for socialization and interaction with other dogs. Always manage every situation so your Bulldog is not allowed to develop bad or fearful behaviors. Never allow him to bully or harass other animals, and vice versa. If other dogs bully your puppy, he could grow into an adult who is fearful of other dogs.

Dogs run, chase, play bite, tug at body parts, yip, yap, body slam, and knock each other down. Most of the time it is great fun for them, provided all the dogs are enjoying the game. How do you tell when a fun game has crossed over into a brawl? Watch the dogs' body language—the dog chasing and the dog being chased. Are your Bulldog's ears up? Is

he returning play or trying to get away? Is your dog nervous or frightened? Is he cowering? Young or very small dogs can inadvertently be injured when tussling with bigger, more powerful ones. In any of these situations, it is always best to err on the side of caution.

GROOMING NEEDS

Overall, the breed does not require a tremendous amount of grooming. Bulldogs have a smooth coat, which makes brushing and bathing them quite easy. However, they are predisposed to some skin conditions, and their numerous wrinkles require daily attention. All breeds, including the Bulldog, are subject to periodontal disease, so regular teeth brushings are recommended.

HEALTH ISSUES

While the breed gets a bit of a bad rap in the health department, it's true that Bulldogs are predisposed to a number of health-related issues, which are discussed in detail in Chapter 8. A significant issue is their compromised airways, which predisposes them to heat-induced illnesses.

TRAINABILITY

A Bulldog does not have the "Send me in, coach!" attitude of other breeds. He will never have the get-up-and-go of a high-drive, high-energy breed. Nor will you ever see him anxiously awaiting or anticipating his owner's next command, as most Border Collies do. That said, the Bulldog does respond well to positive training and reinforcement, but he is independent and famously stubborn, so training him requires a good deal of patience and the ability to keep training routines fun and unpredictable.

CHAPTER 2

FINDING AND PREPPING FOR YOUR BULLDOG PUPPY

Once you have decided the Bulldog breed is right for you, you will need to find the perfect puppy for you and your family. Someone once said, "You don't pick the puppy, the puppy picks you," and there is some truth in that statement. Your Bulldog is going to be around for many years, so you want one who not only melts your heart but grows up to have the qualities and personality you expect. First impressions are helpful because they are instinctive feelings that guide your judgment. However, that special puppy needs to be compatible with you, your family, and your lifestyle, and vice versa. He needs to be healthy, too.

Choosing a puppy, as opposed to an adult dog, means you are starting with a clean slate, so to speak. He will not have any bad habits (yet!), and you can maximize his potential by shaping his character, fostering his personality, and instilling in him all the behaviors he will need to function as he matures. You set your own expectations and manage your puppy so he grows into a well-rounded, well-behaved adult dog.

That said, raising a puppy is a lot of work. Puppies require an enormous amount of time and energy—at all hours of the day and night.

If left to their own devices, they will get into all kinds of mischief—barking, chewing, digging, and peeing from one end of the house to the other. Puppies will also require a good deal of socialization and training—this, in particular, is absolutely necessary if you want to raise a well-behaved, nonaggressive adult Bulldog.

THE RIGHT PUPPY FOR YOU

Before you choose your Bulldog, you must decide which breeders are producing dogs that have a consistent reputation for the traits you desire. Are you looking for a pet-quality companion? A show dog? A performance Bulldog? (Yes, a bit of an oxymoron, but Bulldogs can and do compete in obedience and agility.)

The majority of Bulldogs grow into sensitive, loving companions, but acquiring a Bulldog, or any other dog, on impulse is a bad idea. A well-bred and well-cared-for Bulldog can live to be 8 or 10 years old, with some even living to be 12 years of age. Caring for him is a lot of work because he cannot take care of himself. Bringing a dog into your family, regardless of breed, is a decision that must be seriously considered because you will be making a

If you want a stable, affectionate, devoted pet, look for a Bulldog with a sound temperament and a personality you like.

commitment to provide for all his needs and to love him for his entire lifetime.

Family Companion

Reputable breeders often sell puppies as pet quality or nonshow. This does not mean they are unhealthy or undesirable. It simply means that for whatever reason, they do not meet the breed standard requirements for a conformation dog. A puppy, for example, may have a brown or liver-colored nose, which is a disqualification in the breed ring. He may have a curved or curly tail, which is not allowed. Or his color may be a muddy brindle, which is unacceptable. These are "cosmetic" faults that do not affect his temperament or personality. Everything else considered, he should make the perfect pet companion for the right owner. Also, consider an older puppy or young adult who didn't work out as a show dog. This is

a great opportunity to get a very nice dog at a lower cost. Look for breeders who have a reputation for producing healthy, sound dogs.

Show Dog

Prospective show dogs do not come with a guarantee that they will win when entered in competition, or that they will finish their championship. Winning involves many variables, including structure, movement, conditioning, grooming, handling, and the judge's interpretation of the breed standard. Potential show dogs should be free of disqualifying faults, sound in temperament and structure, and good representatives of the breed according to the standard.

Consider an older puppy, say six to ten months old, as this will give you a better indication of what he will look like at maturity. Look for breeders who have a reputation for producing healthy, sound champions. Expect to pay top dollar for a show prospect.

Performance Dog

Bulldogs are famously stubborn, and that makes training and showing them a bit challenging. That said, obedience and agility prospects should be structurally sound and physically and mentally capable of performing the required behaviors, such as jumping, running, sitting, lying down, and maneuvering agility equipment. Ideally, they should be responsive and willing to work for you. Look for a breeder who has a proven record of producing performance dogs.

Choose Your Puppy Wisely

Regardless of whether you are choosing a pet-quality dog, show dog, or performance dog, you should follow these guidelines:

- Purchase your Bulldog from a reputable, knowledgeable breeder.
- Choose a healthy, active puppy. Avoid lethargic puppies, and ones with runny noses or gunk in their eyes. Avoid puppies that are dirty, smelly, or have open sores. Be smart. Don't let sympathy guide your decision. Taking home a sickly puppy because you feel sorry for him will cost you dearly in the long run.
- Ask to meet the sire and dam. At the minimum, meet the dam, as the sire may not be owned by the breeder and therefore not on the premises.

- Ask for health records—vaccinations, worming schedule, etc.—of the sire, dam, and puppy.
- Ask for a copy of the pedigree.
- Never take a puppy under eight weeks of age. Puppies learn important socialization and coping skills from their mother and littermates. If taken too early, they may develop problems later on.

For the next ten or more years, your Bulldog will depend on you for his food, water, shelter, exercise, grooming, training, affection, and regular veterinary care. He will look to you for companionship. He will also mess up the house, refuse to come when called, and provide plenty of opportunities for public humiliation. The good news is he will provide you with years of unconditional love and companionship—and more laughs than you ever thought possible.

WHERE TO FIND THE PUPPY OF YOUR DREAMS

Purchase your Bulldog puppy from a trustworthy, knowledgeable, and experienced breeder. Breeding purebred dogs is a labor of love, as well as an art and a science. A reputable breeder will gladly answer your questions and help you with the decision-making process. Conscientious breeders also care about the

Meet the Puppy

Bulldogs are very popular, but finding the Bulldog who is right for you will take some time and plenty of investigating. Puppies can be purchased and shipped long distances, be it across the state or across the country. Unless you personally know the breeder, or the kennel has outstanding references, it is always prudent to meet the puppy in person first. This allows you to view the facility and see all the puppies, as well as the dam and possibly the sire. Selling dogs online has become increasingly popular. But online photos will not tell you anything about the puppy's temperament, personality, or health. Unfortunately, not all people who breed dogs are reputable, and the Bulldog you purchase online may be a far cry from what arrives at your doorstep.

long-term welfare of their puppies and adult dogs and work diligently to maintain and improve the quality of their breed. Great care and forethought are put into their breeding programs. Breeding stock is carefully evaluated, and only those dogs representing the best quality of the breed are bred. Puppies are regularly and affectionately socialized to everything they are likely to encounter as adult dogs, and they are evaluated to assess training requirements, competitive potential, and placement options.

Purchasing a Bulldog from someone who understands and cares about the breed goes well beyond the sales transaction. That person will be there to help you through the transition periods, to offer care and training advice, and to help you make serious decisions regarding the overall well-being of your Bulldog. And if for some reason your particular Bulldog does not work out, your breeder is often in a position to either take back the dog, help rehome him, or offer an appropriate solution.

Finding a Breeder

Breed clubs and registries, such as the Bulldog Club of America (BCA), the American Kennel Club (AKC), and the Kennel Club in the United Kingdom (KC) are good places to start your search for a reliable breeder. They also can provide you with overall information on the breed.

Veterinarians are often familiar with local breeders and the health of their dogs. They can usually provide you with the names of one or two people who are involved in showing or dog sports if you are interested in finding a performance- or show-quality dog, and can direct you to a Bulldog breeder in particular.

Dog shows are another good outlet for fact-finding missions because the best indicator of a puppy's temperament is his sire and dam. You can compare the quality of several Bulldogs under one roof, talk to owners and breeders, see how they interact with their dogs, and watch dogs compete in different venues, such as conformation, obedience, or even agility. Information about dog shows can be found at Infodog.com and through local clubs and national registries.

The Interview

A reputable breeder will be concerned whether or not a potential puppy buyer has the time, energy, appropriate facilities, and money to properly care for the puppy. Most breeders will interview potential owners and have them fill out a questionnaire. Some of the questions you might be asked include:

- Have you owned a dog in the past?
- Why do you want a Bulldog? Have you owned one before?
- Are you looking for a pet or a show prospect?
- Do you want a male or a female? Why?
- Are you interested in training or showing?
- Do you have children? If yes, what are their ages?
- Do you have other animals?
- Will this dog be an indoor or outdoor dog? Or a combination of the two?
- Do you live in the city or in the country? Do you live in an apartment or do you own or rent a home?
- If you have a yard, is it fenced?

Questions to Ask the Breeder

Likewise, you will want to interview any breeders you visit as well. Educating yourself about the Bulldog's temperament, genetic diseases, health issues, exercise requirements, grooming, and so forth will allow you to ask informed questions. At a minimum, you will want to know:

- What are the goals of their breeding program? Responsible breeders will gladly explain their goals in detail. Any breeder who can't or won't answer the question or is insulted by it is not the breeder for you.
- How long have they been involved with Bulldogs?
- Do they compete in canine sports, such as agility, obedience, or conformation?
- What local or national clubs do they belong to?
- Are their dogs registered? (Registration alone does not guarantee quality).
- What documents will they supply (i.e., three-generation pedigree, worming

and vaccination schedule, health certificates, etc.)?
- Are they willing to take back the dog if things don't work out?
- What is their refund policy?
- How many litters do they breed yearly? (Most responsible breeders produce only one, two, or three litters a year. Anything more may indicate a problem.)

Documents and Guarantees

When you purchase a Bulldog from a reputable breeder, you should receive, at the very least, the following:

- A sales contract that includes the puppy's

Responsible breeders will want to be assured that a potential puppy buyer has the time, energy, and appropriate facilities to properly care for him.

name, sex, color, date whelped, date of sale, your name, address, and telephone number, as well as the name and address of the breeder, the purchase price of the puppy, and the date you bought and took possession of him. It should spell out the entire purchase agreement, including any conditions and stipulations.

- The puppy's registration paperwork, which allows you to register the dog in your name with the appropriate registration organization, such as the American Kennel Club.
- A three-generation pedigree, which is your Bulldog's family tree—a genetic blueprint that authenticates your dog's ancestry. A word of caution: The pedigree does not guarantee your Bulldog has a shred of show potential or is free of inherited diseases or disorders.
- Health records that indicate the puppy's worming and vaccination schedule,

and any health screening certifications for the sire, dam, and puppy, such as a complete eye examination by a canine ophthalmologist and certification from the Canine Eye Registration Foundation (CERF). Certifications available on a young puppy are limited, but an eight-week-old puppy can be examined to detect congenital heritable eye defects. This is not a lifetime certification, though. Annual examinations are recommended because the health of the eyes can change from one year to the next.

PREPARING FOR YOUR PUPPY

Once you have found the perfect Bulldog, there are many responsibilities you must assume. He needs a safe environment, which means puppy-proofing inside and outside. He also needs quality nutrition, regular training, and routine medical care. He needs hugs and kisses and cuddling and sweet nothings whispered in his ear. Equally important, you need to provide guidance and direction, which means setting up a schedule and reinforcing household rules from day one.

Puppy-Proofing

Puppy-proof your house *before* your Bulldog arrives. Remove or put away anything he is likely to seek out and destroy. Like toddlers, puppies will want to explore their surroundings and try to put everything in their mouths—whether it fits or not. Your puppy is too young to understand that your expensive leather heels are not for teething. Pick up shoes, books, magazines, and pillows. Put poisonous houseplants, prescription bottles, waste baskets, candy dishes, and so forth out of reach. Tuck electrical cords behind furniture or under rugs, or tape them to the baseboards. Many objects, such as shoelaces, buttons, socks,

By the Numbers

Breeders generally send their puppies to new homes between eight and ten weeks of age. Ideally, you should avoid bringing a puppy home when the puppy is less than eight weeks old. Puppies learn important coping and socialization skills from their mother and littermates during this time. Bringing a puppy home earlier than eight weeks means he may lack those necessary skills, and he may grow into a dog who is worried, anxious, or fearful.

Before bringing your new Bulldog puppy home, pet-proof your house and yard to ensure his safety.

A puppy's tummy is small, and it can't hold enough food at one time to meet his growth needs. Therefore he needs to be fed several small meals each day. Regular feeding times also help to facilitate housetraining. Ideally, until he is about four months old, feed him three times a day. After that, feed him two times a day. Some owners opt to feed their dogs once a day. While this schedule may be more convenient, consider that your dog will then need to go 24 hours between feedings. That's a long time. By splitting his meals, he isn't consuming his entire daily caloric intake at one meal. That said, overfeeding can turn a healthy puppy into a fat one. Weight gained in young puppies is not easily lost, and extra weight predisposes a puppy to additional health issues, including diabetes and heart, respiratory, and skeletal problems.

Puppies also have small bladders, with no bladder control until they are six months to one year of age. Therefore your puppy will need to be taken outdoors regularly to eliminate. Ideally, you should take him out at the following times:

- first thing in the morning when he wakes up and at least every hour throughout the day
- about 15 minutes after drinking water
- about 30 minutes after eating
- immediately after waking up from a nap
- when you arrive home
- anytime you take him out of his crate
- anytime he shows signs of having to go
- last thing at night

Puppies are individuals and must be treated as such. You may need to tweak or adjust his schedule to fit his individual needs.

Puppies need plenty of physical and mental exercise, as well as rest. So you will need to establish a regular routine and schedule for playing and resting.

marbles, and paperclips, if swallowed, can cause life-threatening intestinal blockage and may require surgery to remove.

Puppy-proof your yard, garden, and outdoor areas, too. Pick up hoses, sprinklers, poisonous plants, and lawn ornaments that your puppy will likely try to consume. Store containers of poisonous products—antifreeze, fertilizers, herbicides, and the like—on shelves and out of reach. Make sure there are no holes in your fencing or broken gates that an inquisitive puppy is likely to escape through. If your property is not fenced, be sure your puppy is leashed each and every time he goes outdoors. He does not have the mental wherewithal to understand that the street is a dangerous place to be. It is your job to keep him safe.

Setting Up a Schedule

A regular schedule of eating, pottying, playing, and resting for your puppy will make your life easier and his life happier.

Training Tidbit

Ideally, a buckle collar should fit around your Bulldog's neck with enough room to fit two fingers between the neck and the collar. It should not be so tight as to restrict his breathing or cause coughing, nor should it be so loose that it slips over his head. When too loose, the collar can easily snag on objects, such as shrubbery, a fence post, or another dog's paw or tooth, causing the dog to panic and inadvertently hang himself. Equally important, growing puppies quickly outgrow their collars. Be sure to check collar size frequently. Left unchecked, a collar that is too small can become imbedded in a dog's neck, causing serious health issues. Also check your dog's collar regularly to ensure it is not frayed or worn.

BULLDOG SUPPLIES

Basic essentials for your Bulldog include a dog bed, collar and leash, crate, safety gate, exercise pen, food and water bowls, identification, and an assortment of training and chew toys.

Bed

Puppies chew, and a tenacious Bulldog can turn a pricey canine bed into worthless scraps in a matter of minutes. A puppy definitely needs a bed of his own, but it is best to hold off on anything too expensive until he is well through the chewing stage. A large blanket or towel folded over several times or a cozy fleece pad placed in his crate or exercise pen will do the job for the first few months. They are easily cleaned in the washing machine and therefore less likely to develop that distinctive doggy smell.

Collar and Leash

Collars are generally made of leather, nylon, cotton, or hemp, and they come in a variety of styles: buckle, harness, head halter, etc. Ideally, your Bulldog should wear a lightweight nylon or leather buckle collar with proper identification attached. Some experts decry the practice of letting an unattended dog wear a collar 24 hours a day, the theory being that the dog could get it snagged on something and choke to death. This is a genuine concern, and you will need to weigh the pros and cons of a collar. Should you opt against a collar, be sure your dog has a secondary form of identification, such as a microchip.

Nylon collars are inexpensive and work well with puppies because they will need to be replaced several times before your puppy is fully grown.

Leather collars are more expensive than nylon but well worth the investment for adult dogs because they are softer yet sturdier and will last a lifetime if given the right care. Significant differences exist in the quality of these collars. Be sure to select a high-quality leather collar from a reputable manufacturer.

Several types of collars, such as choke chains, prong collars, and martingale collars, work by putting pressure on your dog's neck and throat. While it may be tempting to use these devices on a tough Bulldog, they are best left to professionals because they can cause serious damage to a dog's throat. Taking the time to train your Bulldog to walk properly and not pull without these devices will be much more rewarding to you both.

A head halter goes over your dog's face and applies pressure to the back of the neck rather than the front of the throat. While head halters can be very effective for other breeds, they are not designed for a Bulldog's face.

Some owners choose a harness for their dogs. Keep in mind that a harness will not prevent your Bulldog from pulling, but it will take the pressure off his trachea. A variety of models are available in different shapes, sizes, and materials. It is best to seek professional advice in order to correctly fit your Bulldog with a harness and prevent chafing.

A good-quality leather leash is expensive but well worth the investment. Leather is kinder and gentler on your hands, which is important because you'll be using the leash a lot, and the more you use it, the softer and more pliable the leather becomes. When well cared for, a leather leash will last a lifetime. Nylon leashes are lightweight and relatively inexpensive, but they are not always the best choice for medium or large dogs because they are hard on your hands and can slice your fingers to the bone should your Bulldog lunge or give a good pull. Chain leads are noisy, heavy, and unnecessary. A 5/8- or 3/4-inch (1.6- or 1.9-cm) wide and 4- to 6- feet (1- to 2-m) long leash should provide sufficient strength and control.

Retractable leads are designed to extend and retract at the touch of a button. They provide your Bulldog with plenty of distance on walks without dragging a long line that can get tangled, dragged through the mud, or wrapped around bushes. A retractable lead that extends to 16 feet (5 m) or more allows your Bulldog plenty of privacy to do his business and to sniff and explore countless sights and smells. A finger brake button allows you to stop your dog at any time. If you go this route, be sure to invest in a good-quality retractable lead designed specifically for strong medium-sized dogs.

Crate

A crate is an absolute necessity. Crates come in different shapes, sizes, and materials, each offering its own advantages. Folding wire crates provide good air circulation and help keep dogs cool when temperatures are high. Crate covers, available in a variety of styles, turn any wire crate into a secure den and provide protection from the elements. Other crate types include soft nylon, canvas, or heavy-duty, high-impact plastic kennels that meet domestic and international requirements for airline travel.

Purchase a crate that is big enough for your Bulldog when he is fully grown. Ideally, it should be big enough for an adult Bulldog to stand up, turn around, and stretch out in while lying down. If the crate is too big, it defeats the

A crate, such as the Nylabone® Fold-Away Pet Carrier, is an invaluable housetraining tool.

purpose of providing the security of a den. If it is too small, your Bulldog will be cramped and uncomfortable, and this is neither fair nor humane. During the housetraining stage, a crate that is too large allows a puppy to use one end for sleeping and the other end as a bathroom, which defeats the crate's usefulness as a housetraining tool. Some crates come equipped with a divider panel that allows you to adjust the crate space accordingly. This option allows you to block off a portion of the crate for housetraining purposes, and it can take your Bulldog from the puppy stage through housetraining and into adulthood without the expense of purchasing progressively larger crates.

Exercise Pen

A portable wire "playpen" (or exercise pen) is indispensable for raising a well-behaved puppy. It is ideal for placement anywhere you need a temporary kennel area, such as the kitchen or family room. It is also ideal for safely confining your Bulldog when you cannot give him your undivided attention, such as when you are eating, working on the computer, talking on the telephone, or doing the laundry.

If you place the exercise pen in the kitchen area, or wherever your family tends to congregate, your puppy can get used to his home's many sights, sounds, and smells from the safety of his exercise pen. Most owners prefer the kitchen area because kitchens tend to have washable floors and can easily be cleaned and disinfected if your puppy has an accident.

Food and Water Bowls

Bowls should be easy to clean and made of material that is not potentially harmful, and they should not slip when placed on the floor. You will need two bowls: one for water and one for food. Stainless steel is the best choice

Multi-Dog Tip

For multiple-dog households, be sure each dog has his own food bowl. This allows you to feed the dogs separately (preferably in their own crates) and allows you to monitor who is eating what and how much. It also helps to prevent possessive or guarding-type behavior because even the best of friends are not immune to squabbling when food is around.

because it is easy to clean and dishwasher safe, and some models come with nonskid rubber on the bottom. Ceramic bowls, which can be toxic, and glass bowls can easily break. Plastic bowls are inexpensive, but they are not the best choice. Plastic is not as easily sanitized as stainless steel, can contribute to chin acne, and can harbor bacteria. Tenacious chewers could easily ingest or choke on shredded pieces.

Identification

Even the most conscientious owner can experience the nightmare of a lost dog—that's why making sure your Bulldog is properly identified is crucial.

ID Tags

Your Bulldog must have an ID tag that includes, at a minimum, your name and telephone number. Tags are relatively inexpensive and well worth the investment because they are your dog's ticket home should he become lost or separated from you. Readily available at retail pet outlets, mail order catalogs, and online vendors, they come in a variety of shapes, sizes, colors, and materials, and easily attach to your dog's buckle collar with an S-clip or good-quality split ring. Nameplates that attach directly to your dog's collar are also available; they eliminate the unmistakable, not to mention frequently annoying, jingling noise produced by multiple dangling tags.

Microchipping

Until recently, tattooing was the most widely used method of permanently identifying an animal. Modern technology has given pet owners the latest in identification options—a silicon microchip about the size of a grain of rice that is painlessly inserted under the skin. This microchip contains an unalterable identification number that is recorded on a central database along with your name, address, and telephone number. When scanned via a hand-held electronic scanner, the number can be read and linked to your dog's information. But a microchip will not do your Bulldog any good if it is not registered, so don't forget to do the paperwork and keep your contact information up to date.

A universal scanner can detect and read the numbers of all major brands of microchips. Several state and national registries are available for registering and storing your contact information.

Safety Gates

Safety gates (baby gates are often used) are indispensable and ideal for corralling your puppy. Until he is thoroughly housetrained and well through the chewing stage, you should never give him free access to wander around the house. Baby gates are available in metal, plastic, and wood.

Toys

Bulldogs, like most other dogs, like and need to chew, but because of the breed's unusual bite, a Bulldog can't chew very efficiently. Bulldogs can choke to death on bones and toys more easily than other breeds. Your healthiest and most long-lasting selections will be toys made for your Bulldog's body type and chewing power. Hard rubber and nylon toys, such as Nylabones, are made for real gnawing and gnashing. They exercise your dog's teeth and gums, promoting oral health while relieving the need to chew. Some of these toys are hollow and specially designed for hiding treats in them. Be careful with vinyl or plush toys that contain squeakers or noisemakers. Dogs love them, but tenacious Bulldogs will chew right through the material and may

Toys provide excellent opportunities for exercise, mental stimulation, and interaction between pets and their owners.

swallow the squeaker, which could become lodged in their throats.

Many kinds of edible chews and toys for dogs now provide nutritional enhancement or breath fresheners. Most are strong enough for your Bulldog to get a good chew out of them before breaking into bits that can be eaten. Again, always be on the lookout for small pieces that your Bulldog could choke on. These edible chews and toys should not be substitutes for the more long-lasting chew toys, but they make an enjoyable break for your dog.

Rope toys and tugs are often made of 100-percent cotton and frequently flavored to make them more attractive to dogs. Some have plaque-fighting fluoride floss woven into the rope to deep-clean teeth and gums. Be careful your Bulldog cannot shred the cotton ropes, which may be a potential choking hazard. Rope toys are excellent for tug of war games, too.

BRINGING YOUR PUPPY HOME

Try to make your puppy's trip home and his first experience with his new family a pleasant one. You don't want to be rushed, so plan to pick up your Bulldog on a day when you aren't working and no one has school. If possible, consider taking a few days off so you can be with him and help him to get started on the right foot.

On the ride home, your puppy should be safely crated and not on your lap or loose in the car— and never in the back of an open pickup truck. Many breeders crate train their puppies and give them short car rides to precondition them for the trip to their new homes. Your puppy may whine or cry because he is nervous or

scared. Avoid yelling at him or telling him to be quiet. He won't understand, and you are likely to exacerbate the situation. Line the crate with a few towels in case he has an accident. If possible, ask the breeder whether the puppy can take one of his toys with him because the familiar smell will help him feel calmer.

Once home, allow your puppy plenty of time to freely explore his new yard and potty area. If your yard is not fenced, keep him on leash at all times. To begin training your puppy to potty in a specific spot, take him to that location when you first get home. Calmly praise him when he is in the process of pottying; overly excited praise will cause him to forget what he's doing.

When he has done his business, take him indoors, but be sure baby gates are in place. You do not want him roaming around the house where he can inadvertently get himself into trouble, especially by peeing or chewing.

Introduce other household pets in a controlled and supervised environment. Never put your puppy in a position where he can be bullied, frightened, or bitten by another animal. If your other pets are pushy or bossy,

put your puppy into an exercise pen (ex-pen) and allow them to meet him with a barrier between them. Otherwise, sit on the floor and hold your puppy in your lap. If everything seems fine, let the other animals interact, but continue to supervise. If you have a cat or cats, provide them with plenty of escape routes, such as access to countertops, furniture, other rooms, and so forth. You don't want your puppy's first introduction to a cat to be a scratched nose.

Puppies have short attention spans and tire easily. Provide your Bulldog with a comfortable bed, crate, or ex-pen of his own for sleeping and recuperating. Avoid overwhelming him or allowing your kids or other pets to overwhelm him.

Teach children to approach the puppy quietly and slowly, and don't allow them to grab or bully him or to run and scream around him. Teach them how to properly pick up a puppy. Do not allow very young kids to pick up a puppy without your supervision. They can inadvertently hurt him should they pick him up by his ears or legs or, heaven forbid, drop him.

Surviving the First Night

Your puppy's first night away from the security of his mother and littermates may be difficult. Some puppies adjust more easily than others, but most likely your little guy will be feeling lonely and insecure, and he may whine and cry for a little while after being put into his crate. This is natural. To help make the first night with your puppy more calm and stress free, follow these tips:

- Before putting your puppy to bed, be sure he has been outside to potty and do his business.
- Place his crate next to your bed or that of another family member. Knowing you are close by will help to comfort him. During the night, you can reach down and reassure

Moving to an unfamiliar environment can be an unsettling experience, so give your puppy plenty of time to adjust to his new home and family.

him that you are close by.

- Be sure to put some comfy towels or a soft crate pad and a soft dog toy inside so he can curl up and be comfy and comforted.
- Use an old towel or shirt to wrap around an alarm clock that ticks, and place it into his crate. The ticking sounds can help to calm him. A softly playing radio may also help.

Once tucked into their new beds, some puppies cry for a few minutes before dozing off. Others wail for 30 minutes or more. Avoid taking your puppy out of his crate and putting him into your bed—unless that is where you want him to sleep for the rest of his life. Doing this will reinforce that you will rescue him whenever he cries. Ideally, it is best to ignore his pitiful pleas, provided of course you are certain he is safe and does not need to potty. Grit your teeth and endure, and know that this will pass. It might take a few sleepless nights, but once a puppy settles down he will become quite attached to his crate.

CHAPTER 3

CARE OF YOUR BULLDOG PUPPY

Owning a Bulldog puppy is an enormous responsibility because he cannot take care of himself. For his entire lifetime, which is generally eight to ten years, he will depend on you for his food, water, shelter, exercise, grooming, regular veterinary care, and love. How you care for him will have a significant impact on his growth and development.

FEEDING A PUPPY

Good nutrition is one of the most important contributors to your Bulldog's well-being. Studies indicate that proper nutrition can help prevent disease, promote healthy skin and coat, and provide your Bulldog with optimum health and longevity. Granted, canine nutrition can be complex and frustrating, and a trip down the dog food aisle can be more intimidating than computer science. Sorting nutritional fact from fiction— deciphering kilocalories and metabolizable energy, solving algebraic formulas for rates of energy expenditure, and making sense of food labels—can be a daunting task for even the most experienced dog owner.

Feeding your puppy a well-balanced diet is nothing to be afraid of, though. All it really requires is a basic understanding of canine nutrition, a keen observation of your Bulldog and whether or not his diet is agreeing with him, and, finally, the ability to look beyond slick multimillion-dollar ad campaigns.

This chapter cannot tell you the name of the best dog food available because no one food is the best. Hundreds of types and brands are available, and your job as a responsible dog owner is to find the one that works best for your Bulldog.

What to Feed

A Bulldog puppy has gigantic nutritional demands. He spends a significant part of his day playing, which requires a lot of calories. His body is growing rapidly. His system is building strong muscles, bones, and vital organs and establishing a resistance to disease. As a result, for the first 12 months of his life he needs a specially formulated food that is designed exclusively for his demanding energy and nutritional needs.

How Much to Feed

A puppy's growth rate and appetite are primarily dictated by his genetics, which varies from puppy to puppy, so feeding the correct amount can be a bit tricky. A growing Bulldog needs about twice as many calories per kilogram of body weight as an adult Bulldog. But the feeding guidelines on puppy foods are just that—guidelines. They are not etched in stone, and many dog food manufacturers tend to be overly generous with their proportions. Your veterinarian can help you determine the proper amount to feed.

For the first few days after bringing your puppy home, continue feeding the same type and brand of puppy food he has been eating, provided he has been eating a well-balanced, good-quality food. Depending on where and from whom you acquired your Bulldog, this may or may not be the case.

When to Feed

Because puppies have small stomachs, they need to be fed smaller amounts of food three or four times a day until they are about four to six months old. Thereafter, your Bulldog can be fed two times a day—once in the morning and again in the evening.

Feed your puppy at regular times throughout the day. This not only establishes a schedule for eating and eliminating, but also prevents overeating.

Scheduled Feeding Versus Free Feeding

Feed your puppy at regular times, and pick up and throw away any food that is left after 15 minutes. This regimen of scheduled feeding will help your puppy establish a regular routine of eating and eliminating, which will speed up the housetraining process. Designated feeding times also help with the bonding process because your puppy learns that food comes from you—the pack leader.

Free-feeding, which is putting the food out, leaving it all day, and allowing your puppy to eat at his leisure, does not establish a set schedule for feeding and eliminating and is not recommended. Also, when food is perpetually available, some dogs will overeat or may develop the annoying and potentially dangerous habit of food-bowl guarding. Finally, if you have more than one dog, feeding them separately in crates, kennels, or at opposite sides of the house while they eat is recommended. Otherwise, you will not know for certain whether your puppy is eating or the other dogs are eating for him. Even the best of friends have been known to squabble over food.

The Dangers of Juvenile Obesity

Bulldogs in general are inherently predisposed to a number of respiratory issues, which are exacerbated when they are overweight—even by just a few pounds. Studies indicate that as human's become more obese, so too do their dogs. Bulldogs who are overweight as puppies are more prone to being overweight as adult dogs because juvenile obesity increases the number of fat cells in a Bulldog's body, predisposing him to obesity for the rest of his life.

Extra pounds also contribute to diabetes, increased blood pressure, congestive heart failure, and digestive

If you intend to switch foods, it is best to do so slowly. Veterinarians recommend switching foods over the course of seven to ten days to prevent upset stomachs, vomiting, loose stools, or constipation. To do this, make a mixture of 75 percent old food and 25 percent new food. Feed this mixture for three or four days. Then make a mixture of 50 percent old food and 50 percent new food. Feed this mixture for three or four days. Then make a mixture of 25 percent old food and 75 percent new food. Feed this mixture for three or four days. After that, you can start feeding 100 percent new food.

disorders. Fat works as an insulator, which is great if you're a hibernating bear, but too much fat is going to wreak havoc with a Bulldog's internal and external parts. Extra fat restricts the expansion of a dog's lungs, making breathing difficult. Overweight Bulldogs are less capable of regulating their body temperatures and are therefore more susceptible to heatstroke. They have less stamina and endurance because their heart, muscles, and respiratory system are always working overtime—way beyond what they were designed to do. Additionally, overweight Bulldogs have increased surgical risks and decreased immune functions and are more susceptible to injuries including damage to joints, bones, and ligaments. Simply put, allowing your Bulldog to become overweight subjects him to a diminished quality of life, and he is likely to die at a younger age than his physically fit counterparts.

GROOMING

The Bulldog's coat is straight, short, smooth, and flat, with a fine texture and glossy appearance. While it takes less maintenance than a longhaired coat, it does require regular grooming to keep it in tip-top condition. Regular grooming also allows you to check for bumps, lumps, cuts, fleas, ticks, and the like. Because Bulldogs are prone to skinfold dermatitis, regular grooming allows you to keep the "facial folds" and tail pocket clean and dry. You can also check the feet for cuts, torn pads, broken nails, and interdigital cysts, and examine the mouth for tartar, damaged teeth, or discolored gums.

Grooming, when done correctly, can produce a calming effect, and since most dogs love to be groomed once they've been trained to accept it, this is a great way to spend quality time with your puppy while simultaneously building a strong and mutually trusting human/canine relationship.

Grooming a canine companion, as opposed to the competitive show dog, is a relatively simple process as long as it is done regularly and your dog views it as a positive and enjoyable experience.

Getting Your Puppy Used to Grooming

It is a good idea to start grooming practices right away. If your puppy came from a reputable breeder, he is probably used to being handled and gently stroked. He has probably had at least one bath and may already be accustomed to being brushed and examined, which makes your life much easier. A puppy who is exposed to positive and delightful grooming experiences will grow into an adult dog who takes pleasure in the regular routine. Few things are more frustrating than trying to wrestle a 50-pound (23-kg) Bulldog who doesn't want to be groomed.

Start slow and progress at a rate that is suitable for the age and mental maturity of your dog. Begin by teaching your puppy to stand on a table. If you do not have a grooming table, consider investing in one. Absent a grooming table, any sturdy surface such as a bench or crate top covered with a nonskid, nonslip surface is sufficient. Sitting or kneeling on the floor with a puppy works especially well for the first few grooming sessions, too. Eventually you will want to teach your puppy to lie down and relax on the table. This position is helpful when trimming nails, brushing his tummy, and examining his body for stickers, burs, cuts, hot spots, and such. Bulldogs who learn to relax on a grooming table are more likely to relax on a veterinarian's examination table, making a trip to the vet's office less stressful for all involved.

Puppies have limited attention spans, so do not expect your Bulldog to remain still for extended periods of time. In the beginning you want progress, not perfection. Your goal should be for him to stand or lie still for a few seconds while you verbally praise and reward him with yummy treats. Harsh handling during these learning stages will come back to haunt you when your Bulldog begins resenting the necessary chore. Keep sessions short, combined with a soothing voice and gentle hands. Progress to the point where your puppy will accept having his entire body stroked, then slowly and calmly brush him all over. At first your Bulldog may be frightened, nervous,

Training Tidbit

Always lift a puppy on and off a grooming table and never leave him unattended while he's on it. Bulldogs—especially puppies— can easily injure themselves if permitted to jump on or off tables, countertops, or from anything of significant height. Keeping one hand on your puppy while he's on the grooming table will reassure him that he is safe and prevent him from leaping off and injuring himself.

or unsure. Patience, gentle handling, and plenty of hugs and kisses will help to build his confidence. Just spending a few minutes every day brushing and stroking your puppy will familiarize him with the grooming process and teach him to accept and enjoy it.

Grooming Supplies

This breed does not have high-maintenance grooming needs. However, you will need to invest in a few pieces of equipment, including:

- A soft bristle brush for daily brushing. Bristle brushes don't penetrate as deeply as others (i.e., a pin brush), so they're excellent for a Bulldog's short coat. A boar-bristle brush is expensive but lasts forever. Natural bristle brushes, unlike plastic, nylon, and wire bristles, can lead to better distribution of natural oils.
- A slicker brush for stripping out the undercoat.
- A curry comb, which has stubby rubber nubs, is also ideal for loosening and removing dead hair. A hound mitt, also called a hound glove, grooming mitt, or coat mitt, is also an option.

Some hound mitts have pure horsehair on one side and a chamois, or polishing cloth, on the opposite side.

- A chamois cloth or grooming/glossing mitt (if you don't have a hound mitt with a polishing cloth).
- Nail clippers or a nail grinder.
- Cotton balls for ear cleaning.
- Shampoo and conditioner. Unless your dog has a specific skin condition, such as dry, flaky, itchy skin, choose a good-quality shampoo and conditioner designed specifically for dogs—something nontoxic and shampoo-based so as not to strip the hair of its natural oils.
- Toothbrush and toothpaste specifically for dogs (never use human toothpaste).
- Towels.
- Blow dryer (optional).
- Nonskid, nonslip mat for the tub.
- Grooming table (optional, but highly recommended). A table allows you to easily work without stooping or bending, and to control your dog because he can't easily scoot away. If you plan to show your Bulldog, a grooming table is essential.

While the initial outlay of money can be a bit expensive, it is well worth investing in good professional equipment. In the long run, you won't be replacing brushes and combs every few months, and, when properly cared for, good equipment will last you a lifetime.

HEALTH

Your Bulldog's health is paramount. The breed's predisposition to respiratory issues, including increased risks to anesthesia, makes finding a Bulldog-savvy veterinarian essential. Ideally, you want to find a veterinarian before you bring your new Bulldog home. Flipping through the Yellow Pages or choosing the clinic down the street might be convenient, but the closest or most convenient veterinarian may not be the one best suited to your Bulldog or you. Taking the time to do research and weigh your options may produce better results. However, depending on the area in which you live, your choices may be limited.

Finding a Vet

Finding the right veterinarian is not difficult, but it may take some time and a bit of detective work. The good news is the hard work you invest in today will pay off in the future when you need to put your Bulldog's health and well-being in the hands of someone you trust. To start your search:

- Ask your Bulldog's breeder for a referral. Most reputable breeders know several local veterinarians and specialists.
- Ask friends, family, neighbors, and colleagues who own a pet for a referral.
- Ask for recommendations from local dog clubs, obedience schools, dog groomers,

Having a veterinarian whom you can trust is essential to your Bulldog's health.

or boarding kennels. These people are involved with dogs and will have established a relationship with one or more local veterinarians.

- Check local telephone directories, which may be a good starting point for names, addresses, and telephone numbers of veterinary and emergency clinics in your area.

The Clinic

Visiting clinics can be time consuming, but seeing the premises and meeting the staff in person is well worth your while. When visiting veterinary clinics, don't be afraid to ask for a tour of their exam rooms, x-ray room, operating and recovery rooms, boarding areas, and so forth. If the clinic is busy, you may need to schedule an appointment, which is not an unreasonable request. If the staff or veterinarians refuse to show you their facilities, run, don't walk, to the nearest exit.

Do not be afraid to ask questions while you're there. It's the best way to find a place where you will be comfortable and confident taking your Bulldog. Ask about their regular office hours, holiday and weekend hours, and how emergencies are handled. Find out what type of services they offer (surgeries, hip or elbow x-rays, ultrasound, dentistry, eye exam, endoscopy), and, most importantly, ask whether the veterinarian is familiar with the Bulldog breed.

When visiting clinics, look for a minimum of the following:

- The clinic should be neat and clean. Exam rooms should be cleaned and disinfected between animals.
- The clinic should be organized and run smoothly; a noisy and chaotic place might not be your best bet.
- The waiting area should provide adequate room for separating large and small dogs,

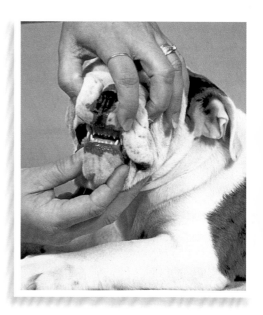

During his first checkup, your puppy will receive a complete physical examination and any necessary vaccinations.

unruly dogs from nervous dogs, and rambunctious dogs from shy dogs.
- There should be a fenced or grassy area for your Bulldog to relieve himself.

The Staff

Like human doctors, veterinarians differ in their bedside manners. Some are very personable, caring, and compassionate. Others are less so. Remember, your Bulldog's life expectancy is eight to ten years, and a good relationship between you and your veterinarian will see you through those years. Otherwise, you will not be comfortable taking your Bulldog there, and he will sense your anxiety.

You should be comfortable talking with the veterinarian and asking questions, and you should never feel rushed. He and his staff should be patient, knowledgeable, and friendly, and they should treat your Bulldog with kindness, respect, and concern. They should be willing to explain the diagnosis, treatment, and expected outcome in layman's terms.

Despite a veterinarian's glowing recommendations and academic qualifications, your personality may differ or clash with his or hers. If this is the case, keep looking until you find the veterinarian who is right for you.

The First Exam

Once you have found a good veterinarian, you should take your Bulldog for his first checkup within 48 to 72 hours of acquiring him. This establishes an initial record of his health. To the untrained eye, a puppy who appears healthy can still have a serious problem. As a new Bulldog owner, you must work with your veterinarian to develop a preventive healthcare plan and schedule routine visits.

Your veterinarian will check your Bulldog's overall condition, including inspecting his skin, coat, eyes, ears, feet, lymph nodes, glands, teeth, and gums. He will listen to his heart and lungs; feel his abdomen, muscles, and joints; and take his temperature. He will ask you about your puppy's daily routine, his eating and elimination habits, and so forth. Jot down any relevant information beforehand so you will have it at your fingertips, such as the type of food your puppy eats; how much and how often he eats and drinks; how often he relieves himself; the

color, shape, and size of his stools; and anything else you may have noticed. The veterinarian also should discuss a preventive healthcare plan that includes vaccinations, deworming, spaying or neutering, and the importance of scheduling routine veterinary visits.

Vaccinations and Infectious Diseases

Vaccines are designed to trigger a protective immune response and prepare a dog to fight future infections from highly contagious and deadly disease-causing agents.

In the simplest of terms, a dog's immune system is like a border patrol, guarding the body against foreign invaders. When a dog is vaccinated or exposed to something foreign or "nonself," such as bacteria, viruses, or parasites, the immune system reacts by producing antibodies or sensitized lymphocytes (a type of white blood cell) that will find and destroy the intruders. These cells not only destroy the organism but also remember what it looked like so they can fend it off in the future, preventing or minimizing illness if the body is exposed to the same organism again. It is this immunological memory that enables vaccines, which purposely contain live, weakened, or dead pathogens, to protect against future disease. Immunization stimulates a dog's immune system to produce disease-fighting

Preparing for Emergencies

Now that you own a Bulldog, you will quickly learn that emergencies never happen between 8 am and 5 pm. It's Murphy's Law with a twist: Anything that can go wrong will go wrong, and it will happen on weekends, holidays, and always after your veterinarian's office has just closed for the day. Therefore, it is prudent to know the location of the emergency veterinary clinic closest to you. Emergency animal clinics handle problems that occur outside of your veterinarian's regular office hours. Most generally, they do not handle routine checkups, vaccinations, or spaying and neutering.

antibodies against infectious diseases.

Strictly a preventive measure, vaccines will not cure a disease. When it comes to viral diseases, no specific treatment or drug will kill the virus once the infection begins. However, according to the American Veterinary Medical Association (AVMA), "vaccines can lessen the severity of future disease and certain vaccines can prevent infection altogether."

Colostrum, which is the first milk secreted from the dam, is rich in antibodies that provide passive immunity to newborn puppies. These maternal antibodies transfer primarily by intestinal absorption from the colostrum during the initial two days of a puppy's life. They have limited effectiveness and do not last too long, generally decreasing during the first few months of a puppy's life. Problems can arise if there are gaps in protection as the milk antibodies decrease and the puppy's immune system is not yet capable of fighting off infection. Vaccinations help to keep these gaps in protection to a minimum while providing optimal protection against disease.

While veterinarians occasionally vary in their vaccination protocol, the standard protocol recommends that puppies receive their first vaccination at eight weeks of age, followed by "booster" shots three to four weeks later, with the last shot given around four months of age. Your veterinarian will set up a continued vaccination schedule for your dog; it may vary from standard protocol, depending on where you live, travel plans, and whether your dog has any underlying diseases, such as immune problems or existing infections.

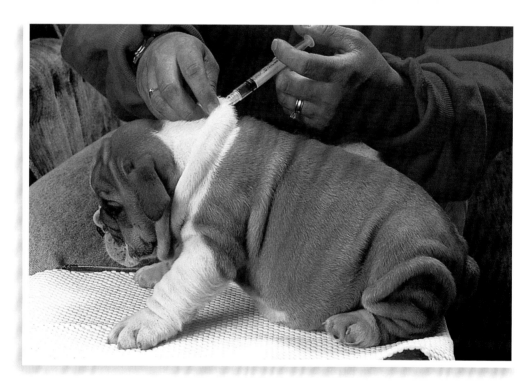

Vaccinations protect your puppy against many life-threatening diseases.

Diseases to Vaccinate Against

The following is a list of viral and bacterial diseases that your veterinarian may recommend vaccinating against—taking into account your lifestyle and the region in which you live.

Coronavirus

Spread through the stool of infected dogs, coronavirus is highly contagious. It is rarely fatal to adult dogs, but frequently fatal to puppies. Symptoms can include vomiting, loss of appetite, and diarrhea, which may lead to dehydration, further endangering puppies. Puppies less than 12 weeks of age are at the greatest risk. Laboratory tests are necessary to differentiate it from the deadly canine parvovirus.

Distemper

A highly contagious viral disease that is similar to the virus that causes measles in humans, distemper is a primary cause of illness and death in unvaccinated puppies. Spread through the air as well as through contact with an infected animal's stool, distemper spreads rapidly through kennels or multiple-dog households, especially if unvaccinated dogs are present. Distemper attacks a wide range of canine organs including the skin, brain, eyes, respiratory, digestive, and nervous systems. Puppies less than six months of age are in the highest risk bracket. Symptoms may include nasal and eye discharge, coughing, diarrhea, vomiting, and seizures.

Hepatitis

Also known as canine adenovirus, infectious canine hepatitis typically affects the liver, tonsils, and larynx but can also attack other organs in the body. It is spread primarily through infected fluids including saliva, nasal discharge, and urine. Symptoms can include a sore throat, coughing, and occasionally, pneumonia. As it enters a Bulldog's bloodstream, it can affect his liver, kidneys, and the appearance of his eyes, which may become cloudy or bluish. More advanced symptoms are characterized by seizures, increased thirst, vomiting, and diarrhea. Unvaccinated Bulldogs of all ages are at risk. However, the disease is most prevalent in dogs less than one year of age.

Kennel Cough

Also known as canine infectious tracheobronchitis or bordetellosis, kennel cough is highly contagious and normally characterized by a harsh, dry coughing or hacking, which may be followed by retching and gagging. The disease is airborne—meaning it is passed through the air—and can spread rapidly among dogs who live together. Dogs at shows, boarding kennels, grooming shops, veterinary clinics, and public or private dog parks are at an increased risk of exposure.

Leptospirosis

A bacterial disease that is transmitted primarily through the urine of infected animals, leptospirosis is caused by organisms that can get into water or soil and survive for weeks to months. Bulldogs, as well as humans, can become infected through contact with the contaminated urine or contaminated water or soil. A dog who drinks, swims, or walks through contaminated water can also become infected. Symptoms can include fever, vomiting, abdominal pain, diarrhea, loss of appetite, weakness, lethargy, stiffness, severe muscle pain, and even death.

Lyme Disease

Caused by a spiral microorganism identified as *Borrelia burgdorferi*, Lyme disease is a bacterial infection that spreads to humans and dogs through the bite of an infected deer tick, also known as the black-legged tick. If infection occurs, the spirochetes migrate from the site of the bite and then invade and penetrate into connective tissues, skin joints, and the nervous system, causing arthritis-type symptoms. However, symptoms may not show up for months after initial exposure to an infected tick. Severity of the disease may vary depending on the dog's age and immune status. Symptoms include fever, shifting leg lameness, swelling in the joints, enlarged lymph nodes, and lethargy. Vaccines are available, but their protection is not absolute.

Parainfluenza

Transmitted by airborne respiratory secretions, parainfluenza is a highly contagious canine respiratory infection. Often associated with other respiratory infections, such as canine adenovirus-2 and bordetella bronchiseptica, parainfluenza is an important component of kennel cough. Diagnosis is generally based on clinical signs that include a fever and a dry unproductive cough, as if a dog were trying to "hack up" something from his lungs. While the virus can be mild, secondary bacterial infection may occur and cause a more severe disease. Treatment may involve a cough suppressant and, if necessary, antibiotics.

Parvovirus

Spread through the stools of infected dogs, parvovirus is a leading viral cause of diarrhea, and a terrible killer of puppies. This highly contagious gastrointestinal disease normally affects puppies more frequently than adult dogs, with the most severe cases seen in puppies younger than 12 weeks of age. Primary symptoms include an odorous diarrhea, oftentimes dark and bloody. Bulldogs can be

If your puppy seems unusually lethargic or has prolonged bouts of diarrhea, take him to the vet right away.

infected with both parvo and coronavirus at the same time, leading to vomiting, dehydration, and in severe cases lowered white blood cell counts. Healthy adult Bulldogs generally survive, but the loss of fluids in puppies and older dogs can lead to rapid dehydration, followed by death within a few hours. Time is of the essence. Seek veterinary attention immediately if you suspect your puppy has been exposed or shows symptoms including vomiting or diarrhea.

Rabies

A highly infectious viral disease that affects the brain, rabies is almost invariably fatal once symptoms begin to appear. All warm-blooded animals—including humans—are at risk. Transmission of the virus is almost always from a bite from a rabid animal. The virus is relatively slow moving, with the average incubation time from exposure to brain involvement (in dogs) being between two weeks to six months. Behavior changes are frequently the first symptom, and infected dogs have trouble swallowing and will drool or salivate. Advanced symptoms include paralysis and convulsions. Always err on the side of caution and seek veterinary assistance immediately if you suspect a wild animal or an infected dog or cat has bitten your Bulldog. Although rabies is incurable, properly vaccinated animals are at a relatively low risk of contracting the disease.

The Vaccination Controversy

Vaccines—and vaccination protocols—have been under fire for quite some time. Countless articles arguing every possible position are readily available. However, decoding the scientific lingo can, unfortunately, be excruciatingly boring, and more than a few people have gone cross-eyed in an attempt to

---

Want to Know More?

For more detailed information about anasarca and other hereditary diseases, see Chapter 8: Bulldog Health and Wellness.

---

do so. Basically, the majority of experts agree that vaccinations are an important part of canine preventive medicine. They are also in agreement regarding puppy vaccinations and the need to vaccinate all dogs against rabies.

Veterinarians used to vaccinate dogs on an annual basis. However, modern science and technology have helped to improve the quality and duration of vaccine immunity. Therein lies the controversy. Some experts believe vaccinating dogs on a yearly basis is no longer necessary because the duration of immunity (DOI) with some vaccines may be as long as three or four years. Also, many unanswered questions remain regarding the long-term health risks associated with vaccination. Questions regarding the necessity of vaccinating for Lyme disease, giardia, or even rattlesnake bites also abound. As a result, some researchers advocate rotating yearly vaccines using a single component vaccine—a vaccine, for example, that contains only parvovirus rather than combination vaccines that contain parvovirus, distemper, and hepatitis. Other veterinarians recommend giving the vaccinations together, but only every three years.

Some vaccinations are an absolute necessity, and new-age medicine and technology will help to keep your Bulldog happy and healthy. However, the controversy surrounding vaccinations is not likely to fade anytime too soon. That's why it is important to know the

Unless you plan to show your dog in the conformation ring, spaying or neutering is a good idea.

options and discuss vaccination protocols with your veterinarian.

Controlling Reproduction

After vaccinations, spaying or neutering is likely to be the next preventive health issue you address with your Bulldog. Unless you plan to show your dog in the show ring, spaying or neutering is a good idea for a number of reasons, including protecting overall health

and limiting the number of unwanted, homeless dogs born through accidental breedings.

Controlling reproduction is important for practical reasons as well. Intact females generally come into season twice a year and require 24-hour supervision during the 23-day estrous cycle. Washable diapers are an option, but they are not foolproof. Nor are they cheap. Intact males are attracted to females in season and will roam for miles in search of one. They are also more likely to mark their territory and fight with other males.

Neutering

Castration, usually referred to as neutering, refers to the surgical removal of both testicles in the male dog. The procedure is performed under anesthesia and provides a number of advantages including:

- eliminating testicular cancer
- decreasing the incidence of prostate disease (more than 80 percent of unneutered dogs develop the disease)
- helping to prevent behavioral problems, such as aggression, roaming, and territorial marking
- eliminating exposure to sexually transmitted diseases

Spaying

Spaying (ovariohysterectomy) is the term applied to the surgical procedure involved in the removal of the uterus and ovaries of a female dog. The procedure takes about an hour, but because it is abdominal surgery that is done under general anesthesia, the veterinarian may require your dog to stay at the clinic overnight. The primary reason for spaying a female is eliminating the nuisance of the heat cycle, which generally occurs every six months, thereby preventing her from having unwanted puppies. Other reasons for spaying a female may be related to diseases of the ovaries and uterus. Additional advantages include:

- reducing or eliminating mammary gland tumors, the most common tumors in unspayed females
- eliminating the incidence of ovarian and uterine infection
- eliminating false pregnancies
- preventing unwanted pregnancies that contribute to pet overpopulation
- eliminating the risks and stresses associated with unnecessary pregnancies
- eliminating exposure to sexually transmitted diseases

While the majority of dogs are altered around six months of age, many veterinarians alter dogs as young as eight weeks of age. Once considered controversial, early spay/neuter procedures are becoming more common. Your veterinarian is the best person to advise you on what age to alter your dog.

The Cost of Breeding

Breeding dogs is a serious business in which anything and everything can go wrong—and "anything" and "everything" are usually expensive. Breeding Bulldogs involves additional health risks and financial expenses because Bulldogs are rarely ever bred naturally. They are bred through artificial insemination, which is costly. You also need to pay for the semen (fresh, chilled, or frozen), the cost of collection, and the cost of having it shipped. These fees are in addition to the agreed-upon stud fee.

Bulldog puppies are delivered by Caesarean section (C-section), which is another costly veterinary bill, depending on where you live and how complicated the operation becomes. None of this guarantees you any live puppies. Nor does it guarantee your bitch will survive the ordeal. Bulldog puppies are also hereditarily predisposed to anasarca, a life-threatening complication, which appears to develop in the later stages of gestation.

Once the puppies are born, you will need to spend many sleepless nights caring for them, making sure the dam doesn't accidentally roll over and crush them. You will need to make sure the puppies are nursing properly and sufficiently. If the mother doesn't accept them for nursing and cleaning, you must become responsible for the entire process.

As they begin to grow, you will need to wean them, housetrain them, and socialize them. You will need to screen potential owners and find good and loving homes for them, which can be difficult. If anything goes wrong, you must take on the responsibility of taking the dog back and keeping him or finding another responsible owner.

Bulldogs are not inexpensive to purchase, but the high price tag and the additional costs for spaying or neutering are a bargain compared to genetic testing, stud fees, veterinary bills, and the like, if you do choose to breed your dog.

CHAPTER 4

TRAINING YOUR BULLDOG PUPPY

Regardless of whether your Bulldog's future is as a loving companion or a competitive superstar, he will need basic obedience training. Practical exercises like walk on leash, sit, down, and come when called will make you and your Bulldog's life more enjoyable. Puppies also need to be socialized, housetrained, and crate trained. All of these commands and behaviors take time to teach, but they can be incorporated into your daily activities in an enjoyable and positive environment. It's also never too early (or late!) to begin your Bulldog's training. Ideally, however, you should start as soon as your puppy comes to live with you. Puppies are young and impressionable and still agreeable to learning. And they have no bad habits to overcome—yet!

TRAINING IS IMPORTANT

Training provides your Bulldog with a basic foundation of obedience skills and manners that allow him to grow into a well-behaved adult dog who can coexist with humans. No doubt his life is more enjoyable because as a well-behaved adult dog, he is more likely to be considered a family member and included in family activities—rather than to be relegated to the isolation of the back yard.

Most important in the training process is understanding that all puppies are individuals. Puppies have their own unique characters, temperaments, and personalities and, as a result of their genetic makeup plus some environmental influences, they will grow into adult dogs who possess their own distinct qualities. If you have children, think how they were all raised with the same amount of love, individual attention, rules, values, and so forth in order to make the most of their personalities and talents. Yet despite their seemingly uniform upbringing, each child is an individual with his or her own special talents, likes, dislikes, quirks, and idiosyncrasies.

A keen understanding of the Bulldog breed—his history and origin—will help you to better understand what makes your puppy tick. Get in the habit of watching your puppy when he is sleeping or playing by himself or with other animals or children. Is he bold? Sassy? Bossy? Lazy? Does he growl at or attack other animals? Does he cower from children? Is he inquisitive?

Understanding your puppy's individual personality will help you to recognize which behaviors you can live with and those that might preclude a long and happy human/canine relationship. If, for instance, your puppy is bossy and pushy, begin right away

Training provides your Bulldog with a basic foundation of obedience skills and manners that allow him to grow into a well-behaved adult dog.

discouraging the behavior of bolting outdoors or grabbing food or toys from your hand without permission. If your puppy is shy or nervous, expose him to safe situations that will help build his confidence, such as encouraging friends to get on the ground and talk to him, play with him, rub his tummy, and kiss his nose. Take him for rides in the car, to the veterinarian's for a cookie and a kiss, or trips to the neighbor's barn—on leash, of course— to see the horses and explore strange smells, sights, and sounds.

Positive Motivation

Bulldogs are not your typical obedience or agility breed. Obviously, they do not have the "Send me in, Coach!" or "get-it-done-right-now" attitudes of Border Collies and Australian Shepherds. Bulldogs are also famously stubborn, but they do respond well to positive motivation and training. Slow-witted is a term often used to describe them, but that is most

unfair. Bulldogs are intelligent, and most love to please their owners, but they do not like to be bullied or browbeaten. Berating them or treating them harshly will not get you far. Bulldogs must be trained and handled with respect, fairness, and consistency.

Ideally, all dog training, be it basic obedience commands or fun games and tricks, should be taught to dogs positively. Positive motivation should not be misinterpreted as being permissive, thereby allowing a dog to run amok and do whatever he wants, whenever he wants. Using positive rewards like yummy treats and fun toys and interactive play does not give a dog permission to be out of control.

The concept behind positive motivation and reinforcement is that when a behavior has favorable consequences, the probability that the behavior will be repeated is increased. For example, if every single time your puppy comes to you he receives a ton of positive reinforcement in terms of verbal and physical

How to Find a Trainer

As previously mentioned, Bulldogs are noted for their independence and stubbornness. Finding a knowledgeable trainer who understands different learning theories as well as the Bulldog breed is very important. To find the right trainer or puppy class for you and your Bulldog:

- Ask your veterinarian, breeder, dog groomer, or dog-owning friends for referrals. Word of mouth is a great tool for uncovering talented and knowledgeable trainers while avoiding problem ones.
- Contact professional organizations that certify or recommend trainers, such as the Association of Pet Dog Trainers (APDT) or the National Association of Dog Obedience Instructors (NADOI). (Certification doesn't guarantee a good or knowledgeable trainer, but it's a starting point.)
- Attend the classes of several trainers to observe their personalities, training techniques, and facilities.
- Look for trainers who focus on rewarding what your Bulldog does right rather than punishing what he does wrong.
- Does the trainer recognize that puppies are individuals? Are the same training methods imposed on all of the puppies, regardless of their breed and mental maturity?
- Puppies learn best in low-risk, stress-free environments. Look for classes that are structured and run smoothly yet still emphasize fun.
- Do the facilities provide a safe learning environment for you and your puppy? Are they well lit, with matted floors and eight to ten puppies per class?
- Are the puppies separated—small puppies from large, young puppies from juniors, the rambunctious from the shy?

Trust your instinct. Your puppy's safety and well-being are paramount. If you feel uncomfortable about the facility or trainer, find another puppy class.

praise and a tasty tidbit or interactive play, he will learn to repeat the behavior because in his mind coming when called is always fun, positive, and rewarding. The dog learns a behavior through positive motivation and reinforcement.

It is worth clarifying that in dog training, positive simply means adding something, such as cheery praise, a favorite toy, or a tidbit of food, that will make a behavior, such as a *sit* or *down*, more likely to occur in the future. If you sit, Mom will reward you with a cookie. Positive does not necessarily mean being nice.

Think about the owner who smiles while she is jerking her dog into a *sit* with a choke chain and then rewards with a yummy tidbit. Is that positive training? Owners or trainers can be upbeat and sweet, but that doesn't mean that they are positive trainers. This is a point worth remembering when you are searching for an obedience trainer.

Without getting too bogged down in the complexities, let's just say that the general concept of positive motivation and reinforcement is teaching dogs without corrections or harsh handling. It's about training dogs primarily or exclusively by positive motivation and reinforcement to instill the behaviors you want. The reward can be a combination of verbal or physical praise coupled with a tasty tidbit of food or your dog's favorite toy.

Successful Training

A successful and key component of training is managing your puppy's environment so that he is not put into a situation where he can get himself into trouble. The majority of your interactions should be positive and fun as you work toward building a solid human/canine relationship by instilling desired behaviors, discouraging undesired behaviors, and fostering his zany personality. Managing your Bulldog so that he does not develop bad habits is critical. Take every opportunity to manipulate the situations so that your dog does the right thing and can be rewarded, which is, of course, the essence of positive motivation. If left to their own devices, Bulldog puppies, like most other puppies and adult dogs, will do what is in their best interest—and that is seldom, if ever, conducive to living in a domesticated environment.

Successful training also includes having a clear picture of what you want to accomplish and a well-thought-out game plan, which includes regular training, socialization, and interaction with your puppy both at home and in public. Additionally, it helps if you start right away—preferably as soon as your Bulldog starts living with you.

Equally important, training must be fun. Maximize your puppy's training by avoiding techniques that are repetitious, predictable, and boring for your dog. Puppies have limited attention spans. As a result, they become bored quite quickly. Use your imagination to be creative and come up with enjoyable-to-him training techniques and games that stimulate your Bulldog's mind and increase his desire to learn.

SOCIALIZATION

Socialization is about exposing a puppy in a positive, safe, and fun environment on a daily basis to all of the things he is likely to encounter as an adult dog. Certain periods in a puppy's life are critical to his social development. What happens within these individual stages has an enormous and significant impact on his future behavior as an adult. Research has shown that puppies are capable of learning at an early age, and they form lasting impressions during these critical periods. These impressions are remembered throughout a dog's life, be they good or bad.

A puppy who is exposed to positive experiences during the socialization period, such as handling, grooming, and different sights and sounds, stands a better chance of developing the socialization skills and coping mechanisms necessary to grow into a mentally sound and confident adult dog. Older puppies who have not been adequately or properly socialized during these periods tend to be more cautious. They generally grow up shy, fearful,

Socialization is critical to your puppy's social development, so introduce him to a variety of new people, places, and pets.

and frequently nervous. As adult dogs, they find it difficult and sometimes impossible to cope with new experiences. This is a disastrous situation for any dog, including Bulldogs.

Socialization is the single most important process in a Bulldog's life. Breeders and owners owe it to their puppies to take advantage of these critical periods to maximize their future, foster their zany personalities, and instill desired behaviors. How much time and energy you invest during this critical period directly impacts the future character of your puppy.

Early Socialization: The Breeder's Role

By the time your puppy is ready to begin his new life at your home, usually at around eight weeks of age, the process of socialization will have already begun. The breeder will have seen your puppy through the neonatal (approximately 0 to 13 days old) and transitional (approximately 13 to 20 days)

periods and halfway through the critical socialization period (approximately 3 to 12 weeks, although some experts consider it up to 16 weeks). During this time, reputable breeders will ensure that their litters are handled daily to accustom them to human contact and imprint trust. Breeders often have a radio or television playing to accustom the puppies to different voices and sounds. Puppies also receive individual attention and are exposed to a variety of sights and smells in a safe and stress-free environment. Many breeders will have accustomed their young puppies to crates, thereby facilitating the crate-training process.

For this reason, you must make careful choices about where you acquire your Bulldog. How your puppy is managed during the neonatal, transitional, and socialization periods has a tremendous impact on how he reacts and interacts to various situations and people as an adult dog.

Your Job

Your job begins the day your puppy arrives at your home. There is much to accomplish and a very small window of opportunity, so it is important to maximize your time and use it wisely. Your Bulldog must learn important socialization skills between 8 and 16 weeks of age. Once this small window of opportunity has passed, it can never be recaptured. Squandering your opportunities during this critical time means that your puppy will suffer in the long run. You run the risk of having your Bulldog develop bad habits and associations that are difficult, if not impossible, to correct later in life.

As the owner of a new Bulldog puppy, you are assuming the role of parent and pack leader. You are assuming an enormous responsibility that includes protecting him from bad or traumatic experiences while simultaneously instilling desired behaviors, fostering his upbeat personality, and providing him with every opportunity to grow into a well-adjusted, mentally confident adult dog.

The importance of maximizing your opportunities during this critical period cannot be overly stressed. Dogs mature faster than humans. On the average, humans take about 18 years to reach maturity, while dogs take about 1 to 1.5 years—depending on the dog. Your eight-week-old Bulldog will be eight weeks old for exactly seven days. The same goes for being 9, 10, 11, 12 weeks old, and so forth. While one week may seem insignificant in the life span of a child, it represents a significant portion of your Bulldog's puppyhood. Once those seven days have passed, they can never be recaptured.

Therefore, if possible, avoid scheduling vacations or extended trips out of town while your puppy is between 8 and 16 weeks of age— unless, of course, you plan to take him with you. Boarding him in a kennel or leaving him in the care of friends or relatives during this time puts your puppy at a serious disadvantage later on in life. You will have missed a prime opportunity to shape his future character and instill all of the behaviors you want your puppy to possess as an adult dog.

How to Socialize

Before taking your Bulldog puppy outdoors and around other animals, consult with your veterinarian about any necessary vaccinations to ensure that he is protected from diseases. Then, in a fun, safe, and stress-free environment, begin exposing him to a wide variety of people, including babies in strollers, toddlers, teenagers, women in floppy hats, and men with tools. Expose him to other animals in the household, the clapping of hands, the jingling of keys, and the clatter of dog bowls. Let him explore a variety of surfaces including grass, cement, gravel, tile, carpet, linoleum, sand, and dirt. He should be exposed to strollers, wheelchairs, shopping carts, vacuums, bicycles, and kids on roller skates and skateboards. A puppy who is not exposed to moving objects may be fearful of them as he gets older. He should be exposed to stairways, paper bags blowing in the wind, wind chimes, and horns honking. Let your puppy play in and around empty boxes, tunnels, and buckets. Allow him to investigate trees, rocks, bushes, branches, leaves, and fallen fruit. He should explore bugs and other animal odors, pastures, wooded areas, city sidewalks, and sandy beaches.

Enlarge your puppy's world and challenge his curiosity by taking him for rides in the car and walks in the park. Take him to the bank, post office, flower shop, veterinarian's office, and outdoor cafe for cookies and kisses.

As your puppy's guardian of safety and

well-being, you will want to protect him from potentially harmful or fearful situations yet not coddle or reward fearful behavior. Observe your puppy's reactions to different situations. Watch his ears and tail and body posture. Is he fearful? Apprehensive? Courageous? Dominant? Submissive? By understanding and reading your puppy's body language, you will be able to evaluate and adjust the situation accordingly. For instance, if your Bulldog was raised in a childless environment, a room full of noisy, rambunctious children may be overwhelming or downright scary. By coddling or otherwise rewarding a puppy who shows fear, you reinforce that fear. Modify or restrict the exposure to one quiet, well-behaved child in the beginning until your puppy's confidence can handle more. When your puppy is brave, praise and reinforce him for being brave and inquisitive. "Good puppy!" or "Look at you. Aren't you brave!"

If you do nothing else for your puppy, you owe it to him to make the time to properly and adequately socialize him during this critical life stage. Yes, it's time consuming, but it is a necessary and obligatory investment. Your puppy's future well-being depends on how much you do—or fail to do—during this critical period.

CRATE TRAINING

Crate training is about teaching your puppy to enjoy—to love—his own special den, which is his crate. Puppies naturally seek the security of a sheltered, secure, or den-like atmosphere, which is why they frequently lie under dining room tables, end tables, chairs, beds, and so forth. A specially designed canine crate provides that security. By crate training a puppy—teaching him to love being in and around his crate—you are capitalizing on his natural den instinct.

By the Numbers

Years ago, the accepted methodology of dog training was that a puppy had to be at least six months old before you began teaching basic obedience skills. That concept has since been debunked, and modern-day breeders, trainers, and animal behaviorists now recognize the important benefits of early training—as early as eight weeks of age.

When used properly by responsible dog owners, a crate is an excellent training tool. Although many owners look upon crates as cruel or inhumane, they really should be viewed from a dog's perspective. Before dogs became domesticated pets, they tended to seek safe, enclosed areas for security and protection. A crate mimics that safe, enclosed environment. Puppies, especially very young puppies, tire quickly and need a lot of sleep during the day. A crate placed in a quiet corner of the kitchen or family room will replicate a dog's natural instinct to seek a safe and secure environment. When properly introduced, a crate becomes a safe zone for your Bulldog—a quiet place all his own to sleep, eat, and retreat from the demands of being a puppy.

A key to successful puppy rearing is to never put your puppy in a position where he can get himself into trouble. Any puppy left unsupervised will develop bad habits. In record time, your adorable Bulldog puppy can pee from one end of the house to the other, ransack the trash, and gnaw the leg off your antique armoire. During those short periods when you cannot watch your puppy closely, a crate prevents him from getting into mischief.

Also, a crate is one of the safest, most successful, and efficient ways to housetrain a young puppy or adult dog. If your Bulldog has an accident in his crate, the mess is much easier to clean and less damaging than when it is in the middle of your expensive Persian rug. A crate is also ideal for keeping your Bulldog safe while traveling. A crated dog will not distract you from your driving responsibilities, teethe on your armrests, ransack the grocery bags, or eat your cell phone. Many motels and hotels, as well as friends and family, are more receptive to dogs provided they are crate trained. As your Bulldog grows and matures,

Most puppies quickly learn to love their crate when it is associated with good things, such as feeding, yummy treats, security, and sleep.

the crate will continue to be his den and safe place for eating, sleeping, and retreating from the often chaotic and noisy world of humans.

How to Crate Train

A crate, like any other training tool, has the potential to be abused. A crate is not intended for 24-hour confinement. Ideally, your puppy or adult dog should never be crated for more than an hour or two at a time. For example, when he is resting, eating, traveling, when you cannot watch him, and so forth. The exception is at night, when he will no doubt be confined for six to eight hours. At night, puppies are generally tired from their busy day of being a puppy and will generally sleep for six or eight hours—if you're lucky. Some puppies need to be let out several times at night to potty. Your Bulldog should live with you and not in his crate. A crate should never be used as a form of punishment. It should provide your Bulldog with a safe, secure environment and be a place that he enjoys.

Most puppies quickly learn to love their crates when they are associated with good things, such as feeding, yummy treats, security, and sleep. To maximize the crate training process, follow these steps.

Make the Crate Attractive

Make the crate attractive to your puppy by placing an old blanket, towel, or rug and a few of his favorite indestructible chew toys, like Nylabones, inside the crate. Remember, young puppies love to chew, so choose toys and blankets that are safe and do not present a potential choking hazard.

Leave the Door Open

Leave the crate door open and allow your puppy to explore in and around the enclosure. If your puppy goes inside the crate, praise him.

"Good puppy!" or "Aren't you clever!" Reward him with a tasty tidbit while he is in the crate.

Encourage With a Lure
If your puppy is reluctant to go inside, encourage him by letting him see you toss a tasty tidbit of food inside the crate, preferably toward the back of it. When your puppy goes inside the crate to retrieve the food, praise him. "Good puppy!"

Feed Him in the Crate
Feed your puppy his meals inside the crate, luring him inside with his food bowl. This will make the crate a positive place for your puppy to be.

Close the Door for a Minute
When your puppy is comfortable being inside the crate and shows no signs of stress, try closing the door for one minute. Open the door and praise your puppy for being brave. "Look at you! You're so brave!"

As your puppy becomes more comfortable with the crate, you can gradually increase the time that he spends there. Never confine him for longer than an hour or two at a time—except at night when he is sleeping.

Don't Reinforce Whining or Crying
If your puppy whines or cries, avoid reinforcing the behavior by letting him out of the crate or coddling him, such as saying "What's the matter, baby?" Wait for him to be quiet for a minute or two before opening the door (provided you are certain that he does not need to relieve himself.)

HOUSETRAINING
The object of housetraining is to teach a puppy to relieve himself outdoors and not on your floors. As a general rule, Bulldogs are no more difficult to housetrain than any other dog. Some puppies can be more difficult to housetrain than others, but that has more to do with the individual puppy than being a reflection on the breed. The key to successful housetraining is commitment, vigilance, and consistency on the part of the owner.

Housetraining is a relatively easy and painless process, yet it often causes owners a great deal of anxiety. Good planning and preparation and your unwavering commitment to the situation will provide your puppy with the best possible start. Crate training, when done properly, helps to quickly and efficiently housetrain a puppy. If your puppy had been born in the wild, most likely he would have lived in a cave or den, and most den animals have an instinctive desire to keep their dens clean. As a result, they avoid eliminating in their dens. A crate serves as your puppy's den. If you watch a litter of puppies, you will notice that around three weeks of age the puppies will begin moving away from the whelping box in order to relieve themselves. A dog's deep-seated instinct to keep his den clean provides the foundation of housetraining via use of a crate. If you take advantage of this natural instinct, you reduce the chance of accidents. As your puppy matures, you gradually teach him to hold his bladder for longer periods of time.

To increase your chances of success while minimizing accidents, you must provide your puppy with a regular schedule of eating, sleeping, and eliminating. Dogs are creatures of habit, and your Bulldog will have an easier time adjusting to his new household and a housetraining schedule if you establish some order and routine in his life.

As a general rule, puppies need to relieve themselves 15 to 20 minutes after drinking, and half an hour to an hour after eating. Pay attention to when your puppy eats and drinks and to what he's doing each time he relieves himself. Knowing what is normal behavior for your puppy means you will know when something is awry. Limit your puppy's food and water intake approximately one hour before you turn out the lights. This helps to ensure his bladder and bowels are empty. Note: Do not restrict water intake during the day, but do avoid allowing your puppy to drink heavily as bedtime approaches.

No Bladder Control

The first step in any successful housetraining program is recognizing that young puppies have very little or no bladder control until around five months of age. Puppies mature at different rates, so your puppy's control may develop earlier or later. A seven- or eight-week-old puppy is equivalent to a four- or six-month-old human baby. You would not expect a young baby to control his or her bladder, and it is unfair to ask your puppy to exercise control that he does not have.

Puppies are most active during the day—running, jumping, training, playing, and exploring. Because of their limited bladder size and lack of control, it goes without saying that they are going to need to relieve themselves many, many times throughout the day. During the night, however, puppies are usually exhausted from their busy day of being a puppy. They are more relaxed; as a result, most puppies can sleep between five and eight hours without having to potty. This varies from puppy to puppy, and in this sense they are not unlike human babies. Some parents

get lucky and their babies sleep through the night. Others are relegated to months of sleeplessness.

If your puppy wakes you up in the middle of the night or the early morning because he needs to go, it is always better to get up with him. The fewer accidents he has in his crate, the less stressful the process will be, and while it may seem like forever, it will not be long before he can hold on all night.

That said, if your puppy wakes you up when he has to go and you find that you simply cannot get up several times during the night—cover an area of the floor with sheets of newspaper. This works particularly well in a kitchen, which usually has a vinyl or linoleum floor. Set up an exercise pen on top of the newspaper and put his crate inside the exercise pen. At night, leave his crate door open. He will have access to his crate for sleeping, and he can also potty on the paper if he needs to go. The exercise pen will keep him confined to a small area. This technique works in a pinch. However, it is always worthwhile to make the effort to get up with your puppy if he needs to go outside, as teaching your puppy to urinate

The object of housetraining is to teach a puppy to relieve himself outdoors and not in places he shouldn't.

indoors on newspaper creates its own set of problems.

Set Up a Schedule

For the first several months—until your puppy begins to develop some reliable bladder control—you must take him outdoors frequently. When you are 100 percent committed to a regular schedule, your puppy will quickly learn that relieving himself occurs on schedule.

As a general guideline—to increase your chances of success while minimizing accidents—take your puppy outdoors at the following times:

- first thing in the morning when he wakes up and at least once every hour throughout the day
- about 15 minutes after drinking water
- about 30 minutes after eating
- immediately after waking from a nap
- when you arrive home
- any time you take him out of his crate
- any time he shows signs of having to go
- last thing at night

Because puppies are individuals and must be treated as such, you may need to tweak or adjust this schedule to fit your puppy's individual needs. No one said that raising a puppy was all fun and no work! Housetraining a puppy is a time-consuming endeavor, but time invested at this stage will make your life easier in the long run. It may seem unnecessary to take your puppy outside every hour to potty, but taking him out on a regular basis is easier, cheaper, and less aggravating than constantly cleaning or replacing carpets. Dogs are either housetrained or they aren't, and the fewer accidents your Bulldog has as a puppy, the faster he will learn to relieve himself outdoors, making him a more reliable adult dog. These steps work equally well when housetraining an adult dog—especially if you have acquired

Taking your puppy outdoors after eating, sleeping, and crate time will increase your chances of housetraining success while minimizing accidents.

a rescue or shelter dog. In these instances, it is always wise to assume that he is not housetrained and begin the housetraining process as if he were a puppy.

How to Housetrain

First thing each morning, when you hear that unmistakable "I gotta go" whimper, let your puppy out of his crate and immediately take him outdoors to a designated spot.

Don't Procrastinate

Do not procrastinate or allow yourself to get sidetracked making coffee, checking your e-mail, or fumbling around for a leash—keep one in a convenient spot. A few seemingly insignificant minutes to you is long enough to guarantee an accident for your puppy. Remember, your puppy has limited bladder control and has been confined in his crate for several hours. He simply cannot wait another two or three minutes while you brush your teeth. He needs to go right now!

Watch Your Puppy

While you are outside, watch your puppy to make sure that he empties his bladder or bowels. Be patient. It may take a few minutes. When your puppy has finished doing his business, calmly praise: "Good puppy!" or "Good potty!" Once you have seen your puppy relieve himself outdoors, you can allow him supervised play indoors. If you take your puppy outdoors and he does not relieve himself, it is important that you put him back in his crate for five or ten minutes and then repeat the aforementioned steps. (If you are not using a crate to housetrain, you will need to keep your puppy where you can watch him like a hawk for those five or ten minutes.) Do this as many times as necessary until your puppy relieves himself outdoors. Never assume that he has done his business. You must see your puppy empty his bladder or bowels. You need to repeat this routine many, many times throughout the day and again just before you go to bed at night.

Take Your Puppy Out

Going out with your puppy and actually seeing him relieve himself has many important purposes. First, if your puppy is on leash, you can take him to the same spot each time he needs to eliminate. This will help establish the habit of using a certain area of your yard. This will also help keep your puppy on track and prevent him from getting too distracted with the potpourri of sights, smells, and sounds. Puppies are naturally curious and easily distracted, but if your puppy gets too distracted and forgets to go, he will feel a sudden urge to go when you bring him back indoors and he

Training Tidbit

Choose a quality food designed for your puppy's needs and try to stick with it, provided there are no problems. Avoid changing brands from week to week, especially during the housetraining phase. Changing foods can upset your puppy's digestive tract and complicate the housetraining process. If you must change foods, do it gradually. Also, cheaper foods are not always the best buy. Premium foods are usually more digestible, often resulting in smaller stools.

is no longer distracted, and the odds are good that he will go on your carpet.

Young puppies, generally under the age of three months, find comfort and security by being close to you. If you leave while your puppy is searching for a spot to potty, he will likely run after you and forget about the task at hand. If you put him outdoors and leave him to his own devices, he's likely to spend most of his time trying to get back in the house to be with you, and, again, he will have forgotten about the task at hand. If you bring him indoors and he hasn't relieved himself outdoors—guess where he's going to potty?

In addition, by going outside with your puppy you can praise him for doing what you want, which is going to the bathroom outdoors. This will help your puppy understand exactly what you want, thereby maximizing the learning process.

By going with your puppy, you can also begin instilling a verbal cue for the command, such as "Go pee" or "Go potty." You can choose a separate word for urinating and defecating. Use the correct chosen verbal cue each time your puppy is in the process of urinating or defecating; otherwise you will teach him the wrong association. The words should be said in a calm but encouraging tone of voice. If your voice is too excitable, your puppy is likely to forget what he is doing and run to see what you are so excited about.

Where owners often run amok is by thinking that their puppy is housetrained when it is only wishful thinking on their part. Puppies between the ages of eight and ten weeks do not show signs of having to urinate. When they have to go, they go right away—often stopping

to urinate in the middle of their play session. It is unrealistic to expect your puppy to stop what he is doing and tell you when he needs to go outside. More often than not, your puppy will not realize that he has to go until he is already going. Your job for the next six months or longer, depending on the puppy, is to keep an eye on him and anticipate his bathroom needs.

Recognize the Signs

Around 10 or 12 weeks of age, a puppy will start to exhibit signs—warning signals that he is about to urinate or defecate—by circling, making crying noises, sniffing the floor, arching his back, or standing by the door. This is where owners get overconfident and think that they are home free. These are signs that your puppy is learning, not that he is housetrained. Now more than ever, you need to remain diligent and stick to the program. Teach him which signal to use when he needs to go outside by reinforcing any or all of the signals. For instance, if he stands by the door, take him outdoors. If he relieves himself, praise him. "Good potty."

Accidents Will Happen

It is in your own and your puppy's best interest to keep indoor accidents to a minimum. However, few owners escape puppy rearing without an accident here and there. If an accident does happen, consider it just that: an accident. Also, consider it your fault and resign yourself to being more observant in the future. Never scold or hit your puppy and never, ever rub his nose in the mess. Those are not housetraining techniques—they are crimes in progress. Punishing, yelling at, or otherwise berating your puppy will only confuse him and prolong the housetraining process.

Dogs live in the moment. Young or old, they do not have the mental wherewithal to

To make housetraining easier for your Bulldog, choose a spot in your yard where you want him to eliminate and take him to that same area every time.

When Accidents Mean Something Else

Accidents are bound to happen during the housetraining process. However, in some instances, inappropriate elimination may be caused by a medical issue. You should seek veterinary assistance if you observe any of the following conditions:
- change in color or odor of urine
- change in frequency of urination
- sudden change in the number of accidents
- sweet or foul odor to the puppy

associate the punishment they are receiving with an earlier act of urinating on the floor. When you scold or tell off your puppy, he will display a submissive response. Your puppy is reacting to your mannerisms and tone of voice. Many owners tend to believe that their puppy's submissive demeanor is because he understands that he did something wrong. They often say, "He knows what he did wrong. He even looks guilty!"

Scolding, punishing, or berating your puppy is counterproductive to building a solid, trusting, and mutually respectful relationship. A puppy who lives in fear of you is likely to grow into an adult dog who is anxious and frequently worried. If he potties on the floor and you scold him when you get home ten minutes or two hours later, he is likely to become anxious and perhaps fearful of being left alone, which can exacerbate urinating in the house or cause him to develop all sorts of unwanted behaviors as he grows into an adult dog. Be smart. Stick to a reliable housetraining protocol.

BASIC OBEDIENCE COMMANDS

Puppies and adult dogs learn through repetition and consistency. To provide your puppy with a basic foundation of obedience skills and manners that allow him to grow into a well-behaved adult dog and coexist with humans, you must be consistent with your expectations. As previously mentioned, Bulldogs are famously stubborn and independent, but they learn faster when the rules stay the same.

The first step in teaching any exercise is to have a clear picture in your mind of what you want to teach. If you are teaching your Bulldog to sit, have a clear picture in your mind of what a sit looks like. This may seem simple, if not downright silly, but if you cannot visualize it in your mind, how can you teach it? More important, how can your puppy learn it? Many owners have different ideas of what a *sit* or a *down* or even a *come* command represents. Some owners are happy if their dog comes on the eighth or ninth command. Others want their dog to come the first time he is called. The choice is yours.

Dogs are naturally curious and love to explore and test their boundaries. Therefore it is best to begin your dog's training in a familiar environment that has a limited amount of distractions, such as your house or yard. This is especially helpful if you are training a young puppy.

Your Bulldog must also trust you and should never feel that he must worry about how you are going to react from day to day. For instance, it is unfair to allow an eight-week-old puppy to jump on you today but scold him for doing so tomorrow when his feet are muddy. He does not have the mental ability to understand that his feet are muddy and your designer skirt is expensive. If you do not want your adult Bulldog jumping on you, you should discourage the behavior from day one when he is a young, impressionable puppy. It is equally unfair to allow your adorable puppy to get up on the furniture today but reprimand him for the same behavior when he is a 50-pound (23-kg) adult dog. It is unfair to feed your dog at the table every night, then act mortified and correct him when he begs your in-laws for tidbits of steak and potatoes. Think ahead and decide which behaviors you will or will not accept and which behaviors you can or cannot live with for the next eight to ten years.

Puppies have limited attention spans and are easily distracted by kids playing, toys lying around, birds flying overhead, a bug on the ground, cows mooing, horses whinnying, and so forth. It is unreasonable to expect a young puppy to ignore all of the distractions and focus entirely

Want to Know More?

To learn some intermediate training commands, see Chapter 9: Bulldog Training.

on you. "It's a bit like taking a child to Disneyland for the first time and expecting her to learn logarithms," says English dog trainer Annette Conn, author of the book *It's a Dog's Life*.

The *Come* Command

Come is one of the most important commands you can teach your dog. A reliable *come* command can save his life if he gets loose, runs toward traffic, chases another dog, bolts out the car door, and so forth. The goal is to teach your puppy to come to you reliably, willingly, and immediately—without hesitation—upon hearing the command while in a wide range of situations, such as at the park, in the neighbor's

Come is a must-know command for every dog.

yard, at a friend's house, in an emergency, or any time he gets loose. In your dog's mind, the word come should never mean "Okay, I hear you. I'll be there as soon as I finish chasing this bug." You want your dog to understand that when you say "Come!" it means "Stop what you are doing and run back to me as fast as you can—right now." In the beginning, you teach this behavior with fun games and tasty rewards. Ideally, as he grows into an adult dog, you want him to come to you because he wants to be with you—not just because you have a cookie. This is why it is so important to connect with him mentally—to establish a strong human/canine bond.

Never use the come command for anything your Bulldog might dislike or to end playtime. When you call your puppy, do something silly with him when he gets to you, such as a quick game of tug or a fun trick, or reward him with a tasty tidbit and then let him run off and play again. Owners often make the mistake of calling their puppy only when it is time to go in his kennel or to put his leash on and go home. In these situations, your puppy will quickly learn that come means the end of his freedom, and he is likely to avoid you the next time he is called.

How to Teach It

When teaching the come command, call your puppy only when you are absolutely certain that he will respond. For example, if you call your puppy when he is excited about greeting another dog, when a family member has just come to visit, or when he is eating his dinner, he will be too excited and distracted to respond to your command, and you will inadvertently be teaching him to ignore you. In the early stages, when your puppy is learning the come command, wait until the excitement has subsided and then call him to you. If you must

have your puppy during these times, it is better to go and get him rather than call him to you.

Equally important, take advantage of opportunities where you can set him up to succeed by calling him back to you when he would be coming to you anyway, such as when you have just arrived home and he is running toward you, or when you have his dinner or a tasty tidbit. Let him know how clever he is when he gets to you. "What a good come!"

A puppy who views come as a fun game is more likely to develop a reliable response to the command. If this behavior continues throughout his puppyhood, and you remain excited and enthusiastic each and every time he comes to you, you will have a strong and positive response to the behavior as he grows and matures into an adult dog.

You can use an informal game like "Find me!" to begin teaching come in a positive, fun, and exciting manner. This game capitalizes on a dog's natural chase instinct and is an excellent game for instilling the come command in young puppies.

1. Start with a pocketful of tasty tidbits.
2. Rev your puppy up by showing him a yummy treat and then toss the treat down the hallway or across the living room.
3. As your puppy runs for the treat, you run in the opposite direction and hide behind a chair or door as you say his name enthusiastically.
4. When your puppy finds you, make a big fuss. Get on the floor, roll around, and lavish a potpourri of kisses and praise on him. "Good come!" or "You found me!"
5. Repeat the game several times throughout the day, but not so many times that your dog becomes bored.

You can also play this game outdoors. Be sure to play in a fenced area to protect your dog from harm or prevent him from running off.

When you are in your yard with your dog and he stops to sniff the grass or explore a bug—duck behind a tree or bush, clap your hands, and say his name in an exciting tone of voice.

When your dog gets to you, greet him with plenty of hugs, kisses, and praise, "Good come!" or "Good boy!" It is not necessary for your dog to sit before he gets a treat. If you insist on your puppy's sitting first, you will not be rewarding the most important part of the exercise, which is coming to you.

The *Down* Command

Down is another important command. Your Bulldog may need to lie down on the vet's exam table, while you brush or scratch his tummy or check his coat for stickers, or when you want to massage his sore muscles. As your puppy matures and thoroughly understands the *down* command, use it when you are watching television, preparing dinner, reading quietly, or when friends come to visit and you do not want your dog directly involved in what you are doing at that moment.

How to Teach It

Teaching the *down* command can be a bit more challenging than the *sit* because it is considered a submissive position for some dogs. If your puppy has an independent personality, this exercise will take a bit more patience and persistence on your part. Do not give up! Remember, puppies learn through repetition and consistency.

1. Begin by kneeling on the floor so that you are at eye level with your puppy.
2. With your puppy standing in front of you, hold a tasty tidbit of food in one hand.
3. Let your puppy sniff the treat. Move the treat toward the floor between his front feet.
4. When done correctly, your puppy will plant his front feet and fold his body into the *down* position as he follows the treat to the ground.
5. When his elbows and tummy are on the ground, give the *down* command.
6. While your puppy is in the *down* position, reward him with the treat and calmly praise him: "Good down."
7. Release your puppy with a release word, such as "free" or "okay," and repeat the exercise three or four times in succession, three or four times a day.

The *Sit* Command

Think of the many situations where your Bulldog will need to know how to sit—at the vet's office, waiting to be fed, waiting to cross the street, or waiting while you open any door.

To reinforce training, always acknowledge your puppy for doing what you've asked with praise, treats, a big hug, or enthusiastic pats on his chest.

He will need to sit when you put his collar on or take it off, when you want to check his coat for stickers or burs, or when you want to brush him or trim his nails. The *sit* command increases his vocabulary and instills order in both your lives.

How to Teach It

Teaching the *sit* command is relatively simple.

1. Begin with your puppy on leash. This is especially helpful if your dog, like most other puppies, has his own agenda, tends to wander off, or is easily distracted.
2. Start with your leash in one hand, a tasty tidbit in the other hand, and your puppy standing in front of you. (Hold the tidbit firmly between your thumb and index finger so that your dog cannot get it until he is in the correct position.)
3. Show your puppy the tidbit by holding it close to and slightly above his nose.
4. As he raises his nose to take the food, slowly move the treat in a slightly upward and backward direction toward his tail, keeping it directly above his nose. (If your puppy jumps up or brings his front feet off the ground, the treat is too high. If he walks backward, the treat is too far back or too low.)
5. At this point, your puppy's hips should automatically sink toward the ground. As they do, give the *sit* command. While your puppy is sitting, praise him with "Good sit!" and reward him with the tidbit. (Give the *sit* command as your puppy's rear end hits the ground. Saying it too soon will teach the wrong association.)
6. Release your puppy with a release word, such as "free" or "okay," play with him for a few seconds, and repeat the exercise three or four times in succession, three or four times a day.

Leash Training

Your puppy should never associate his leash and collar with a barrage of corrections or nagging. He should view walking on leash as something fun that he does with his owner.

How to Teach It

To begin:

1. Always teach this exercise on a buckle collar, never a choke chain.
2. Attach a leash (or thin long line) to his collar and allow him to drag it around. Don't worry if he picks it up and tries to carry it around. In fact, put a command to the behavior. "Have you got your leash?" eventually becomes "Get your leash!"
3. When your puppy is happily dragging the leash, pick it up and start walking forward, encouraging your puppy to walk close to your left side by talking sweetly to him and luring him with a tasty tidbit from your left hand. (This is easier if the leash is in your right hand.)
4. When you have walked a few steps with your dog on your left side, reward him with the tidbit of food. Remember to verbally

praise and offer the food reward when he is close beside your left leg. This will encourage him to remain in position.

5. Once your puppy is comfortable walking beside you, you can begin teaching a more formal "walk nicely on leash."

To help facilitate the process and keep the "game" fun, keep these simple tips in mind:

1. Only reward sensible walking. If your puppy is jumping and lunging for the food, hold the food lower and in front of his nose, but do not give it to him until he takes two or three steps without jumping.

2. If your puppy is not interested in following you, slow down and be more obvious with the lure. You may need to get a tastier lure, such as boiled chicken, hot dog, liver, or leftover steak.

3. If your puppy freezes on the spot and won't move, do not drag him around or force the issue. Try this: Drop the leash and run away while clapping your hands. Very young puppies like to follow their owners. Most likely, he will see you running away and try to catch you. When he does, praise him for catching you. "Good boy!" Nonchalantly pick up the leash, start walking, and encourage him to walk close to your left side by luring him with a treat and talking sweetly to him. Take two or three steps and reward your dog.

PUPPY KINDERGARTEN

If your Bulldog is between two and five months of age, a puppy kindergarten class is an ideal environment for exposing and socializing him to the many things he will encounter in his adult life. Puppy classes will help your Bulldog continue to expand on his knowledge of canine communication and the social skills that he learned from his canine mother and while interacting with his littermates. A puppy class allows him to continue learning to communicate and interact with other dogs in a low-risk and stress-free environment.

Puppy classes should not be a free-for-all, where puppies play on their own while their owners socialize on the sidelines. A well-structured puppy class will begin teaching basic obedience skills, including fun puppy *recall* games, *sit*, *down*, and name recognition. You will learn how to read canine body language, how to train your puppy, and how to recognize problems early on before they become annoying ingrained habits that are difficult to break.

If you want your Bulldog to go anywhere with you, he'll have to learn to walk politely on leash.

PART II

ADULTHOOD

CHAPTER 5

FINDING YOUR BULLDOG ADULT

There is no denying that puppies are cute and irresistible, but there is a lot to be said for acquiring an adult Bulldog. Generally speaking, Bulldogs are considered to be physically mature adults around 12 to 18 months of age. However, some dogs are not mentally mature until 24 or 36 months of age. Acquiring an adult dog makes sense for a number of reasons—especially for the novice or first-time owner—because an adult dog's personality is already developed. What you see is what you get. All of his good (and bad) habits are already in place. With close observation, interaction, and help from a knowledgeable dog person, you should be able to determine the quality of his disposition and whether he will suit your personality and life. Is he timid? Aggressive? Nervous? Happy? Spoiled rotten? Does he get along with other animals? How is he with children?

THE ADVANTAGES

Advantages to acquiring an adult Bulldog include:

- Adult dogs generally do not need 24-hour supervision, as do puppies.
- Adult dogs do not require as much time and energy.

By the Numbers

Veterinarians often estimate a dog's age by the wear and tear on his teeth. While this can provide a reasonable guesstimate, it isn't 100 percent accurate because the condition of a dog's teeth can be influenced by the size and breed of the dog, his diet, and his chewing habits.

- Some adult dogs are already crate trained, housetrained, socialized, and obedience trained.
- Most adult dogs are beyond the chewing stage (although older dogs often chew as a result of boredom or anxiety).
- Rescued dogs appear to have a profound sense of appreciation and a deeper bond with their owners. (While there is no scientific data to support this theory, many experts claim that it's true.)

Adult dogs do not require as much time and energy as puppies do.

THE DISADVANTAGES

Despite all of the positive reasons for acquiring an adult Bulldog, doing so also comes with a few disadvantages including:

- Some adult dogs have social, emotional, medical, and behavioral issues, such as dog-to-dog aggression issues, fear phobias, or trust issues.
- They may lack socialization and obedience training, which can be the primary cause or exacerbation of the abovementioned issues.
- They may not be suitable for placement with kids or other animals.
- Adult dogs with behavioral or medical issues may require significant amounts of your time, energy, and financial resources.

- Old dogs can learn new tricks, but many ingrained behaviors are managed, not cured.

MALE OR FEMALE?

Choosing between a male and a female usually comes down to personal preference. Some people are attached to the strength and masculinity of a male dog. Others love the femininity and light refinement of a female. Generally speaking, females tend to mature physically a bit earlier than do males. As a result, females might be more serious or emotionally more mature at a younger age. However, both males and females can make sweet, loving companions, and there are pros and cons to both sexes. If you already

Want to Know More?

If you have your heart set on a puppy, see Chapter 2: Finding and Prepping for Your Bulldog Puppy for some pointers on how to go about it.

own a dog—regardless of the breed—and are thinking of adding a Bulldog, consider a dog of the opposite sex who is (or will be) spayed or neutered. If, for example, you already have a male dog, consider a female and vice versa. Dogs of the opposite sex are less likely to create chaos and turmoil in terms of fighting and squabbling, and some females—despite your best intentions—simply will not live happily together.

When it comes to choosing an adult Bulldog, knowledgeable breeders and experienced dog people know the capabilities of both sexes and are your best bet when choosing a dog who suits your temperament and lifestyle.

WHERE TO FIND AN ADULT BULLDOG

An older Bulldog is well worth your consideration if you are looking for a companion. Adult dogs become available

Some adult dogs are already housetrained, socialized, and obedience trained.

Rescuing an adult Bulldog is a good option for many prospective owners.

Multi-Dog Tip

Dog training is about compromise. Each dog is an individual, and sometimes you don't always get the behaviors you want. Rather than lumping all of your dogs into the same category, focus on what each of your dogs does right. Focus on the positive aspect of each dog. Focus on their individual strengths and what behaviors you can improve for each one. Enjoy each of your dogs for who they are individually. Let them be themselves rather than trying to make them into something they are not and never will be.

for a number of reasons, but finding the perfect one may take some time and a bit of detective work.

Breeders

Many reputable breeders have one- or two-year-old show prospects who did not pan out for a variety of reasons but would make exceptional pets in the right home. Breeders often have limited space, and they may have retired show dogs they need to place. Older dogs are often returned to breeders because the owner moved or is no longer able to keep them. Many of these dogs are well bred and have been well cared for, yet for one reason or another they need to be placed in a good home. Oftentimes breeders are looking to place these dogs in a good home for a reasonable cost.

Training Tidbit

If you are unsure of your adopted dog's training, it is always safe and wise to assume that he has no training, and begin his training as if he were a puppy. That said, occasionally, due to the stress and confusion of being surrendered to a shelter, a trained Bulldog may temporarily forget previously learned obedience commands, as well as his housetraining. In these instances, never scold or reprimand a Bulldog. Simply start from step one, as if he had no training whatsoever. Once established and confident in their new home, most Bulldogs remember their previous training.

Newspaper Ads

If you see a Bulldog advertised "Free to Good Home" in the local papers, it's usually code for "The dog has bad habits, he's driving me crazy, and I don't want him anymore." These dogs are often lacking in direction, management, and love and have been allowed to develop annoying habits. In the right hands, they can make wonderful pets, but go into it with your eyes wide open.

Also, adult dogs offered for sale at reduced prices, for a "relocation" fee, or accompanied by a request for last-minute shipping fees should be considered red flags. Dognapping has become a problem in many areas of the country, and stolen Bulldogs, as well as other breeds, are often sold to unsuspecting people via newspaper ads.

Rescue Organizations

Rescuing an adult Bulldog is a good option for many prospective owners. Bulldog rescue volunteers work tirelessly to educate the public, as well as rehabilitate and place purebred Bulldogs in loving, permanent homes.

Many wonderful and loving Bulldogs are surrendered to rescue organizations because their owners did not understand the breed or the special attention and requirements that come with flat faces and wrinkles. Many Bulldogs are given up or abandoned after they outgrow the cute puppy stage. Some Bulldogs in rescue have been abused or mishandled. Others have been accidentally lost or voluntarily relinquished to animal shelters or rescue groups by their owners or their owners' families because of personal illness, death, or other changes in circumstances.

Rescuers carefully evaluate the Bulldogs in their care via temperament testing. They then place the Bulldogs in experienced foster homes where they receive veterinary attention, obedience training, socialization, grooming, and lots of love until they can be placed in a permanent home.

For additional information, contact the Bulldog Club of America Rescue Network at (BCARN) www.rescuebulldogs.org.

Shelters

Bulldogs of all ages find their way into humane societies for a number of reasons. Most adult dogs surrendered to shelters tend to be between one and two years of age. However,

Don't Buy Stolen Bulldogs

Dognapping is a problem in many areas of the country. Bulldogs, as well as other breeds, are stolen and sold to unsuspecting pet owners. Puppies or young Bulldogs are often the target, which makes it doubly important to not leave your puppy unattended in the yard. To protect your dog, as well as ensure that you are not buying a stolen Bulldog, the American Kennel Club (AKC) recommends the following tips:

- Don't buy dogs from the Internet, flea markets, or roadside vans. There is no way to verify where an animal purchased from any of these outlets came from. Websites and online classifieds are easily falsified, and with roadside or flea market purchases, not only do you not know the pet's origin but you will never be able to find or identify the seller in case of a problem.
- Newspaper ads may be suspect as well. Reputable breeders and responsible dog lovers looking to sell or rehome their Bulldog will be able to provide background information and identification on their pet, such as a microchip, AKC or other registration paperwork, veterinary receipts, and so forth.
- Seek out reputable breeders or rescue groups.
- Demand proper papers on the puppy or adult dog. Ask for the AKC Litter Registration Number and contact AKC customer service to verify the registration authenticity of the dog.

Shelter personnel screen Bulldogs for temperament and placement before they become eligible for adoption.

it's not unusual for older Bulldogs, say five, six, or seven years old, to end up in an animal shelter. By no means are they genetically or behaviorally inferior. Granted, some may have medical or behavioral issues, but it's not unusual for expensive, well-bred Bulldogs to end up in a shelter.

Many Bulldogs are surrendered or abandoned by their owners. Others living in abusive conditions are confiscated by animal control officers and turned over to shelters.

Lost or stray Bulldogs are often taken to a shelter by caring and compassionate dog lovers. Shelter personnel screen Bulldogs for temperament and placement before they become eligible for adoption. Many shelter dogs facing euthanasia are rescued by Bulldog rescue organization volunteers and placed in foster homes for further adoption. Shelter dogs often can and do make excellent companions, provided they are given proper care and training.

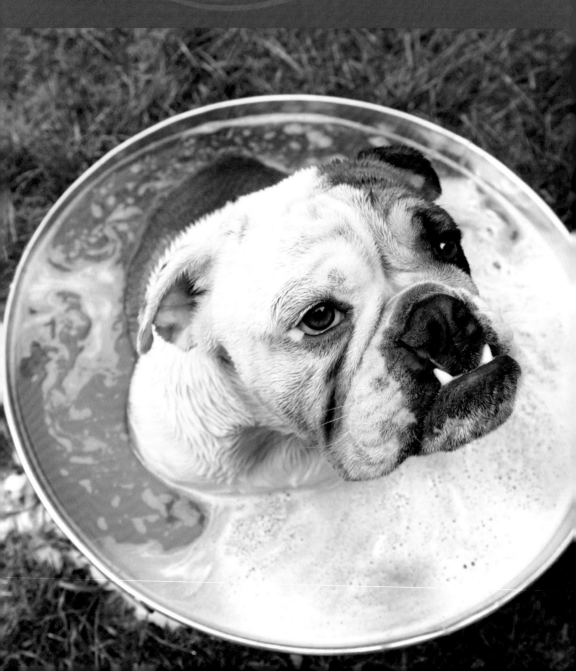

CHAPTER 6

BULLDOG GROOMING NEEDS

Grooming goes beyond keeping your Bulldog's coat and skin in tip-top condition. Grooming is a complex social behavior of many animals. Studies indicate that grooming can provide environmental enrichment for dogs as well as other domestic pets. Dogs often groom themselves by licking, rolling, scratching, and shaking debris from their coats. They occasionally groom each other by licking a sibling's ears or eyes. Grooming also builds a bond between you and your dog that enriches the human/canine relationship.

Grooming also allows you to check his entire body for lumps, bumps, cuts, rashes, dry skin, fleas, ticks, stickers, and the like. You can check his feet for cuts, torn pads, and broken nails and examine his mouth for signs of trouble, including tartar, broken teeth, and discolored gums.

Most Bulldogs love to be groomed, making this necessary chore a great way to spend quality time with your dog. Equally important, regular grooming allows you to quickly recognize when something is amiss.

THE BULLDOG'S COAT

Someone once said, "Give me a square dog with a good coat, and in three hours I'll carve you out a top Kerry" (meaning the well-coated Kerry Blue Terrier). A Bulldog's coat is straight, short, and flat, which means that it isn't terribly difficult to groom, but it also means that no amount of grooming will hide his structural faults in the breed ring. Despite his lack of "coat," the breed still requires regular grooming to stimulate the natural oils and keep the skin from becoming diseased. For the companion Bulldog, as opposed to the show dog, grooming is a relatively easy process that starts with a good brushing.

BRUSHING

Breeders, owners, and handlers have their own routine, established habits, idiosyncrasies, and favorite products and equipment when it comes to grooming. You too will establish your own personal preferences as you develop your own grooming knowledge.

Despite their short coats, Bulldogs still shed, which is a natural process in which strands of hair die, fall out (shed), and are replaced by new hairs. Brushing helps whisk away those dead hairs, promotes and distributes natural oils, and brings out the shine and natural luster in a dog's coat.

For most Bulldogs, a soft bristle brush, such as a boar-bristle brush or a hound mitt is usually sufficient for whisking away pieces of debris, dust, dirt, and dead hair. A curry comb, which has stubby rubber nubs, is also ideal for loosening and removing dead hair. Natural bristle brushes, unlike plastic, nylon, and wire bristles, can lead to better distribution of natural oils.

How to Brush

To brush your Bulldog properly, follow these quick tips:

1. Start with your dog standing on a grooming table or suitable surface. This position will allow you to reach all parts of his body, including his tummy, inner legs, and chest. If you don't plan to show your dog or if he prefers sitting or lying on the table, that's okay too.

2. Before brushing, spritz the coat with a coat dressing, coat conditioner diluted with water, or plain water. This will protect the hair and control static as you brush.

3. Start with a curry comb or an appropriate hound mitt to remove loose and clumped hair. Begin at your dog's head, brushing in long strokes toward the tail and then down the sides and legs. Some experts

suggest backward brushing—brushing against the direction of hair growth—but some dogs find the process uncomfortable and annoying. Incorrect brushing or poor grooming equipment can damage a dog's coat and skin, causing irritation and making the entire process unpleasant.

4. Next, repeat the abovementioned steps using a soft bristle brush to brush away loose hair and debris.

5. Follow with a rubdown using a polishing or chamois cloth, or a grooming/glossing glove.

6. Finish the coat and add shine by applying a small amount of a specially designed coat dressing or coat oil.

Once-a-week brushings are usually sufficient, but a five-minute once-a-day once-over with a soft bristle brush, grooming glove, or curry comb is ideal to keep your Bulldog's coat brilliant and gorgeous.

While brushing, pay particular attention to the condition of his coat and skin. A Bulldog's coat is a reflection of his health. A healthy coat begins on the inside with proper nutrition. Is the coat healthy? Or is it dull, brittle, and lackluster? Is the skin dry and flaky? Does it smell bad or have that unmistakable doggy odor? Do you see bare spots or hot spots (inflamed skin)? Any of these conditions could be a sign of inadequate grooming, illness (including allergies), parasitic infestation, or an inadequate diet. When in doubt, a veterinarian can diagnosis any problems and recommend suitable treatments.

BATHING

How often your Bulldog requires bathing depends on where you live, how much time he spends outside, and how dirty he gets. Like kids, some Bulldogs have a knack for getting dirtier than others. Bulldogs who are being

The Bulldog's coat is straight, short, and flat, which means that it's not too difficult to groom.

exhibited or campaigned in the breed ring will require bathing more than a companion pet. The same goes for obedience and agility Bulldogs. A Bulldog should be cleaned and groomed before any competition.

Most Bulldogs are amenable to baths. Some are not. If yours is not, condition him slowly with plenty of verbal praise and yummy rewards to accept the necessary chore.

In hot climates, you may be able to bathe your dog outdoors with a garden hose, provided the water is not too cold. Otherwise, a rubber mat on the bottom of a bathtub, utility sink, or shower stall will provide secure footing and prevent him from slipping. If possible, lift him in and out of the tub, as Bulldogs slip easily and your dog may injure himself. Consider investing in a screen that fits over the drain opening, which will help keep your dog's hair from clogging your drain.

Unless your dog has a specific skin condition, such as dry, flaky, itchy skin, choose a good-quality shampoo and conditioner designed specifically for dogs—something nontoxic and shampoo-based rather than detergent-based so as not to strip the hair of its natural oils. Do not use human shampoos, because the pH balance is different for dogs. Many shampoos and conditioning products are available, from all-purpose to medicating to herbal to color enhancing, so do not be shy about asking for help when choosing shampoos and conditioners.

Gather all of your supplies together before you start. You never want to leave your Bulldog unattended in a tub while you search for supplies. Bulldogs can easily drown in a small amount of water. Also, they can easily injure themselves trying to "escape" out of the tub.

How to Bathe

Start by placing large cotton balls in the ears to prevent water and soap from leaking into the ear canal. Some dogs object and will vigorously shake their heads, dislodging the cotton. If this is the case and your dog persists in shaking, forget the cotton and simply be careful not to get water into his ears, and avoid using soap around his ears too.

1. Saturate your dog's coat with warm water. Be sure to keep an eye on the water temperature. If it's too hot, it can burn his skin. If it's too cold, he may get chilled. Because of the Bulldog's facial features, water can trickle down and get into his

How often your Bulldog requires bathing depends on where you live, how much time he spends outdoors, and how dirty he gets.

nose, so take care not to get water in there.

2. Apply a dab or two of shampoo, working it into his coat with your fingers or a rubber massage tool designed specifically for dogs. Scrub from head to toe, being careful to avoid the eye area. Don't overlook his belly, the inside of his hind legs, under his arms, and behind his ears. Pay special attention to his wrinkles and tail pocket.

3. To clean around his eyes, wipe the area with a damp cloth. If you prefer, use a small dab of tearless shampoo to gently wash around the head and eye area. Even though it's tearless, avoid getting any in your dog's eyes.

4. Rinse his entire body thoroughly with tepid or lukewarm water until the water runs clear. Pay special attention to his wrinkles—

making sure that you rinse away all of the shampoo. Rinsing is the most important part because residual shampoo can irritate the skin as well as leave a dull film on the coat. If necessary, shampoo and rinse again to be sure that your Bulldog is squeaky clean.

5. If you are using a coat conditioner or skin moisturizer, follow the directions carefully.

6. If possible, let your Bulldog shake off any extra water, then towel dry him thoroughly and remove the cotton balls from his ears.

If the weather is warm enough, allow your Bulldog to air dry. Or use a blow dryer specifically designed for dogs. (Most human dryers are too hot for dogs. If you go the blower route, use the lowest possible setting. Bulldogs have sensitive skin, and you can easily burn them with a dryer that is too hot.) Be sure to dry all of his wrinkles, as wet wrinkles can lead to infection. Also, avoid cage drying, which involves putting your Bulldog in a crate with a dryer blowing into the crate. Bulldogs can overheat in cage-drying situations.

EAR CARE

The key to preventing ear problems is to keep the ears clean and to know the difference between a clean-smelling ear and a problematic ear. A healthy ear should have a clean, healthy doggy smell—somewhat resembling the smell of beeswax. Honey-colored wax in the ear is normal, but a crusty dark substance may indicate problems, such as ear mites.

How to Care for the Ears

An infected ear has an unmistakably foul odor. Ear infections are serious and should never be ignored or taken lightly. If your Bulldog's ears have a discharge or smell bad; or if the canals look abnormal, red, or inflamed; or if your dog is showing signs of discomfort, such as depression or irritability, scratching or rubbing his ears or head, shaking his head or tilting it to one side—these are signs of a problem. Seek veterinary attention right away. An ear infection left untreated can cause permanent damage to a dog's hearing.

To prevent problems, examine your Bulldog's ears regularly for wax, ear mites, and other irritations. To clean your dog's ears, follow these quick steps:

1. Place a few drops of ear-cleaning product specifically designed for dogs into the ear canal, and gently massage the base of the ear for about 20 seconds. This helps soften and loosen the debris.

2. Let your dog have a good head shake to

The key to preventing ear problems is to keep the ears clean.

eject the cleaning solution and debris from the ear canal.

3. Apply some ear-cleaning solution onto a clean cotton or gauze pad or cotton ball. Gently wipe the inside leather (ear flap), and the part of the ear canal that you can see.

Remember the old adage "Never stick anything smaller than your elbow in your ear"? The same concept applies to dogs. Never stick cotton applicator swabs or pointed objects into a dog's ear canal because this can pack the debris more deeply rather than remove it. More important, you risk injuring the eardrum should you probe too deeply.

EYE CARE

Healthy dog eyes are moist and clear. Any redness or swelling or discharge may be indications of an eye infection. Occasionally, dust and dirt particles cause eye irritation, which can lead to conjunctivitis—an inflammation or infection of the mucous membrane (conjuctiva) that surrounds the eyelid and eyeball. Conjunctivitis can occur unilaterally (in one eye) or bilaterally (in both eyes). Conjunctivitis can also be caused by a viral infection such as canine distemper or by bacterial eye infection, disorders of the tear ducts, eyelid infections, or corneal diseases.

How to Care for the Eyes

To properly care for your dog's eyes:

1. Keep eyes clear of mucus at all times.
2. Use a sterile eye wash and/or eye wipes to keep the eye area clean. Several eye solutions specifically for dogs are available at most pet stores.
3. To rinse out your dog's eye (or eyes), carefully squirt a mild eye solution specifically for dogs into the eyeball area.

TEARSTAINS

Tear staining is a common problem with some Bulldogs. Tears are bactericidal, meaning that they kill the bacteria that can cause eye infections. Normally, tears are constantly produced and drain through small ducts in the eyelids. The brownish stain is due to tears spilling out over the lid, lying on the surrounding hair, and mixing with facial bacteria. In pronounced cases, a crust forms in the corner of the eye and on top of the skin, which can, in some instances, cause small ulcers. Bacteria grow in the moist, tearstained fur around the eye. Bacteria can then travel into the eye, causing eye infections.

Yeast infections can also exacerbate the problem. Yeast live normally on your dog's skin. When conditions change and become favorable to the proliferation of yeast—such as your Bulldog's damp, wrinkled face—he can get a canine yeast infection, including the "red yeast," which looks and smells awful.

Healthy Bulldog eyes are moist and clear, with no redness, swelling, or discharge.

Something as simple as hair acting like a wick, drawing the tears out of the eye, can cause an overflow of tears. More serious causes include an irritant, such as dust particles, or an allergy, or an abnormal eyelid or eyelash that turns inward and rubs against the surface of the eye. Inflammation or ulcers of the eye or inflammation of the duct or a blocked tear duct can also cause tear overflow.

These conditions are painful and need to be examined by your veterinarian. Oral antibiotics may be prescribed, and in some instances tear duct surgery may be necessary.

How to Eliminate Tearstains

Reddish-brown tear stains are most noticeable on dogs with light-colored coats and heavy wrinkles. They present a real grooming challenge. Commercial products are available, or you can try making your own:

1. Mix hydrogen peroxide and cornstarch to form a paste.
2. Apply carefully to the stain (being careful to avoid the eye).
3. Let the area dry, and then brush off.
4. Apply daily. Stains should lighten or disappear within several weeks.

NAIL TRIMMING

Nail care is a necessary part of dog ownership. Few Bulldogs, especially those who spend the majority of their time indoors or on grass when outdoors, will wear down their nails naturally. Ideally, a dog's nails should not touch the ground. This allows a dog to stand squarely and compactly on the pads of his feet. Nails that are too long interfere with a dog's gait—making walking awkward and painful. Long nails can be broken, torn off, or snagged and can scratch furniture, hardwood floors, and skin. Torn or broken nails can cause a Bulldog a great deal of pain and discomfort, and they may become infected, which can require veterinary attention to remove the nail completely.

As with other aspects of grooming, introduce your Bulldog to the practice of nail care at a young age. With any luck, the breeder will have started nail clipping as part of the socialization process. In the early stages, you may need

Grinding the Nails

Rather than clipping the nails, some owners opt to grind them with a professional nail grinder. Others use a combination of clippers, grinders, and files. A grinder has a motor-driven abrasive round drum. Corded or battery-operated, grinders grind and file away the unwanted nail. A grinder eliminates the possibility of nipping the quick. But grinders are not without risk. The abrasive tip—similar to sandpaper—spins at a high speed. If used incorrectly, a grinder can apply too much pressure or file too close to the quick, causing the dog a good deal of discomfort. These types of instruments make whirling noises, and the vibration on the dog's nails can take some getting used to. If started at a young age, many Bulldogs will accept it as part of the grooming process, especially when it's coupled with plenty of verbal praise and yummy treats. Furthermore, many dogs who hate their nails clipped don't mind a grinder, and vice versa. Available at most pet-supply stores and online vendors, they aren't cheap, but they are handy.

someone to hold your Bulldog. But once you get used to it, trimming your dog's nails is no more difficult than trimming your own. When in doubt, ask a veterinarian, groomer, or breeder to show you how to do it properly. Or have a professional trim them regularly, which can mean once a week or once a month or somewhere in between, depending on the dog.

How to Care for the Nails

Dogs have a blood vessel—known as the "quick"—that travels approximately three-quarters of the way through the nail. Your Bulldog may have white or black nails or a combination. Black nails can make it difficult to differentiate between the quick and the hook—the dead section of nail that extends beyond the quick. Clipping a dog's nails too short can cut the quick and cause bleeding. However, learning how to do it properly, using the correct equipment, and having a dog who accepts having his feet handled will go a long way toward reducing the odds of inadvertently nipping the quick.

Nails can be trimmed with one of several varieties of nail trimmers or grinders. A nail file can be used to smooth the rough edges of the nail. Rear nails are shorter and require less trimming than those on the front feet.

When doing the front feet, it's helpful to have the dog sitting. For the rear feet, have the dog standing. (If all else fails and it's easier to trim the nails with your dog lying down, that's okay too.)

Bulldogs who don't spend a lot of time outdoors wearing down their nails naturally will need to have them trimmed.

1. Lift and hold one foot about 4 to 6 inches (10 to 15 cm) or so off the ground so that you can see the nail clearly.
2. Hold the paw firmly but without squeezing. Press lightly enough to separate the toes.
3. Begin by trimming off the hook of the nail. Trimming within approximately 2 millimeters of the quick will reduce the chance of cutting into the quick. Cut dark nails in several small cuts to avoid nipping the quick. If necessary, then take off the remaining dead nail in smaller bits.
4. File the nails to remove any rough or ragged edges (optional).

If you happen to nip the quick, it will bleed like crazy. Use a bit of styptic powder or pencil containing silver nitrate (available at pet-supply and drug stores), or even corn starch, to stop the bleeding. Simply coat the end of the nail generously with styptic powder and keep the paw elevated until the bleeding stops.

DENTAL CARE

The importance of high-quality dental hygiene cannot be overstated. If left unattended, your Bulldog can develop periodontal disease, a progressive disease that can, in advanced cases, lead to decayed gums, infection, and liver,

kidney, and heart damage. And like humans, dogs do experience painful toothaches, although some dogs may not physically exhibit signs of pain or the signs may be subtle and therefore overlooked by some owners.

Dental problems in dogs begin the same way they do in humans—with plaque. Plaque is a mixture of salivary glycoproteins—a colorless, translucent adhesive fluid—and it is the major culprit in periodontal disease. Plaque begins with the accumulation of food particles and bacteria along the gum line. Germs present in plaque attack the gums, bone, and ligaments that support the teeth, but routine home care can help remove this plaque. Left untreated, minerals and saliva combine with the plaque and harden into a substance called tartar, or calculus. As tartar accumulates, it starts irritating your dog's gums and causes an inflamed condition called gingivitis, which is easily identifiable by red, inflamed gums.

In the early stages, periodontal disease is generally reversible provided your Bulldog receives veterinary attention along with sufficient and regular brushings at home. Otherwise, the process continues to erode the tissues and bones that support the teeth, which can lead to pain and tooth loss. If the tartar is not removed, the cycle continues to repeat itself, encouraging even more bacterial growth. The tartar builds up under the gums and causes the gums to separate from the teeth; this causes even larger pockets in which more debris can collect.

Brushing your Bulldog's teeth on a regular basis will remove plaque but not tartar. If your dog already has a tartar buildup, he will need to see a veterinarian to have it removed and his teeth inspected, cleaned, and polished. In most advanced stages, damage from periodontal disease is considered irreversible because bacterial infection destroys a dog's gums, teeth, and bones. Treatment, which can include difficult and extensive surgeries, will not reverse the damage, but it will help prevent further progression, additional pain, and discomfort to your Bulldog, and will guard against bacteria entering the bloodstream, causing secondary infections that can damage his heart, liver, and kidneys.

In addition to home care, a good dental hygiene program includes an annual veterinary examination to check for potential problems, such as plaque and tartar buildup, gingivitis, periodontal disease, and fractured or abscessed teeth. A professional dental cleaning, also known as prophylaxis or prophy, may be recommended. While the dog is anesthetized, his mouth is flushed with a solution to kill bacteria, the teeth are cleaned to remove any tartar and then polished, inspected, and flushed again with an antibacterial solution, and fluoride is applied. In most cases, x-rays will also be taken. Fractured teeth may require reconstructive surgery, not unlike that which people receive, such as root canals and crowns. Because Bulldogs have increased risks when it comes to anesthesia, your veterinarian is the best person with whom to discuss options and alternatives.

How to Brush the Teeth

Preventing periodontal disease means keeping your Bulldog's teeth clean. The process is relatively simple and requires nothing more

Good oral hygiene is necessary to your dog's overall health.

than a small number of fairly inexpensive supplies and a few minutes of your time. You will need a pet toothbrush, gauze for wrapping around a finger, or a finger toothbrush, which simply slides over your finger, and some toothpaste designed specifically for dogs. If you decide to use a pet toothbrush, be sure to get one specially designed for a Bulldog's mouth. Do not use human toothpaste. It is not designed for dogs and can upset their stomach. Most canine toothpastes are formulated with poultry or malt-flavored enhancers for easier acceptance.

As with other aspects of grooming, it is much easier to begin introducing oral hygiene to a puppy, but it is never too late to begin—just progress slowly and at a pace suitable for your Bulldog.

1. Start by using your finger to gently massage your dog's gums.
2. Put a small dab of doggy toothpaste on your index finger and let your dog lick it. Praise him for being brave.
3. Apply another dab on your finger, gently lift up his lips and massage his gums. Ideally, it is best to massage in a circular motion, but in the beginning you may need to be satisfied with simply getting your finger into your dog's mouth.

Remember to keep a positive attitude, praising and reassuring your Bulldog throughout the process. It's helpful if you avoid wrestling with your dog or restraining him too tightly. This will only hamper the process and

Want to Know More?

For more information on how sensitive Bulldogs are to anesthesia, see Chapter 3: Care of Your Bulldog Puppy.

By the Numbers

It is estimated that 80 percent of dogs over the age of three years have some stage of periodontal disease.

make him resistant to the necessary routine. Depending on your dog, it may take a few days or a few weeks for him to accept your fiddling about in his mouth. With any luck, he will eventually come to look forward to the routine. That is the long-term goal. It is possible that he may never come to enjoy it, but it is important that he learns to accept it.

Once your dog is comfortable with this process, follow these quick steps:

1. Let your dog lick some toothpaste off the toothbrush or gauze pad; again, praise him for being brave. This will help accustom him to the texture of the brush or gauze while building his confidence.
2. As before, lift the lips and expose the teeth. Most owners find it easiest to start with the canine teeth—the large ones in the front of the mouth. They are the easiest to reach, and you should be able to brush them with little interference or objection from your dog.
3. Once your dog is accustomed to having you brush a few teeth, progress to a few more, and then a few more until you have brushed all 42 teeth (or 28 teeth, if you have a puppy).

Ideally, you should brush your Bulldog's teeth on a daily basis. Like anything else, the hardest part is getting started. Once you accustom your dog to having his teeth brushed, incorporating the practice into your

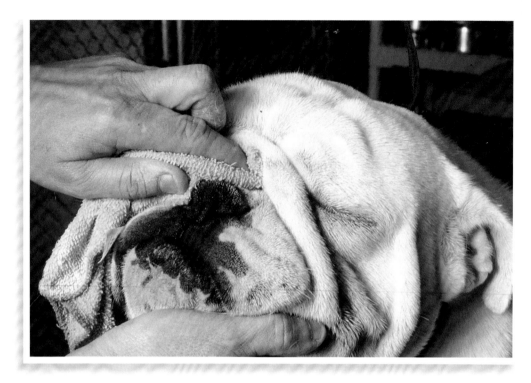

A Bulldog's wrinkle folds are prone to irritation and infection and need to be kept clean and dry.

daily schedule is no more difficult or time consuming than brushing your own teeth.

WRINKLE CARE

Wrinkles are characteristic of a Bulldog's physical appearance and charm, but those wrinkle folds are prone to irritation and infection and need to be kept clean and dry. How often a Bulldog's wrinkles need cleaning depends on the dog. Hot, humid weather exacerbates the problem by producing conditions that allow bacteria to collect. Problems arise when air cannot get to the bottom of the wrinkles to allow adequate ventilation for the skin to air and dry out. As a result, the skin in the folds accumulates an excessive amount of sebaceous (oily or greasy) material, which provides a breeding ground for skin bacteria to proliferate, causing skin fold dermatitis. The skin becomes red, raw, inflamed, or infected; in some cases a smell may be present, as well as an accumulation of "goop" in the wrinkles.

How to Care for the Wrinkles

You can't go wrong cleaning the wrinkles daily. However, depending on your dog, three or four times a week may be sufficient.

1. Use a soft, damp cloth to wipe the folds. Or mix a drop of shampoo in a cup of water and use a damp cloth or cotton balls dipped in the solution to clean the folds.
2. Be sure to rinse the wrinkles well to prevent additional irritation. Aloe baby wipes with lanolin also work well, and they are convenient and disposable.

3. Thoroughly dry the wrinkles with a dry cloth or paper towel when finished. If the skin looks irritated, use a cream, ointment, or petroleum jelly to soothe the skin.

TAIL POCKET CARE

Some Bulldogs have a tail pocket—a thick fold of skin surrounding the base of the tail—that needs to be cleaned regularly to prevent bacteria from accumulating.

How to Care for the Tail Pocket

1. Use a damp soft cloth to wipe the pocket. Or mix a drop of shampoo in a cup of water and use a damp cloth or cotton balls dipped in the solution to clean the folds.
2. As with facial and body wrinkles, the tail pocket needs to be dried thoroughly after cleaning.
3. Apply an ointment when finished. An antibiotic or antifungal ointment may be necessary if irritation or tail infections are an issue.

FINDING A PROFESSIONAL GROOMER

For any number of reasons, some owners opt to take their Bulldogs to professional groomers. There's nothing wrong with this, but finding the right groomer is important. As with most anything else involving dogs, it will take a bit of detective work. To find the right grooming shop, follow these quick tips:

1. Visit the shop.
2. Are the groomers experienced with Bulldogs and the importance of wrinkle care?
3. Are the groomers kind and patient with the dogs? Are the dogs handled carefully?

Multi-Dog Tip

If you have multiple dogs, grooming is an excellent way to spend individual quality time with each of them. Ten or fifteen minutes daily with each dog also helps reinforce the human/canine bond. When acquiring a new dog, be sure not to neglect your resident dog's grooming requirements. Daily grooming sessions will bolster his ego, make him feel good, and remind him that he's still an important and valuable member of the family.

4. Is the shop clean? Does it smell dirty? Some shops have a "salon" smell of wet dogs, but it should not smell dirty or be dirty.
5. Are the floors, tubs, and grooming tables clean? Has the previous dog's hair been swept up? Are there dirty towels lying around? Are the towels being used on your dog clean and freshly laundered?
6. Are the crates or kennels clean? They should be stainless steel or of a surface that is easily cleaned and disinfected. Are there enough crates/kennels for all of the dogs? Do the dogs have to share a crate /kennel with another dog?
7. Does the shop use high-quality products?
8. What is their cancellation policy? Some shops are booked months in advance. Don't be surprised if you're charged for cancelling without having given 24 hours' notice.
9. What are the hours? Is there an additional charge if you're late picking your dog up or dropping him off?

CHAPTER 7

BULLDOG NUTRITIONAL NEEDS

Bulldogs, like most dogs, love to eat—and feeding time is no doubt their favorite time of day. Many are real chow hounds, while a few can be slow or finicky eaters. However, feeding your adult Bulldog is more important than simply satisfying his hunger and filling up his tummy. Good nutrition is essential to a happy, healthy dog. A high-quality, well-balanced diet provides optimum energy to fuel his body physically and mentally.

Granted, one would think canine nutrition is simple, but it's not. It's complex. Tricky. And frequently frustrating. There is a bewildering variety of dog foods available in every conceivable shape, size, and formula—all claiming to be "the best." Yet, no one food is the best. Hundreds of types, brands, and options are readily available, with a number of them being good-quality foods. Your job as a responsible dog owner is to find the food best suited for your Bulldog's individual nutritional needs. This requires a bit of detective work on your part, but isn't your Bulldog worth the extra effort?

Thanks to the Internet, canine nutrition has experienced a great increase in public awareness in the last 15 years or so, and veterinarians and owners are becoming more informed about the relationship between diet and disease. It goes without saying that you shouldn't believe everything you read on the Internet, but it can be an excellent starting point and resource guide for deciphering the complexities of canine nutrition and putting you on the path to finding the best food for your Bulldog.

THE BUILDING BLOCKS OF NUTRITION

When it comes to nutrition, not all dogs are created equal. Bulldogs are predisposed to cystinuria, which often requires reduced dietary protein, increased water, or wet food. Some dogs have allergies to different food sources, such as beef, chicken, or fish, which can cause an array of troubles, including scratching and intestinal gas. Others are sensitive or intolerant to poor-quality ingredients and grain-based diets. Identifying food allergies can be difficult and usually requires a trip to a veterinary dermatologist.

One of the most important requirements in feeding your Bulldog is to meet his individual nutritional needs.

One of the most important requirements in feeding your Bulldog is to look at his individual nutritional needs and then feed a diet that provides the correct combination of nutrients. What works for one Bulldog may not work for another because a dog's nutritional needs will change depending on his age, environment, housing conditions, exposure to heat or cold, overall health, and the emotional and physical demands placed on him. Some Bulldogs are more active than others, and the more active the dog, the more energy he burns. Therefore, some Bulldogs require a higher

intake of nutrients to fuel their bodies. To help your Bulldog's complex system run efficiently, it is important to find the diet that provides the correct balance of nutrients for his age, lifestyle, and individual needs.

Your Bulldog's diet is likely to change several times over the course of his lifetime. Yet the nuts and bolts of canine nutrition remain the same. There are six basic elements of nutrition: carbohydrates, fats, minerals, proteins, vitamins, and water.

Carbohydrates

Dogs are omnivorous animals, meaning that they eat both animal, plant, and vegetable foods, and they get most of their energy from carbohydrates. Carbohydrates are the energy foods that fuel your Bulldog's body. Scientific research indicates that up to 50 percent of an adult dog's diet can come from carbohydrates. They are often referred to as protein-sparing nutrients because the action of carbohydrates (and fats) in providing energy allows protein to be used for its own unique roles.

Soluble carbohydrates consist mainly of starches and sugars and are easily digested. Insoluble carbohydrates, better known as fiber, resist enzymatic digestion in the small intestine. Fiber, while important to the overall process, is not an essential nutrient.

Carbohydrates are introduced into the diet primarily through vegetable matter such as legumes and cereal grains such as rice, wheat, corn, barley, and oats. Unused carbohydrates are stored in the body as converted fat and as glycogen in the muscles and liver. In the absence of adequate carbohydrates, your Bulldog's system is able to utilize fat and protein as a form of energy. However, protein is less efficient because the body does not make a specialized storage form of protein as it does for fats and carbohydrates. When protein is used as an energy source—rather than to do its unique job of building muscle, regulating body functions, and so forth—a dog's body must dismantle valuable tissue proteins and use them for energy.

Fats

Fats and oils are the most concentrated sources of food energy in your Bulldog's diet. Fats account for approximately 2.25 times more metabolizable energy—the amount of energy in the food that is available to the dog—than do carbohydrates or proteins. Fats play an important role in contributing to your dog's healthy skin and coat and aid in the absorption, transport, and storage of fat-soluble vitamins. Fats also increase the palatability of foods, but they contain more than twice the calories of proteins and carbohydrates. Fats in your Bulldog's diet should be regulated. Dogs seldom develop the cardiovascular problems that humans do, but consuming too much fat can result in excess calorie intake, which is not good for your Bulldog's health or waistline.

Minerals

Minerals do not yield sources of energy, but they are important in the overall nutritional equation because they help regulate your Bulldog's complex system and are crucial components in energy metabolism. Minerals are classified as macro minerals or micro minerals, depending on their concentration in the body. Micro minerals, or trace elements, include iodine, iron, copper, cobalt, zinc,

Fats play an important role in contributing to your dog's healthy skin and coat.

Different dog breeds reach maturity at different ages. Generally speaking, smaller breeds tend to reach adulthood sooner than do large-breed dogs. Your Bulldog is likely to reach adulthood around 12 months of age. That said, the age of physical maturity—as opposed to mental maturity—varies from Bulldog to Bulldog, with some Bulldogs reaching maturity sooner or later than others.

manganese, molybdenum, fluorine, and chromium, which dogs need in very small amounts. Macro minerals are needed in large quantities and include sodium, potassium, magnesium, calcium, and phosphorus.

Essential nutrients are those that your Bulldog must obtain from food because his body cannot make them in sufficient quantity to meet his physiological needs. Getting too much or too little of a specific mineral in their diets can upset the delicate balance of dogs' systems and cause serious health problems, including tissue damage, convulsions, increased heart rate, and anemia. Never attempt to supplement minerals in your Bulldog's diet without advice from a veterinarian.

Proteins

Proteins are compounds of carbon, hydrogen, oxygen, and nitrogen atoms arranged into a string of amino acids—much like the pearls on a necklace. Amino acids are the building blocks of life because they build vital proteins that build strong muscles, ligaments, organs, bones, teeth, and coat. Protein also defends the body against disease and is critical when it comes to the repair and maintenance of all of the body's tissues, hormones, enzymes, electrolyte balances, and antibodies.

There are ten essential amino acids that your Bulldog's body cannot make on its own or make in sufficient quantities. These amino acids must be obtained through his diet. To make protein, a cell must have all of the needed amino acids available simultaneously because the body makes complete proteins only. If one amino acid is missing, the other amino acids cannot form a partial protein. If complete proteins are not formed, the body's ability to grow and repair tissue is reduced and limited.

Vitamins

A dog's body does not extract usable energy from vitamins, but they are essential as helpers in the metabolic processes. Vitamins are vital to your Bulldog's health and available in food sources, but they can be easily destroyed in the cooking and processing of commercial dog foods. Nearly every action in a dog's body

Infectious agents, such as *Giardia* and *E. coli*, can be transmitted through contaminated water. To reduce the risk of disease, train your Bulldog to refrain from drinking from puddles, streams, or ponds because the water could be contaminated with parasites that could make him ill.

Nearly every action in a dog's body requires the assistance of vitamins.

requires the assistance of vitamins, and certain vitamins are dependent on other vitamins. Vitamin deficiencies or excesses can lead to serious health problems, such as anorexia, artery and vein degeneration, dehydration, muscle weakness, and impairment of motor control and balance.

Vitamins fall into two categories: water-soluble (B-complex and vitamin C) and fat-soluble (A, D, E, and K). Unlike humans, dogs can make vitamin C from glucose, so they do not need to acquire it in their diet. All other water-soluble vitamins must be replenished on a regular basis through diet. Fat-soluble vitamins are absorbed and stored in the body, which makes oversupplementation potentially dangerous. Seek expert advice before supplementing your dog's food.

Water

Water is the single most important nutrient needed to sustain your Bulldog's health. Water regulates a dog's body temperature, which is essential because of the breed's predisposition to heat-induced illnesses. Water also plays an important part in supporting metabolic reactions and acts as the transportation system that allows blood to carry vital nutritional materials to the cells and remove waste products from your dog's system—another important element considering the breed's predisposition to uroliths (stones).

The amount of water a dog needs to consume daily will vary from dog to dog, depending on growth, stress, environment, activity, and age. Your Bulldog's need for water increases as he expends more energy during work, exercise, play, or training because dissipation of excess heat from his body is accomplished largely by the evaporation of water through panting. Plus, the warmer the weather, the more water a dog needs to consume. If your Bulldog eats primarily dry dog food, he will need access to fresh water to help aid in digestion.

Rather than trying to estimate your Bulldog's daily water requirement, provide him with access to an abundant supply of fresh, cool drinking water at all times. When dogs have free access to water they will normally drink enough to maintain the proper balance of body fluids. If you have less than desirable city water or are concerned about fluoride, chlorine, or lead in your water supply, consider a filtration system or try boiling water or purchasing bottled water for your Bulldog.

WHAT TO FEED YOUR BULLDOG

From convenient commercial foods to healthy home-cooked meals, finding the right diet for your Bulldog can seem overwhelming, but it's well within the capabilities of most dog owners. The most important thing to remember is to find a diet that works for you and your Bulldog. Again, you will need to do a bit of detective work, but the long-term results are well worth the effort.

Commercial Foods

Commercial foods are undoubtedly the most convenient foods to buy, store, and use. They are readily available, and when compared to homemade diets, they are less time consuming. That said, the commercial dog food industry is a multibillion dollar a year business. Manufacturers spend a significant amount of time and money researching and developing dog food products and then spend a lot of money advertising them in a manner to convince you to buy a particular brand. This is not necessarily bad, but it is important to keep in mind if you are choosing a food because of its creative advertisements and fancy packaging rather than your dog's nutritional requirements.

Commercial foods tend to be classified into two broad categories: canned or dry, with semi-moist foods falling into a subdivision of dry foods.

Canned Foods

Many of the same ingredients—meat and fat ingredients, vitamins, minerals, amino acids— that are found in canned foods are also used in dry and semi-moist foods but not at the same level. Canned foods are high in moisture (water) content—approximately 75 percent. As a result, they generally contain higher levels of meat, poultry, or fish products and animal by-products. A meat-based formula, for example, may contain 24 percent to 75 percent meat and/or meat by-products. Some canned foods contain textured protein (either soy or wheat gluten based) with a structure that mimics

Canned foods are high in moisture content, and they generally contain higher levels of meat, poultry, or fish than other commercial dog foods.

Dry food, or kibble, is a popular choice among dog owners.

meat. According to the *Nutrient Requirements of Dogs and Cats*, these products have "all but replaced earlier fortified "all-meat" formulas because of the reduced costs and the improved nutrient profiles possible with meat-textured protein combinations." Because of the heat and pressure involved during canning, some destruction of critical nutrients is highly likely.

Designed to be fed alone as a complete and balanced diet, canned foods are highly palatable, and most dogs love them. They tend to be more expensive than dry foods, and they require refrigeration after opening. Some owners choose to supplement dry foods with canned foods. According to experts, the addition of canned foods may improve the acceptability or palatability of dry foods, but the nutritional value of a well-balanced dry dog food is not likely to be enhanced.

Dry Foods

Dry foods are a popular choice among owners. Hundreds of brands and options are readily available, which can be confusing and frustrating. Formulas range from special condition formulas to breed-specific formulas. Formulas for puppies, adults, and overweight dogs are readily available. Naturally wild formulas and no-grain formulas and formulas with every possible meat source, including poultry, fish, beef, venison, and buffalo, are available at most pet food outlets. Although dry foods used to be easy on the pocketbook—and many brands still are—some high-end premium foods average more money per pound than ever before.

Dry foods, commonly called "kibble," contain about 10 percent final moisture (water) content. While many dry foods are

Stick With Premium Foods

Buying a premium food is more expensive than a bargain or generic-brand food, but in the long run it makes good nutritional and economic sense. Across the board, premium foods tend to be nutritionally complete, meaning that they have all of the required nutrients in balanced proportions so that your Bulldog is getting adequate amounts of all required nutrients. Premium foods are also developed to provide optimal nutrition for dogs during different stages of life, such as puppy, maintenance, active, and senior diets. The initial investment for premium foods is a bit higher on a per weight basis, but because they tend to be higher in digestibility and nutrient availability, less food is required per serving.

grain-free, most contain a high percentage of carbohydrates in the form of grains and are formulated using cereal grains, cereal grain by-products, soybean products, animal by-products, fats, oils, vitamins, and micro and macro minerals.

Extrusion is the primary processing method for most dry foods marketed today. In the simplest of terms, extrusion involves the mixing of ingredients that are then cooked and formed into pellets or expanded into nuggets of varying shapes and sizes, which is done more to satisfy the anthropomorphic desires of owners because dogs don't care about the shape of their food.

The extrusion process results in moderate to high levels of gelatinization of dietary starch. According to the *Nutrient Requirements of Dogs and Cats*, by gelatinizing part or most of the starch, the site of starch hydrolysis (digestion) occurs in the upper gut, resulting in better utilization by the dog and reduced digestive upset. However, high heats used in the processing stage can destroy valuable nutrients

Dry dog foods typically contain 5 to 16 percent crude fat, with the majority of the fat being sprayed on during post-processing. Some foods are also spray coated with various protein digest and/or flavors to increase their acceptability and palatability.

Some prescription foods are recommended to help improve dental hygiene through chewing and grinding, which aids in the removal of dental plaque. However, this does not eliminate the need for regular dental care.

Semi-Moist Foods

Semi-moist foods contain many of the same basic ingredients as dry-expanded products. However, they usually contain meat or meat by-product "slurries," which are incorporated prior to or during the extrusion process. Ingredients can include fresh or frozen animal tissues, cereal grains, fats, and simple sugars. Semi-moist foods also contain propylene glycol, which is an odorless, tasteless, slightly syrupy liquid used to make antifreeze and de-icing products. Propylene glycol is generally recognized as safe by the U.S. Food and Drug Administration (FDA) for use in dog food and other animal feeds. It is used to absorb extra water and maintain moisture, and it's also used as a solvent for food coloring and flavor.

The high sugar content generally increases palatability of semi-moist foods, and they tend to be less offensive-smelling than canned foods. However, sugar levels in dog food cause spikes in blood sugar levels and contribute to obesity. High sugar levels may aggravate an existing or borderline diabetic condition.

Semi-moist foods contain about 25 to 35 percent moisture. They are generally marketed in sealed and/or resealable pouches with the sizes being convenient for feeding as a single meal.

NONCOMMERCIAL DIETS

Commercial diets are relatively inexpensive and provide your dog with a balanced, no-fuss diet. That said, you may opt to feed a noncommercial diet, which includes home-cooked or raw diets. Before jumping in, carefully consider the pros and cons of both, and consult your vet to make sure that your Bulldog is getting all of the nutrition he needs.

Bones and Raw Food (BARF) Diet

It's not difficult to find proponents and opponents on both sides of the controversial issue of whether a BARF diet is best for dogs. Ask a dozen people and each one is sure to have a different opinion, with most people being totally in favor of it or totally against it. Few people are middle of the road on this topic.

A raw diet may include dairy items such as cottage cheese and eggs.

BARF, also known as "biologically appropriate raw food," is based on the premise that raw bones and foods, such as organ and muscle meats and cottage cheese, eggs, vegetables, and fruits, are more suitable than highly processed "commercial" dog foods. Drying, freezing, heating, or canning foods, according to proponents, robs food of its nutritional components. By returning to a more natural lifestyle and feeding a pure diet, they hope to mimic or replicate what wild dogs might have eaten long ago, so they feed foods that they believe dogs are evolutionarily suited to eat.

Proponents claim that their dogs are healthier, with tartar-free teeth and gorgeous coats. Despite the fact that many of the reputed health and therapeutic benefits of raw diets are empirical—meaning that they are based on owner observation and trial and error rather than scientific validation—feeding a raw diet is becoming increasingly popular among owners and breeders. To meet the increasing demand, several companies are now marketing raw diets, and these diets are readily available at a variety of pet stores, dog-show vendors, veterinary clinics, and online vendors.

Opponents cite the increased health risks because dogs, like humans, are susceptible to internal parasites and food-borne illnesses caused by organisms such as *Salmonella, Campylobacter,* and *E. coli* carried in raw meat, poultry, eggs, and unprocessed milk. A study published in 2009 notes that dogs who were fed raw meat were more likely to shed *Salmonella* in their feces than dogs who were not, and that *Salmonella* may contaminate the household environment and serve as a source of infection to humans. The study also cited the multifaceted risks, including

Feeding a raw diet should be undertaken only after doing a great deal of research and consulting your vet.

potential health concerns for people handling the food, people handling feces from animals fed raw diets, people handling food bowls, and animals exposed to animals who are fed raw diets.

One challenge that arises with this type of diet is finding a good source of healthy raw meat and bones and then achieving the correct balance of nutrients—water, vitamins, minerals, protein, carbohydrates, and fats—in the right amounts and doing so on a routine basis. Dogs who eat raw bones are, according to some experts, highly susceptible to choking or damaging their stomachs. Both of these situations can be life threatening.

Feeding a raw food and bones diet works for some owners, but it takes considerably more effort than opening a can of food or pouring some kibble from a bag. Feeding this type of diet should be undertaken only after a great deal of research and understanding, and it is highly recommended that you work closely with a veterinarian or certified canine nutritionist.

Home-Cooked Diet

Feeding a home-cooked diet is often easier said than done. It requires a good deal of knowledge about canine nutrition, as well as an abundance of time and energy. Home-cooked diets are a time consuming, labor-intensive, potentially expensive, and complicated process. The previously mentioned concern of bacterial infections, parasites, and food-borne illnesses for both dogs and humans handling and eating raw foods also exists.

It is tricky, albeit not impossible, to prepare a canine diet on a routine daily basis that is complete and balanced and contains the proper ratio of nutrients. Doing so requires owners to become well informed about their dog's nutritional requirements. It's also helpful if you understand the important aspects of diet formation, which include the knowledge and application of energy, amino acids, mineral, and vitamin requirements for each dog, as well as the selection of specific ingredients and amounts that contribute required and available nutrients to the diet so that the level of each required nutrient is met in the amount of diet consumed on a daily basis. Commercial companies and consulting nutritionists use a computer-based "linear programming" process. You too can purchase such a program, but they aren't cheap. Computer-savvy owners may be able to use a spreadsheet program with linear program capabilities to formulate diets.

The nutritional value of raw ingredients will fluctuate depending on their sources, and supplementing with vitamins and minerals is usually necessary. However, that can be harmful to your dog if too much or too little or the wrong combinations of supplements are used. Be sure to consult with a veterinarian or certified veterinary nutritionist to make sure that the meals you cook contain the proper proportions of proteins, fats, carbohydrates, vitamins, and minerals.

PRESCRIPTION DIETS

Prescription diets are special-formula diets prepared by dog-food manufacturers and are normally available only through a licensed veterinarian. They are designed to meet the special medical needs of dogs, such as low-protein and mineral diets for kidney disease; low-protein, magnesium, calcium, and phosphorus diets for bladder stones; lamb and rice-based diets for food-induced allergies; and low-calorie foods for weight-reduction diets, and so forth.

SUPPLEMENTS

Your Bulldog's system is complex. To run efficiently, it must receive the proper amounts of nutrients in a balanced ration. Many experts say that if you are feeding a quality diet that is complete and well balanced, supplementing is not required or recommended.

Treats should be fed in moderation to help keep your Bulldog trim.

Technically, a supplement is anything that is given in addition to your dog's feed. It can include something as simple as adding yogurt, brewer's yeast, vegetables, a few pieces of leftover steak, or half a cup of chicken broth to increase the palatability of your dog's food. While these tidbits are not likely to upset your Bulldog's nutritional balances—provided they account for less than 10 percent of your dog's caloric intake—too many tasty tidbits, gravies, and other gastronomic delicacies can add unnecessary calories, resulting in harmful excess weight. To prevent problems, always consult your veterinarian before using supplements.

TREATS, BONES, AND CHEWS

Countless products designed for dogs to chew are readily available. And while Bulldogs love to chew, keep in mind that the breed's jaw structure can make them especially vulnerable to choking. Therefore, you should always exercise precautions and choose your dog's treats carefully.

That said, many treats currently available are

Multi-Dog Tip

When indulging your dogs with chew toys, be sure to separate your pets, such as putting them in their individual crates, ex-pens, separate rooms, or one indoors and one outdoors to prevent any squabbling. Bulldogs are sweet, but even the best of friends have been known to squabble over bones.

manufactured and processed using the same extrusion system for commercial dog foods. When choosing treats, read labels carefully and choose treats that are low in fat, sugar, and salt. Small pieces of fruit or fresh veggies are good alternatives to store-bought treats. Home-baked treats can be yummy and low in fat. Remember, treats should be a reward for the performance of desired behaviors, such as coming when called or sitting or for performing a fun trick. They should never be a substitute for well-deserved hugs and kisses. Also, they should not represent a significant portion of a dog's typical diet. Too many treats will increase his caloric intake and waistline.

Most dogs love bones, but they can also be hazardous to their health. Cooked bones are dangerous because they easily splinter and can damage a dog's throat and digestive system. Uncooked bones of the large cow hock variety, along with the popular cow hooves, are the primary cause of broken teeth in dogs. Fresh hooves, such as those from the recently trimmed hooves of horses and cows, are more pliable than the varieties available in feed stores. However, they can still present choking hazards. Someone once said something along these lines: "If you do not want me to hit you in the knee with a toy, then you should not give it to your dog to chew." The point being: If it's hard enough to hurt your knee, it's probably hard enough to break your dog's tooth.

Pigs' ears, which are basically pigskin and cartilage, usually dried and smoked to prevent decay, aren't likely to cause dental fractures. However, reports indicate that some may harbor bacterial pathogens, such as *Salmonella*.

Anything a dog chews into tiny bits and swallows, such as rawhide chews, pigs' ears, bones, the fuzz on tennis balls, etc., bears some risk of causing gastrointestinal upset or blockage. Some treats, such as rawhide, can also cause upset tummies due to the basting flavors added to them.

WHAT AND WHEN TO FEED YOUR ADULT

Adult foods, often called maintenance diets, are specially designed foods that satisfy the energy and nutritional needs of adult dogs who have reached maturity. These diets are designed to provide the proper quantities of nutrients to support a mature Bulldog's lifestyle. Bulldogs who are more active than the average dog, or who are under physical or emotional stress, and lactating bitches have different nutrient requirements than the average couch potato. Canine nutritionists are a good source of information when determining the type of food to choose.

Ideally, adult dogs should be fed twice a day—preferably in the morning and evening, such as 8 am and 5 pm, although this may vary depending on your work and/or lifestyle. As with puppies, follow a protocol of scheduled feeding—meaning put the food down for about 15 minutes. Any leftover food should be picked up and refrigerated or discharged, depending on the food type.

OBESITY

Most adult Bulldogs would rather go for a ride in the car than take a walk around the block, and their sedentary tendencies make them

---

Want to Know More?

For more information on puppy nutrition, see Chapter 3: Care of Your Bulldog Puppy.

Preventing Bloat

Do not feed or water your Bulldog either right before or right after exercise to prevent indigestion, or worse, possible bloat. Bloat can cause the stomach to twist or turn on itself, trapping food and gases and eventually cutting off blood supply to the organ. This condition is very painful and may quickly become life threatening. It can sometimes result in death if veterinary treatment is not obtained immediately.

particularly prone to obesity. As previously mentioned in Chapter 3, canine obesity predisposes a dog to serious health problems, with studies indicating that 20 to 40 percent of dogs are considered obese. Medically, obesity is defined as a "pathological condition characterized by excessive fat deposition leading to modifications to various bodily functions." On a quantitative level, obesity is defined as being 15 percent overweight as compared to optimal weight. The problem

is that it's difficult to mathematically define obesity because it's difficult to define optimal weight, as dogs vary in their size, bone structure, and muscularity. Generally speaking, owners shouldn't need a mathematical equation to determine whether their dog is overweight. His appearance alone should be a good indicator. Putting your hands on your dog and feeling his neck, ribs, and hips is an ideal way to assess his weight.

Run your fingers up and down along his ribcage. You should be able to feel the bumps of his ribs without pressing in. Also run your hand over his croup (his rump). You should be able to feel the bumps of his two pelvic bones with little effort and without pressing down.

Some owners think that if they can feel their dog's ribs he's too thin. Not so. Bulldogs should be fit and lean—not too skinny and not too fat. When looking at your Bulldog from the side, his abdominal tuck—the underline of his body where his belly appears to draw up toward his hind end—should be evident. When standing over your Bulldog and viewing him from above, his waist—the section behind his ribs—should be well proportioned. Your veterinarian can help you determine the ideal weight for your Bulldog and develop a long-term plan to condition his body and provide him with a longer, healthier, and happier life.

Bulldogs should be fit and lean—not too skinny and not too fat.

CHAPTER 8

BULLDOG HEALTH AND WELLNESS

Bulldogs, as a whole, have special needs—many resulting from their charming physical traits. Your Bulldog's life will be shaped, influenced, and prolonged by the excellent health care and daily companionship you provide. Unfortunately, however, regardless of your best efforts, your Bulldog may develop health problems. Just as you are a reflection of your parents' genetic contributions, your Bulldog is the sum of his genetic makeup. His genes lay the foundation for his size, markings, structure, and temperament, and they will dictate his overall health. This makes acquiring your Bulldog from a reputable and knowledgeable breeder doubly important.

THE ANNUAL VET EXAM

Annual checkups help a veterinarian keep tabs on your dog's health and catch problems such as diabetes, kidney problems, and cancer early on before they become severe medical issues. Protocol differs from veterinarian to veterinarian, but an annual checkup should include but may not be limited to checking the following:

- overall health, including temperature, weight, coat and skin condition, ears, eyes, feet, limbs, and heart, respiratory, and urinary functions
- behavior changes in temperament or normal behaviors, problems with barking, chewing, digging, and so forth
- blood tests for older dogs, those with medical conditions, and those receiving medications
- dental health, including mouth odors, pain, broken teeth, and related ailments.
- exercise, including how often, what types, and changes in your dog's ability to walk or exercise
- nutritional requirements, including increases or decreases in appetite or water consumption, obesity, and special diets
- parasite prevention
- spaying or neutering
- vaccination status and requirements

PARASITES

Despite improved medications and topnotch sanitary practices, it is highly likely that sometime within your Bulldog's life he will

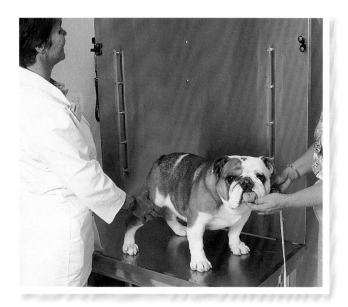

Annual checkups help the vet keep tabs on your dog's health and catch any problems early.

suffer from an internal parasite (like worms) or external parasite (like ticks and fleas) and you will need to deal with them. If left unchecked, parasites can cause debilitating and life-threatening problems.

Internal Parasites

Known as endoparasites because they live inside a dog's body, heartworms, hookworms, roundworms, tapeworms, and whipworms are the most common internal canine parasites. Deworming medications are available at local pet stores and retail outlets; however, they differ drastically in their safety and effectiveness in expelling worms from the body. Therefore the wise choice is to have a veterinarian diagnose the specific type of internal parasite and then prescribe the proper deworming medication.

Heartworms

An 1847 issue of *The Western Journal of Medicine and Surgery* published the first description of heartworms in dogs in the United States. Since then, heartworms have been found throughout the United States, with the most frequent occurrence being on the seacoast in the southeastern United States. However, all dogs, regardless of their age, sex, or habitat, are susceptible.

Of all of the internally parasitic nematode worms, which group also includes hookworms, roundworms, and whipworms, heartworms are potentially the most dangerous. Mosquitoes transmit heartworm disease when they suck blood from an infected dog and then bite a healthy dog, thereby depositing infective larvae through the bite wound. The larvae grow inside the healthy dog, migrating through the dog's tissues into the bloodstream and eventually into the dog's heart, where they grow into adult worms. Heartworms become fully grown about six or seven months after infection. As mature adults, the worms mate and the females release their offspring (microfilariae) into the bloodstream. Their life span in dogs appears to average between five and seven years. A severely infected dog can have several hundred heartworms in his heart and vessels, completely filling and obstructing the heart chambers and the various large blood vessels leading from the heart to the lungs.

Signs: In many cases, signs may not appear until the damage is extensive and the disease is well advanced. First symptoms usually include a chronic cough and exercise intolerance, with advanced symptoms including abnormal lung sounds, enlargement of the liver, and temporary loss of consciousness due to poor blood flow to the brain. Some dogs accumulate fluid in their abdomens and take on a pot-bellied appearance. In some situations, dogs may die of sudden heart failure.

A blood test is used to detect the presence of adult antigens in the blood. Radiographs (x-rays) and ultrasounds (echocardiography) of the dog's heart and lungs may be taken to determine the severity of the infection and to develop a prognosis. If your dog is diagnosed positive for heartworms, an intensive course of action must follow.

Treatment: The protocol your veterinarian chooses will depend on the severity of infection and whether or not your Bulldog's kidney and liver functions can tolerate the treatment. It generally consists of a two-step process, as the adult worms and microfilariae must be killed separately. Treatment is long and risky, but it can be successful if the infestation is diagnosed early. Dogs with more severe heartworm disease run an increased risk of complications, and the mortality is greater. When the worms die, they can lodge in the arteries and capillaries of the lungs, creating blood clots, which can present additional life-threatening problems.

Prevention: The best "cure" for heartworm is the prevention of the disease. Preventive medications are available, but they must never be given to a dog who is already infected with worms. Always consult with your veterinarian before starting any preventive treatment for heartworms.

Hookworms

Adult hookworms have teeth-like structures (hooks) that attach to the lining of your Bulldog's intestine, feeding on his oxygen-carrying blood. They damage the lining and then migrate to a new location. Because hookworms produce an anticoagulant in their saliva, a dog's blood may not clot at the site where the hookworm attaches. Hookworms are voracious bloodsuckers, and when they move from one site to another to reattach themselves, the first site may continue to bleed—sometimes seriously.

Eggs are passed in the dog's feces, where they hatch into larvae. Infestation occurs when larvae enter a dog's body, which happens in several ways. Burrowing through the skin, larvae migrate through the lungs and trachea, where they are coughed up and swallowed—eventually ending up in the intestinal tract. Ingestion can occur when a dog ingests contaminated food or water, when he licks his contaminated feet, or when he eats an infected transport host. A puppy can become infected

Multi-Dog Tip

In multi-dog households, it is a good idea, if possible, to separate pets if you suspect any of them have a contagious issue, such as canine scabies or any of the infectious diseases, such as kennel cough, distemper, or a similar ailment.

when larvae migrate to the uterus or mammary glands of a pregnant bitch, thereby infecting the fetuses or nursing puppies. Once inside the dog, larvae attach themselves to the intestinal wall, mature, mate, and produce eggs, thus completing the life cycle.

Signs: By feeding on a dog's blood, hookworms can rapidly cause anemia. Typical symptoms include pale gums, weakness, and sometimes black, tarry stools. Vomiting and diarrhea may also occur. A dog's coat may be dull and dry, and a young dog's growth may be stunted. In severe infestations, a dog may cough or develop pneumonia as the larvae migrate through the lungs. Hookworms are small, .5 to .75 inches (1.5 to 2 cm) long and are rarely detected in the stool because of their ability to firmly attach themselves to the intestinal wall. Finding eggs in the feces provides a primary diagnosis.

Treatment: Treatment involves a dewormer. Two or three treatments are generally recommended, as most wormers kill only the adult worm—not the larvae. In severe cases, electrolyte and fluid therapy, iron supplements,

a high-protein diet, and blood transfusions may also be recommended. Some year-round heartworm preventive/intestinal parasite combination products also kill hookworms and help prevent future infections. Always consult your veterinarian before giving any dog a heartworm preventive.

Roundworms

Common parasites of the canine digestive tract, roundworms live and feed in a dog's small intestine. Occasionally found in adult dogs and people, they are most common in puppies, with most puppies requiring deworming at an early age. Puppies can become infected several ways—including being born with them. A pregnant dog who has encysted larvae in her tissues can pass them to her puppies if the larvae migrate through the uterus and placenta and infect the puppies (aka *in utero* transmission) via entering the lungs of the unborn puppy. After he is born, he will cough up and swallow the larvae, and they will then mature in his intestines. Puppies can also become infected while nursing if

If your Bulldog appears lethargic or not like his normal self, take him to the vet.

the roundworm larvae enter the mother's mammary glands.

Adult dogs usually become infected when they eat an infected animal, such as a rodent, when they ingest soil contaminated with roundworms, when they come in contact with infected feces, or when they snack from the cat's litter box. If the larvae are passed in a puppy's feces before they can mature, the mother dog can become infected when she licks the puppy.

Signs: Roundworms feed off partially digested intestinal contents, thereby damaging the intestinal lining and robbing the dog of vital nutrients. In severe infestations, puppies may be thin and have a potbellied appearance. The coats may be dry, dull, and rough- looking. Some puppies have intestinal discomfort and cry as a result. Diarrhea or constipation and vomiting are also frequent symptoms. In some cases, a cough may develop because of the migration of the larvae through the respiratory system.

Treatment: Roundworms are diagnosed by a microscopic examination of eggs in the dog's feces. Treatment involves a wormer that kills them. Puppies can be dewormed as early as two or three weeks of age. Adult dogs should receive annual fecal examinations. Regular fecal examinations—three to four times a year—should be considered, depending on the risk of exposure. Some year-round heartworm preventive products also kill roundworms and help prevent future infections. Always consult your veterinarian before giving any dog a heartworm preventive.

While generally not life threatening, tapeworms are a problem because they attach to your dog's intestinal wall to absorb nutrients.

Tapeworms

While generally not life threatening, tapeworms are a problem because they attach to your dog's intestinal wall to absorb nutrients and can grow to 2 feet (0.5 m) or more in length.

Tapeworms consist of a head and then a number of segments containing female and male reproductive systems and a large numbers of eggs that break away from the rest of the worm and are passed in a dog's feces. Sometimes visible on the dog's rectum or in his stools, they look like grains of uncooked rice or cucumber seeds.

Unlike the nematode worm group (whipworms, roundworms, and hookworms), tapeworms must go through an intermediate host. They are acquired when a dog ingests an intermediate host, with fleas or lice being the most common intermediate hosts in dogs and cats. In certain species of tapeworms, rabbits and livestock can be the intermediate hosts.

Signs: There are multiple species of tapeworms that infect dogs. Tapeworms generally do not cause any symptoms unless they are present in high numbers. Some dogs will scoot their rear ends along the ground. In some cases, diarrhea may be present. In severe infestations, your Bulldog may exhibit abdominal discomfort or nervousness.

Treatment: Finding the moving segments, dried segments, and occasionally eggs in the feces via microscopic examination will confirm a diagnosis. Getting rid of tapeworms can be difficult because it requires successfully eliminating the head of the tapeworm; unless the head is eliminated, the worm will regrow a new body. Treatment involves a wormer that kills the specific species of tapeworm. While single doses are generally sufficient, an additional dose may be required, depending on the species.

Whipworms

Whipworms get their name from the whip-like shape of the adult worm. They are common in dogs and found worldwide. However, they are most prevalent in warm, humid climates. They are rare or nonexistent in arid, very hot, or very cold regions. Both larval and adult whipworms are normally found only in the intestines. Dogs become infected when they ingest food, grass, or water that is contaminated with whipworm eggs. If your Bulldog buries his bone in the dirt, he can pick up eggs from the infected soil. The eggs are swallowed and hatch in his large intestine, and in about three months the larvae mature into adults that attach to the intestinal lining and burrow their mouths into the intestinal wall, where they feed on blood. Adult worms lay eggs that are passed in the feces.

Signs: The symptoms vary, depending on the extent of the infestation. Mild infestations may produce no obvious symptoms in healthy individuals. Larger infestations, however, can result in diarrhea, mucus, and blood in the stools, loss of weight, and inflammation of the intestinal wall. Anemia is possible if hemorrhaging into the intestine occurs.

Treatment: Detecting whipworms can be difficult because whipworms do not continually shed eggs. A negative stool sample does not mean that your Bulldog does not have whipworms. It simply means that no eggs were found in that sample. Stool samples collected on different days may be necessary for positive identification. Treatment generally consists of a wormer that is effective against whipworms.

External Parasites

Bulldogs are susceptible to skin irritations, including those caused by fleas, which are external parasites. One bite from these pesky creatures can cause itching and scratching for days. Therefore it behooves you to practice strict flea prevention and eradication protocol and to protect your dog from external parasites in general.

Fleas

In North America, *Ctenocephalides felis*, also known as the domestic cat flea, is the most common flea responsible for wrecking havoc with your Bulldog. Slightly smaller than a sesame seed and generally brown or black in color, these wingless bloodsuckers are responsible for spreading tapeworms to dogs and causing serious allergy dermatitis.

Check your Bulldog for fleas and ticks after he's been playing outside.

Want to Know More?

If you're wondering how to find the perfect vet for your newly adopted adult dog, see Chapter 3: Care of Your Bulldog Puppy.

Treatment and Prevention: Fleas pass through four stages: the eggs, the larvae, the pupae (cocoons), and the adults. These stages can be completed in as little as 12 days or as many as 190 days. Eggs hatch into wormlike larvae about two to seven days after the eggs are laid. Larval development occurs in protected microhabitats that combine moderate temperatures with high relative humidity. Flea larvae spin cocoons and develop into pupae. Cocoons can be found in soil, on vegetation, in carpets, on animal bedding, and so forth. About 80 percent of the pupae emerge as adults at 80.6°F (27°C) and 2 percent relative humidity. Delayed emergence occurs when there are no emergence stimuli, such as increased temperatures. Adult *C. felis* can remain dormant in the cocoon for up to 30 weeks at 51.8°F (11°C) and 75 percent relative humidity. This pre-emerged adult in the cocoon is the most resistant to insecticides.

Adult fleas hatch within seconds and can survive several days before taking a blood meal. Mating occurs after the fleas have fed, and egg production begins within 48 hours after the female takes her first blood meal. During peak production, females are capable of producing 40 to 50 eggs per day but average 27 eggs per day for an average of 50 days. However, fleas are able to sustain egg production for more than 100 days.

The advent of once-a-month topical treatments makes eradicating fleas a breeze compared to 15 years ago. You mustn't become complacent, however. You need to keep on top of the pesky buggers. Flea control includes not only killing fleas but preventing reinfestation, which is often problematic. Also, flea control regimens must be personalized based on the severity of the infestation, the number of household pets, and your personal finances.

To eliminate fleas and prevent reinfestation, try these steps:

1. Start by bathing your dog and any other household pets that can serve as hosts, such as other dogs, cats, and ferrets.
2. Clean everything your dog has come in contact with. Wash his dog beds and blankets, and mop up floors. Vacuum all carpets, rugs, and furniture. Immediately dispose of vacuum bags because eggs can hatch in them.
3. If necessary, remove dense vegetation near your home, dog yard, or kennel area. These spaces offer a damp microenvironment that is favorable to flea development.
4. Treat other outdoor areas as well, including lawns, dog houses, and so forth with a safe product.

Flea (and tick) preventives are available as adulticides, which kill adult fleas on contact, and insect growth regulators (IGR), which inhibit or interrupt the life cycle of the flea, preventing it from reaching maturity and subsequently reproducing. Many over-the-counter and "natural" products, such as garlic, brewer's yeast, and sulfur, as well as flea dips, shampoos, flea collars, and even ultrasonic flea collars are readily available. Whether or not these products successfully eradicate fleas (and ticks) is debatable. Many of these products have been around for years, but remember that many commercial and "natural" products may be toxic. They may irritate your Bulldog's skin or cause health problems.

Mites and Mange

Mites are related to spiders. Bulldogs appear predisposed to two types of common mites—*Sarcoptes scabei* and *Demodex canis*. A third mite—*Otodectes cynotis*—is common in many dog breeds and is thought to account for about 10 percent of all canine ear inflammations.

Demodectic Mange: Demodectic mange is a skin disease caused by a microscopic mite—*Demodex canis*. Some breeds—including the Bulldog—are predisposed to canine demodicosis. Small numbers of demodex mites normally inhabit the hair follicles and sebaceous glands of dogs and are passed from a mother to a puppy in the first week or so of life.

Microscopic examination of deep skin scrapes from the affected areas is the primary form of diagnosis. Two forms of the disease exist: localized and generalized. Localized demodicosis is the most common, occurring in dogs under one year of age and involving five or fewer lesions. Lesions can appear as crusty red skin with hair loss, and may have a greasy or moist appearance, with most of the lesions being confined to the muzzle, eyes, and other areas around the head. Prognosis is good, with 90 percent of the dogs self-curing without any treatment. Ten percent will go on to develop the generalized form, which requires treatment. Generalized demodicosis is a more severe version of demodectic mange and is characterized by diffuse hair loss, red skin, and lesions on the head, neck, stomach, legs, and feet. A secondary bacterial infection aggravates the lesions, and this is the worst part

Several types of ear mites can wreak havoc with your Bulldog.

of the disease. In severe cases, dogs can become quite ill, developing lethargy, fever, and loss of appetite.

The prognosis for generalized demodicosis depends on the age of the dog at the time he develops the disease. For puppies, long-term prognosis is good because once the mites and infection are treated, there is less than a 50 percent chance of recurrence. With adult dogs—dogs older than one to one and a half years of age—prognosis is guarded and usually requires treatment for the rest of their lives, with success dependent on the dog's tolerance to medications, any underlying cause, and the owner's commitment and adherence to treatments. Generalized demodicosis may require extended aggressive treatment that generally include an insecticidal dip, anti-parasitic drugs, antibiotics, and follow-up visits to a veterinarian every four to six weeks to assess the infection and revise therapy, if needed.

Sarcoptic Mange: Scabies is a highly contagious skin disease caused by a microscopic burrowing mite—*Sarcoptes scabei*. Burrowing mites burrow into the skin, forming tunnels in which they lay their eggs. Eggs hatch, producing six-legged larvae that emerge, develop into nymphs, and then become adults. Highly contagious among dogs, scabies is spread by direct contact.

Typical symptoms include pruritus (itching), with scratching leading to subsequent erythema (redness of the skin due to inflammation), papular eruptions, sores, crust formation, and frequent secondary bacterial infection. Symptoms generally begin on the chest and abdomen and frequently affect the ears and the area around the eyes, elbows, and legs.

Microscopic examination from deep skin scrapings can provide a definitive diagnosis. However, mites are often difficult to find,

and scrapings from a number of sites may be necessary but still uneventful. All in-contact dogs must be treated. If left untreated, the infection spreads, causing the skin to become wrinkled and thickened, with most dogs experiencing extensive hair loss. It may become a severe generalized dermatitis. Treatment consists of special shampoos, dips, oral medications, or injections.

Ear Mites: Several types of ear mites can wreak havoc with your Bulldog, with the most common being *Otodectes cynotis*. These mites live deep in the ear canal near the eardrum, feeding on epidermal debris and tissue fluid from the superficial epidermis. Symptoms include intense irritation, with some dogs scratching around their ears and/or shaking their heads. With more advanced infestations, bleeding in the ear canal is common, which produces a thick reddish brown crust (resembling coffee grounds). Ear mites are highly contagious, and transmission is made through direct and indirect contact.

Left untreated, ear mites can severely damage the ear canals and eardrum and can cause permanent hearing loss. Treatment includes topical ear formulations, as well as spot-on and systemic formulations, as ear mites can live outside the ear and are found all over a dog's body—including his feet, hind end, and tail. Due to their highly contagious nature, treating all pets in the house is recommended. Treatment of the house and yard is usually not necessary, as mites do not survive off the dog.

Ringworm

The term ringworm is a bit deceiving, because a worm doesn't cause it at all; the condition is caused, instead, by a group of specialized fungi. While not too common, it is highly contagious in dogs, cats, and humans. Spores from infected animals are extremely hardy—living for years after being shed into the environment. Transmission is by direct contact with an infected dog or contact with an item that is contaminated with the spores, such as kennels, grooming equipment, bedding, or even the environment where an infected dog has visited. More common in puppies, ringworm is uncommon in adult dogs unless they are immunosuppressed, have poor nutrition, or are kept in high-density populations.

Signs: Lesions may appear on any part of the body and usually consist of small circular areas of alopecia. Vesicles and pustules may be seen early in the infection. Unlike as with humans, the lesions on a dog's skin are rarely the classic ring shape.

Diagnosis is made through multiple methods. Approximately 50 percent of the time, *M. canis* will fluoresce green when stimulated by certain wavelengths of UV light (known as a Wood's lamp). Additional testing, such as a microscopic examination of hair for spores, a fungal culture, or a biopsy may be necessary to make a definitive diagnosis.

Treatment: Ringworm in dogs is often self-limiting and may resolve within a few months. However, treatment will speed recovery, decrease the spread of lesions on the dog, and decrease the risk of transmission. Treatment generally includes topical antifungal creams or shampoos and/or systemic antifungals.

Ticks

There are approximately 850 species of these bloodsucking parasites that burrow into your Bulldog's skin and engorge themselves with blood, expanding to many times their size. They are dangerous because they can secrete a paralysis-causing toxin and can spread serious diseases, such as Lyme disease, Rocky Mountain spotted fever, Texas fever, tularemia, babesiosis, and canine ehrlichiosis. Ticks can be infected with and transmit more than one disease, so it's not uncommon to see a dog

Highly contagious among dogs, scabies is spread by direct contact.

Ticks live in wooded or grassy areas, where your Bulldog is most likely to pick one up.

infected with more than one disease at a time. In severe infestations, anemia and even death may occur.

Wooded or grassy areas and overgrown fields are areas where your Bulldog is most likely to pick up ticks. Ticks commonly embed themselves between the toes, in the ears, and around the neck but can be found elsewhere on the body. Each species has its own favored feeding sites on your Bulldog.

Controlling ticks on your Bulldog is similar to the process for controlling fleas. Some of the once-a-month topical treatments for fleas also kill ticks, but make sure that you check with your veterinarian first. Just as with eradicating fleas, you need to treat your yard, house, doghouse, dog blankets, and your dog with a product specifically designed for ticks. Over-the-counter products are available, such as sprays, foggers, powders, dips, shampoos, and collars. Unlike fleas, ticks are not susceptible to cold weather, so you will need to treat your yard late into the fall and early winter. Again, many of these products may be toxic. It is important to read all labels and follow directions carefully. When in doubt, consult your veterinarian before purchasing and using any tick-control products.

Avoiding tick-infested areas during the peak tick season helps. When walking your dog, do not allow him to wander off designated paths or near low overhanging branches and shrubs where ticks are likely to be waiting for an unsuspecting Bulldog to pass by.

BULLDOG-SPECIFIC HEALTH ISSUES

While responsible breeders are working to control, and in many instances eliminate, health problems, it's highly likely that your Bulldog will experience one or more health problems during his lifetime. The more common issues and the ones you should be most concerned about include allergies, cystinuria, eye and skin problems, hip dysplasia, and respiratory problems.

Allergies

Two of the most common allergenic skin diseases in dogs worldwide are flea allergy dermatitis (FAD) and atopic dermatitis (AD).

Flea Allergy Dermatitis (FAD)

Flea allergy dermatitis, also known as bite hypersensitivity, tends to be most prevalent during the summer, when fleas are most rampant and annoying. One bite from this tiny pest can make your dog's life (and yours!) miserable and plunge him into a vicious cycle of biting, scratching, and licking.

Fleas feeding on your Bulldog inject saliva that contains different antigens and histamine-like substances, resulting in irritation and itching sensations that can range from mild to downright nasty. The severity of FAD is dependent on the number of fleas feeding on a dog and the amount of antigen injected.

Dogs with FAD usually itch over their entire bodies, experience generalized hair loss, and develop red, inflamed skin and hot spots. Frequently restless and uncomfortable, they usually spend the majority of their time scratching, digging, licking, and chewing their skin. It's a miserable and agonizing situation for dogs.

Treatments vary and can be multifaceted. Of primary importance is a strict flea control program. Rapid-acting topical and systemic anti-flea products are available and can help diminish symptoms. Veterinarians frequently recommend hypoallergenic or colloidal oatmeal-type shampoos to remove allergens, and topical anti-itch creams to soothe the skin. These products can provide immediate short-term relief but are not always a long-term solution. Fatty acid supplements, such as omega-3 and -6 found in flaxseed and fish oils, are proving helpful in reducing the amount and effects of histamine. In some cases, veterinarians prescribe corticosteroids to reduce itching.

Atopic Dermatitis (AD)

Atopic dermatitis (AD) is a skin condition caused by a genetic predisposition and hypersensitivity to environmental allergens that usually include tree, grass, and weed pollens, dust mites, and mold spores—all

Atopic dermatitis is a skin condition caused by a genetic predisposition and hypersensitivity to environmental allergens, including tree, grass, and weed pollens.

The mean age of dogs at the time of cystinuria stone removal is 4.8 years plus or minus 2.5 years. The majority, 98 percent, are male dogs. Nearly all stones, 97 percent, are removed from the lower urinary tract.

of which are lightweight and move freely and easily through the air. Exposure to these allergens triggers an immune system response, causing itchy and inflamed skin and sending your Bulldog into a vicious cycle of chewing, scratching, digging, and biting at his skin.

Unfortunately, Bulldogs, along with a number of other breeds, are at risk for developing AD. Depending on where you live and the allergens your dog is sensitive to, symptoms may be seasonal or nonseasonal. Some dogs show symptoms year round, with exacerbations at certain times of the year, such as during the summer and fall seasons when pollen activity is high. The age of onset is generally between one and three years. Some Bulldogs may show symptoms as early as six months of age, but it is very uncommon for dogs under six months to exhibit symptoms. Veterinarians must resort to a process of elimination—looking first at the dog's history (age, breed, sex, affected areas of the body, response to previous treatments, etc.); clinical symptoms (scratching, biting, chewing, inflamed skin, hair loss); and then rule out other conditions, such as food allergies, flea infestation, parasites, and mange, which have similar overlapping symptoms.

Although incurable, AD in many cases can be controlled using multifaceted treatments, such as immunotherapy, drug therapy, and desensitization. A veterinarian may also prescribe corticosteroids for itching. Reducing your Bulldog's exposure to triggering allergens, combined with the use of household air filters, hypoallergenic shampoos, topical anti-itch creams, and polyunsaturated fatty acids (omega-3 and omega-6 fatty acids) supplements can help when combined with medical treatment. Whirlpool therapy with an anti-itching shampoo is proving helpful as well, with one study indicating that dogs improved by 50 to 90 percent.

Cystinuria

Bulldogs are among approximately 70 breeds that appear genetically predisposed to cystinuria, a disease involving a disorder of the amino acid transport of cystine, which, along with other amino acids, is absorbed through the intestines, filtered through the kidneys, and then reabsorbed by special kidney transporters. Most "healthy" dogs reabsorb about 97 percent of the cystine. In cystinuria, a failure of the kidney to reabsorb cystine leads to excess cystine in the urine, predisposing the dog to the formation of cystine crystals and uroliths. Only a small amount of cystine above the normal concentration predisposes a dog to the formation of cystine crystals, uroliths, and urinary obstruction in acidic urine. When too much cystine accumulates in a dog's urine, it predisposes the dog to cystine crystals and painful uroliths (stones) that can lead to kidney, bladder, and other urinary tract obstructions. Obstruction, which can be fatal, occurs when no urine or very little urine can pass.

Statistics are not available on the prevalence of the condition in the breed; although one study showed that Bulldogs were 32.2 percent more likely to develop cystine uroliths than other breeds. A second unrelated study showed Bulldogs were 40.7 times more likely than other breeds to develop cystine uroliths. Males are more commonly affected than females, as males have a narrower, less dilatable urethra, and when urine passes over the os penis, stones can get lodged and cause an obstruction. Females rarely obstruct because they have no narrowing of the urinary pathway. Owners should frequently check their dogs, especially males, to make sure that they are urinating without any problems. Whenever a Bulldog exhibits any sign of difficult urinating, a

Bulldogs are prone to several eye problems.

veterinarian should be consulted immediately.

Evaluating clinical signs, as well as the dog's history of recurrent urinary tract infections, blood in the urine, and straining or difficulty urinating, provide a preliminary diagnosis. A microscopic urinalysis examination and an inexpensive cyanide-nitroprusside urine test are also used. Ultrasound and radiography are used to detect stones. Elevated cystine levels indicate that a dog may be at increased risk for forming stones; however, cystine excretion can vary. Low cystine levels do not prove that a dog does not have cystinuria, and the absence of stones does not preclude a dog from developing stones in the future. A definitive diagnosis comes from mineral analysis of stones retrieved during urination or surgery.

Treatment is multifaceted and generally includes increasing urine volume and giving thiol-containing drugs that help to increase the solubility of cystine in the urine. Modifying the diet by reducing dietary protein and increasing water intake helps. Feeding wet food rather than dry food may help as well. If dry food is fed, plenty of water must be given. If blockage occurs due to cystine stones, treatment may include surgically removing the stone, flushing the stone out through a catheter (urohydropropulsion), breaking stones into small pieces (lithotripsy), or creating a new opening in the urethra to allow a male to urinate more like a female.

Eye Problems

Bulldogs, like many other breeds, are prone to several eye problems that pose serious risk to your dog's health.

Distichia and Ectopic Cilia

Distichia are abnormal eyelashes emerging from the meibomian glands (oil glands at the rim of the eyelids). It occurs in many breeds, but brachycephalic dogs, including Bulldogs, appear predisposed to the condition.

Ectopic cilia (or atypical distichia) are also hairs growing from oil glands on the eyelids, but the lashes protrude from the inner surface of the eyelid and are very painful, often causing corneal ulcers. Ectopic cilia generally affect young adult dogs or older puppies.

Dogs may be asymptomatic, or in more severe cases, may have considerable irritation, an overflow of tears (epiphora), a swelling, inflammation, twitching of the eyelid (blepharospasm), infection of the membrane lining of the eyelids (conjunctivitis), or an inflammation of the cornea (keratitis). Treatment may include topical lubricant ointments, or in severe or recurrent cases, the offending eyelash is surgically removed.

Entropion and Ectropion

Entropion is a condition in which the lower eyelid, along with the eyelashes, rolls into the eye, leading to possible damage and ulcerations of the cornea. One or both eyes may be involved, and in rare cases the upper eyelid may also be affected. Symptoms include squinting and redness and inflammation of the eye. Some dogs will scratch at the eye, possibly causing further damage. Surgery is the only treatment.

Ectropion is a condition in which the lower eyelid rolls outward, causing a looseness or drooping of the eyelid, which results in the exposure of an abnormally large amount of conjunctival lining. Resulting problems include chronic conjunctivitis and irritation to the cornea. Unless very pronounced, ectropion

Bulldogs are predisposed to interdigital pyoderma, an infection that occurs in between the toes. Signs include lameness and persistent licking at the feet.

does not lead to severe diseases of the eye itself. Mild cases are often treated with eye drops or salves. Severe cases require surgery to remove excess tissue.

Keratoconjunctivitis Sicca (KCS)/Dry Eye

A common condition in Bulldogs, KCS is a condition in which there are not enough tears produced in the eye. The mode of inheritance has yet to be identified. However, the majority of KCS cases are thought to be caused by a dog's own immune system. Other causes include but are not limited to canine distemper virus, congenital gland hypoplasia, chronic conjunctivitis, hypothyroidism, diabetes, Cushing's disease, and facial nerve paralysis.

Symptoms include irritation, pawing at the eye, squinting, sensitivity to light, a thick mucoid discharge from one or both eyes, and conjunctivitis. In many cases, chronic or recurring irritation, infection of the conjunctiva and cornea, and corneal ulcers may occur. Diagnosis is through observation of clinical symptoms—particularly in breeds predisposed to KCS. A definitive diagnosis is made via a Schirmer Tear Test (STT), which is used to measure tear production, as well as the basal and reflex components of the tear film.

Treatment generally includes managing this frustrating, painful, and potentially blinding condition through tear stimulants and artificial tear replacements. In some cases, surgery to decrease corneal exposure may be necessary.

Prolapsed Third Eyelid Gland (PTEG)/Cherry Eye

Dogs have a third eyelid that slides over the surface of the eye for protection. Located deep within the tissues of the third eyelid is a gland known as the third eyelid gland (TEG). The TEG produces 40 percent of the tear volume to the surface of the eye. Normally, the TEG is hidden out of sight and anchored to the tissues of the eye socket by ligaments. Prolapsed third eyelid gland (PTEG), also known as prolapse of the nictitans gland, or by the slang term "cherry eye," occurs as a result of weak ligaments that allow the third eyelid gland to pop out of its normal position, looking like a round pink object—or cherry—in the inside corner of the eye.

Thought to be an inherited condition, it is a common occurrence in Bulldogs and can occur in one or both eyes. The prolapsed TEG should never be removed. Treatment involves surgically repositioning and suturing the TEG into place. Surgical complications are minimal, and the recurrence rate for Bulldogs is about 10 percent. If left untreated, the risk of developing dry eye greatly increases.

Skin Problems

Bulldogs can experience a number of skin-related problems, including interdigital pyoderma and skin fold dermatitis.

Interdigital Pyoderma or Furunculosis

Interdigital furuncles (furuncles being a fancy word for boils) are painful nodular lesions located in the interdigital webs of dogs. Frequently, albeit incorrectly, referred to as interdigital cysts, these lesions are areas of deep nodular granulomatous inflammation or dermatitis. They are almost never cystic.

The condition results primarily from a deep infection caused by the bacterium *Staphylococcus intermedius*. The short bristly hairs located on the webbing between the toes, which get trapped in the furuncles and act as a foreign body, predispose many breeds, including Bulldogs, to the condition. Hair is very inflammatory, and the short shafts of hair are easily forced backwards into the hair follicles during walking or running. In

The Bulldog's facial skin folds make him susceptible to skin fold dermatitis.

chronic conditions, scar tissue may form and entrap hair material, worsening the prognosis. Furuncles are usually painful, and a dog may show obvious lameness and may lick or bite at the lesions.

Diagnosis is based on clinical diagnosis, as well as a fine needle aspirate to confirm the presence of inflammatory infiltrate, as well as skin scrapings to rule in or out *Demodex* mites. Treatment usually consists of topical and systemic treatments, including foot soaks in warm water with or without an antibiotic solution, and oral antibiotics. Antihistamines may help to relieve itching, if present. In some instances, surgery may be required to identify and remove foreign bodies.

Skin Fold Dermatitis

Skin fold dermatitis is an inflammatory condition associated with superficial pyoderma, resulting from abnormal surface-to-surface contact of skin folds and/or mucous membranes. Skin folds may be congenital or they can be acquired through obesity or aging. The overlapping of skin causes physical abrasions, an increase in temperature, lack of ventilation, and an abnormal accumulation of skin secretions. Because air cannot get to the bottom of the wrinkles—allowing adequate ventilation for the skin to air and dry out—skin in the folds accumulates an excessive amount of sebaceous (oily or greasy) material, which provides a breeding ground for skin bacteria to proliferate and produce breakdown products that cause skin fold dermatitis.

Symptoms include red, raw, inflamed or infected skin. In some cases, a smell may be present, as well as an accumulation of "goop" in the wrinkles. Treatment generally consists of a daily cleaning of the wrinkles with a damp cloth. Baby wipes with aloe work well because the aloe soothes the skin. Be sure to thoroughly dry the folds when finished. Your vet may recommend an antiseptic product or an astringent combined with topical steroid preparations to dry the area and reduce inflammation. Systemic antibiotics along with steroids may also be recommended in severe cases to reduce infection and inflammation. Recurrent and progressive lesions may require surgery, which involves surgically removing the skin fold and permanently correcting the abnormal environment.

Respiratory Problems

Compared to other breeds, Bulldogs, as well as other brachycephalic breeds, have a shortened skull. The breeding for these exaggerated features has resulted in a number of respiratory problems because as the face and nose bones are shortened, the dog's respiratory anatomy also changes, causing anatomic abnormalities. Not every Bulldog has breathing problems, but many do. As a result, many Bulldogs have difficulty swallowing, have an increased susceptibility to heat-induced illnesses, and have increased anesthetic risks. Therefore it's a good idea to understand the common respiratory problems so that you can keep your

Some Bulldogs, because of their narrow trachea and nostrils, are more prone to respiratory problems.

Signs of Respiratory Distress

Symptoms of brachycephalic airway syndrome vary but generally include:

- collapse
- exercise intolerance
- gagging, coughing, or snorting
- labored and/or noisy breathing
- open-mouth breathing
- restlessness

If you suspect respiratory distress, always err on the side of caution and seek immediate veterinary attention.

Bulldog safe and help him to breathe easier.

Brachycephalic airway syndrome is a collection of physical abnormalities, with the most common problems being stenotic nares and elongated soft palate. Your Bulldog may experience one or more of these abnormalities.

Stenotic Nares

Stenotic nares is the medical term for narrowing of the nostrils—or pinched nostrils. These malformed nostrils are narrow or collapse inward, making it difficult for dogs to breathe through their noses. As a result, dogs are forced to breathe through their mouths. Surgically removing a wedge of tissue from the nostrils allows better airflow through the nose.

Elongated Soft Palate

The soft palate is a soft tissue suspended from the rear of the hard palate; it serves as a mobile flap—closing off a dog's airway (nasopharynx) during swallowing to prevent foods and liquids from entering the nasal cavity. Due to the Bulldog's facial structure, oftentimes the soft palate is too long (elongated) and it extends into the back of the throat, blocking the airway.

Treatment involves surgically shortening the elongated soft palate so that it no longer protrudes into the throat.

Heat-Induced Illnesses

Another complicating factor associated with a Bulldog's compromised airway is a predisposition to heat-induced illnesses. A number of seemingly "normal" situations can lead to your dog's overheating, which can kill him.

The average body temperature of a dog is 101.5°F (38.6°C), with a normal range between 100° and 102°F (37° and 39°C). These are core temperatures and are based on rectal thermometer readings. While temperatures can vary throughout a dog's body, the core temperature is what a dog's body uses to maintain constant internal conditions, also known as homeostatic condition, and includes blood pressure, blood chemistry, and body temperature. Heat-induced illnesses occur when a dog's normal body mechanisms cannot keep his temperature within a safe range.

Unlike humans, dogs do not sweat. Their primary cooling mechanisms are panting and conduction. When overheated dogs pant, they breathe in and out through their mouths. They inhale cool air, and as the air moves into their lungs, it absorbs heat and moisture. When they exhale, the hot air passes over their wet tongues and evaporation occurs, enhancing and maximizing heat loss and cooling their bodies. Some Bulldogs, because of their narrow trachea and nostrils, cannot exchange air as quickly as other breeds. When they start to overheat, they begin to pant more rapidly, which may add stress. As previously mentioned, this added stress can cause swelling of the throat, making panting less effective for cooling your Bulldog. Conduction, a secondary method of

If your Bulldog begins to pant more rapidly and seems restless, he may be overheating. Get him to a cool place immediately.

cooling, occurs when a dog lies down on a cool surface, such as a tile floor, grass, or wet concrete. The heat from his body is transferred to the cool surface.

The specific heat-related health issues that you should be aware of are heat exhaustion, heat prostration, and heatstroke.

Heat Exhaustion

Heat exhaustion is the least severe of the heat-related illnesses. However, it must be taken seriously. Often referred to as a mild case of heatstroke, it is characterized by lethargy and an inability to perform normal activities. If your Bulldog overheats, get him to a cool environment immediately, such as an air-conditioned room. Lower his temperature by

submerging his body in cool (not cold) water (keep his head elevated above the water) or by applying cool water to his body with a shower or hose. Place him on a wet towel to keep him cool, or use a fan. If he will drink on his own, give him water or a hydrating solution. Do not force water, because he is likely to choke. Seek veterinary attention to verify that permanent damage did not occur.

Heat Prostration

Heat prostration is the next level and is considered a moderate case of heatstroke with a dog's body temperature around 104° to 106°F (40° to 41°C). Possible signs include rapid panting, red or pale gums, weakness, vomiting, mental confusion, and dizziness.

Seek immediate veterinary attention. Dogs with a moderate case of heatstroke can often recover without complicating health problems.

Heatstroke

Heatstroke is the most severe form of heat prostration and occurs when a dog's body temperature is over 106°F (41°C). Symptoms include rapid panting, collapsing, inability to stand up, red or pale gums, thick and sticky saliva, weakness, vomiting (with or without blood), diarrhea, shock, fainting, or coma. This is a life-threatening medical emergency that can result in multiple organ-system dysfunction, including the respiratory, cardiovascular, gastrointestinal, renal, and central nervous systems. Immediate veterinary assistance is essential.

Hip Dysplasia (HD)

Hip dysplasia is a defect in the conformation of the hip joint that can cause weakness and lameness to a dog's rear quarters, resulting in arthritis, severe debilitating pain, and crippling. More specifically, it is a failure of the head of the femur (thighbone) to properly fit into the acetabulum (hip bone). The resulting arthritis is frequently referred to as degenerative joint disease, arthrosis, or osteroarthritis. HD is considered to be a polygenic inherited disorder, meaning that it is probably controlled by an unknown number of genes. Environmental factors such as nutrition and exercise may also be contributing factors, although this is highly debatable among experts.

While HD is mostly associated with medium- and large-breed dogs, the Orthopedic Foundation for Animals (OFA) rates Bulldogs with the highest prevalence of hip dysplasia based on OFA data of at least 100 evaluations from January 1994 through December 2008, with 73.6 percent of Bulldogs considered dysplastic and only 0.2 percent rated excellent.

Symptoms vary, making it difficult, if not impossible, to predict when or even whether a dysplastic Bulldog will show symptoms. Some dogs may be asymptomatic—showing no pain whatsoever. Others may exhibit mild to severe lameness. Caloric intake, exercise, and weather can influence the appearance of symptoms that may include a decrease in activity, walking or running with an altered gait, resisting movements requiring full extension or flexion of the rear legs, stiffness and pain in the rear

According to the Orthopedic Foundation for Animals (OFA), Bulldogs have the highest prevalence of hip dysplasia.

legs after exercise or first thing in the morning upon rising, difficulty rising from a lying or sitting position, and balking at using stairs.

A preliminary diagnosis is generally made through a combination of a physical examination and x-rays and by ruling out other problems, such as hip and spine disorders, ruptured cruciate ligament, Lyme disease, and so forth. That said, most Bulldog owners do not x-ray hips, the reason being that in order to do so, the dogs must be anesthetized, and as previously mentioned, Bulldogs, because of their brachycephalic features, have increased anesthetic risks. Treatment varies and can include nutraceuticals, such as glucosamine, chondroitin, and methylsulfonylmethane (MSM), or over-the-counter drugs, such as buffered aspirin. Your veterinarian may also prescribe a pain reliever. Surgery is an option for many breeds, but because of the Bulldog's brachycephalic features, he may or may not be a good candidate.

GENERAL HEALTH ISSUES

Other health problems that you may encounter with less frequency but remain of great concern to Bulldog owners and breeders include anasarca, aortic stenosis, and skeletal disorders.

Anasarca

Anasarca puppies, also referred to as walrus puppies, or occasionally water puppies, rubber puppies, or swimmer puppies, are born with a lethal and abnormal amount of fluid under their skin. A discouraging lack of knowledge exists, and much of what experts do know is speculative. The life-threatening condition appears to develop in the later part of gestation; puppies can be born up to four or five times their normal weight as a result of the excess fluid. One or all of the puppies may be affected. Survival rates are low, and due

to the abnormally large size of the puppies, a Caesarean delivery is always necessary. In Bulldogs, the condition is known to be hereditary, although the mode of inheritance is unknown.

While survival rates are low, some water puppies do survive provided they receive immediate veterinary treatment, including administering a diuretic and potassium, as well as elevating the puppy's temperature to 100°F (37.7°C) and gently massaging the puppy to stimulate circulation.

Aortic Stenosis

Bulldogs are prone to aortic stenosis—a narrowing of the pathway for blood leaving the heart. One of the more common forms is subaortic stenosis (SAS), or subvalvular aortic stenosis. The "sub" of subaortic identifies the constriction as being located just below the aortic valve. The narrowing (stenosis) caused by the abnormal formation of nodules or a fibrous ridge or ring of tissue results in a partial obstruction of blood flow. Think of SAS in terms of water running through a garden hose. If you put your thumb over the end of the hose, making the opening smaller, the water speed increases as the same volume of water tries to pass through the restricted opening. In the same way, an SAS-affected heart must work harder to pump the same volume of blood. This causes the muscle in the wall of the left ventricle to thicken, leading to an irregular heartbeat, which can cause a lack of blood to the heart, congestive heart failure, or sudden death.

SAS is an inherited condition that develops soon after birth, with the disease progressing as the puppy grows. Not all dogs develop severe forms of SAS, and those with a mild case may not show symptoms until they are several years old. A heart murmur, which is caused by blood being pumped across the stenosis into the aorta, is the primary symptom.

Less common symptoms include weakness, exercise intolerance, or temporary loss of consciousness. The condition is difficult to diagnose; most veterinary cardiologists use Doppler echocardiography, which measures the flow of blood across the stenotic opening.

Mildly affected dogs are usually asymptomatic and can often live full lives without treatment. Dogs with moderate to severe cases are expected to have shortened life expectancies. Treatment generally consists of medications. Surgery can be performed at some universities, but it is expensive and the mortality rates are high—as high as 50 percent, according to some reports.

Cancers

Any number of cancers can affect dogs, including the Bulldog breed. Three of the more common cancers include hemangiosarcoma, lymphosarcoma, and mammary gland tumors.

Hemangiosarcoma: This is one of the more frustrating canine cancers due to its aggressive and highly malignant nature. Symptoms are often subtle or non-existent until the final stages, with some dogs succumbing to the disease within days of the initial diagnosis. Clinical signs depend on the tumor size, localization, presence of metastasis, or rupture of the tumor. Symptoms may be nonspecific, such as lethargy and weight loss, or more specific, including shortness of breath, abdominal effusion, hypovolemic shock, or

The incidence of malignant mammary tumors in unspayed females is higher than any other cancer.

sudden death secondary to tumor rupture and hemorrhage. Once diagnosed, the prognosis is poor, with the inevitable outcome being fatal despite aggressive surgical, drug, or radiation treatment.

Lymphosarcoma: This cancer is caused by a cancerous proliferation of lymphocytes (cells that normally function in the immune system). Most dogs are asymptomatic; however, 20 to 40 percent show symptoms of vomiting, diarrhea, loss of appetite, lethargy, weakness, pale mucous membranes, anorexia, or weight loss. Multi-drug chemotherapy is the treatment of choice by most veterinarians.

Malignant Mammary Tumors: The incidence of malignant mammary tumors in unspayed females is higher than any other cancer. They are the most common tumors in unspayed female dogs between five and ten years of age. In females spayed prior to their first heat cycle, malignant mammary cancer is very rare—.05 percent. In females spayed after their second heat, the risk jumps to 26 percent. Mammary tumors are rare in male dogs, but they do occur, and they are very aggressive and have a poor prognosis. Tumors generally appear as a solitary nodule and more commonly as multiple masses. With early detection and prompt treatment, many tumors can be successfully treated. Surgery is the recommended treatment, unless the dog is very old. Early spaying—before a female has her first heat cycle—is the best prevention. A direct and well-documented link exists between the early spaying of females and the reduction in the incidence of mammary cancer.

Skeletal Disorders

Elbow Disease: Anatomically, a dog's elbow joint is similar to a human's. A complicated yet efficient hinge-type joint, it is created by the junction of three different bones: the radius, ulna, and humerus. These bones fit and function together with little room for error, and all the parts must work harmoniously for maximum soundness and efficiency. Anything that alters the elbow configuration will affect a dog's ability to use his leg correctly.

Elbow disease—frequently referred to as elbow dysplasia or elbow incongruency—is really a syndrome for different elbow abnormalities. Symptoms for all of them are similar and can include a weight-bearing lameness in the front legs that persists for more than a few days, reduction in range of movement, and pain when a veterinarian manipulates the joint. Your veterinarian may recommend a set of x-rays and in some cases a computed tomography (CT) scan or exploratory surgery to establish a definitive diagnosis. Treatment varies, depending on the diagnosis.

Patellar Luxation: Patellar luxation is a medical term used to describe a slipped or dislocated kneecap. The problem is a concern for breeders of Bulldogs, as well as small and toy breeds. There are three major components involved in luxating patellas: the femur (thighbone), patella (kneecap), and tibia (second thigh). The three components come together at the stifle, the anatomical equivalent of the human knee. A Bulldog's kneecap, which is very similar to a human's kneecap, is the flat, moveable bone at the front of the knee. Its job is to protect the large tendon of the quadriceps muscle while it is used to straighten the stifle.

Here are things that can go wrong, resulting in a luxated patella: The groove is shallow and not well developed, or the femur and tibia are not properly lined up so that the patella rests securely in the grove. In these instances, there is little to prevent the kneecap from shifting or slipping out of place and riding on the inner surface of the femur. In addition, the lack of stability of the patellar tendon can cause the kneecap to slip out of place. Either of these conditions, or a combination of the conditions, can result in a dislocated kneecap.

Patellar luxations are a congenital condition, meaning that the structural changes that lead to luxation are present at the time of birth. The actual dislocation may not be present, but the writing is on the wall, so to speak. In addition, luxated patellas are thought to be inherited, but the exact mode of inheritance—the genes that cause the abnormality—is not yet known.

Diagnosis is relatively simple and includes palpation of the joint and manual luxation of the kneecap when a puppy is around four to six months of age. Patellar luxation is graded on a scale of one to four, depending on the severity. Surgical correction to correct the alignment is frequently the recommended treatment, coupled with a program to keep extra weight from exacerbating the problem.

ALTERNATIVE THERAPIES

Alternative therapies are perhaps one of the more fascinating topics of canine health, as they are steadily gaining popularity in the treatment of a variety of canine ailments from cancer to chronic pain to behavioral problems. As the demand for alternative medicine for humans has grown, many owners are looking outside of the traditional approaches and exploring "alternative" treatment options for their dogs.

Alternative medicine is a broad term used to describe anything other than conventional medical treatments and practices. The term itself is a bit misleading because it suggests performing one treatment in lieu of another option. To counter any confusion, the more popular terms "complementary therapy" or "complementary and alternative veterinary medicine" (CAVM) are frequently used. Some practitioners who use both CAVM and traditional Western medicine use the term "integrative medicine."

Traditional medicine is rooted in science, physics, chemistry, and biology, and its practices are backed by scientific data. While some alternative medicine has been around for thousands of years, the evidence for it comes less from clinical trials and more from the anecdotes and testimonials of veterinarians and dog owners.

The topic of alternative or complementary medicine is too complex to cover in this limited amount of space. The following brief descriptions are intended to familiarize you with some of the more popular treatments.

A note of caution: Alternative medicine does not replace traditional veterinary medicine or surgery but can provide a valuable alternative or complementary method of care. The American Veterinary Medical Association (AVMA) has established guidelines for veterinary acupuncture, chiropractic, homeopathic, and holistic medicine. Equally important, alternative and herbal do not mean harmless. The Food and Drug Administration (FDA) does not regulate herbs and natural supplements. They can cause side effects or result in cross-reactions if combined with other supplements or medications. Quality control is also a major concern. Consumerlab.com, an independent testing facility, provides analyses of many popular products. To prevent problems, always consult your veterinarian.

Acupuncture

An age-old traditional Chinese medicine (TCM), acupuncture involves the insertion of very fine needles into specific points in the body. In China it has been used to treat animals for nearly 4,000 years. In North America it is not as readily accepted, but its

Acupuncture involves the insertion of very fine needles into specific points in the body.

acceptance as a valid treatment for dogs is growing. Dogs with skeletal disorders, such as arthritis and hip dysplasia, have been successfully treated. So too have dogs with allergies, gastrointestinal, respiratory, urinary, and musculoskeletal disorders, as well as chronic or severe pain.

The length and frequency of treatment depends on the problem and condition of the dog.

For additional information, contact the American Academy of Veterinary Acupuncture (AAVA) at www.aava.org and the American Veterinary Medical Association (AVMA) www.avma.org.

Chiropractic Therapy

A holistic approach to the treatment of many health and locomotion problems of dogs, chiropractic manipulation involves the movement of the joints to correct alignment and to return the body to homeostasis. Chiropractic treatment is based on the principle that the body can heal itself when the skeletal system is correctly aligned. When the spine is even slightly displaced, nerves become irritated. Chiropractors feel for irregularities (subluxations) and adjust them, which restores correct vertebral alignment. Veterinarians can be licensed by the American Veterinary Chiropractic Association (AVCA). Human chiropractors can also work on your Bulldog, but like veterinarians, they need special training in animal chiropractic care.

For additional information, contact the American Veterinary Chiropractic Association (AVCA) at www.animalchiropractic.org.

Herbal Medicine

Herbal medicine focuses on using plants and other natural ingredients to enhance well-being. It emphasizes therapies that are designed to optimize systems' functions and correct immune, digestive, and metabolic deficiencies. Traditional herbal remedies are based on standard formulas created thousands of years ago, which reportedly have antibiotic, antifungal, and even anticancer properties. Proponents of herbal medicine believe that prescribing whole plants provides both synergistic and safety advantages. Some of the more common herbal remedies include

Herbal medicine focuses on using plants and other natural ingredients to enhance well-being.

chrysanthemum, cinnamon, garlic, pumpkin, and curry.

Holistic Medicine

Holistic medicine differs from homeopathy, although some confuse the terms or use them interchangeably. Holistic medicine focuses on the whole animal rather than the disease. The holistic approach uses both conventional and alternative treatments. The underlying philosophy of holistic medicine is that symptoms reflect the underlying healthy status of the energy field. Symptoms that an individual has are the result of the energy field's attempting to heal the underlying imbalance. Holistic practitioners use all of the symptoms an animal currently has and has ever had in the past to find and treat the individual's underlying predisposition to illness.

Homeopathic Care

Homeopathy follows the "law of similars" principle, or "similar cures similar," meaning that a substance that could produce symptoms in a healthy person could cure an ill person with the same symptoms. Hence, the word homeo (similar) pathy (suffering), or homeopathic. Theoretically, the principle is similar to that of inoculations. A vaccine, that purposely contains live, weakened, or dead pathogens stimulates a dog's immune system to produce disease-fighting antibodies against infectious diseases. Homeopathic remedies are theorized to stimulate recovery in a similar manner.

For additional information, contact the American Veterinary Medical Association (AVMA) at www.avma.org or the Food and Drug Administration (FDA) at www.fda.gov.

Massage

Touch is an essential component of the human/canine relationship. Massage therapy involves the physical manipulation of muscles and tendons and can increase blood supply, improve circulation, produce physical and psychological changes, relieve pain, and produce a healing effect. It can result in improved range of movement and a better performance for canine athletes.

Tellington-Touch, or TTouch, is one of the more popular techniques developed by Linda Tellington-Jones. Based on circular movements of the fingers and hands all over the body, the Tellington Method utilizes a variety of techniques of touch, movement, and body language to affect behavior and performance, and to increase an animal's willingness and ability to learn in a painless and anxiety-free environment. The TTouch organization offers a two-year certification program.

Currently, no states require testing before

becoming a canine massage therapist. Before selecting a practitioner, ensure that he or she has received training specifically for working with dogs, as well as anatomy, physiology, and hands-on training. Be certain that your dog is comfortable with the person and that the person knows how to handle him. As always, trust your and your dog's instincts.

EMERGENCY CARE

Hopefully, you will never have to deal with anything more serious than a few bumps and bruises with your Bulldog. However, owning a Bulldog means that you must be prepared for myriad calamities and medical emergencies.

First aid is not a substitute for veterinary attention, but knowing the difference between a minor situation and a life-threatening emergency, and knowing what to do, may save your dog's life until he receives veterinary care. When in doubt, always err on the side of caution and contact your veterinarian or 24-hour emergency clinic. Here are a few—but certainly not all—of the more common situations you are likely to encounter.

You should know basic first aid and have the proper equipment on hand in case your Bulldog should ever have an accident.

Bee and Insect Bites

Bee and other insect bites can cause swelling, redness, and itching. An allergic reaction or a bite from a poisonous spider, such as a black widow or brown recluse, can cause life-threatening complications including facial swelling, vomiting, difficulty in breathing, and collapse. In those instances, seek immediate veterinary attention.

For less severe cases, if you can locate the stinger, pull it out with tweezers, or try to scrape it out with a stiff material, such as the edge of a credit card. Avoid putting pressure on a venom sac, as this can inject more venom into the dog. Apply cool compresses to the bite area. A baking soda and water paste applied to the area will neutralize some of the venom. Do not administer any medications without consulting a veterinarian.

Dog Bites

Dog fights are dangerous for both dogs and humans, especially when you try to intervene. Punctures are most common, as are lacerations, but it's not uncommon for a dog's ears to get ripped or completely torn off in the process. Depending on the severity of the bite and whether your dog is agreeable, you might attempt to clip the hair around the wound and clean it with hydrogen peroxide, but do not bandage it. Consult your veterinarian about antibiotics to prevent infection. Chances are the veterinarian will want to see your dog.

Choking

Dogs can choke on any number of items, from disemboweled doll parts to buttons to dog bones. Any obstruction of your dog's airway is a life-threatening emergency and must be dealt with immediately to prevent brain damage or death. The symptoms of choking vary; however, the most common signs include a coughing, gagging, or retching noise and pawing at the side of the face. Your Bulldog's tongue may turn blue, and he may collapse. If he can get some air around the obstruction, seek veterinary attention immediately.

If he cannot get air around the obstruction, work on clearing his airway. If possible, pull your Bulldog's lower jaw open and tilt his head upward. If an object is visible, try to remove it with your finger without pushing it deeper. Use extreme caution to avoid being bitten. Regardless of how friendly your dog might be, a panicked choking dog is likely to bite as a reflex mechanism. Once you have cleared your dog's airway, have him examined by a veterinarian as soon as possible.

Diarrhea

Diarrhea can occur if you overfeed your dog, if you change his normal food from one brand to another too quickly, or if there is a change in water while traveling. (That's why it is always prudent to carry your own water or purchase bottled water.) Unclean feeding bowls, stress, and allergies can also cause diarrhea. It can also be a symptom of intestinal parasites or disease.

Equally important, know what your Bulldog's normal stools look like. When you know what is normal, you are more likely to recognize when something is not normal. Normal feces vary in color and consistency depending on the individual dog and his diet. Normal color usually ranges from light brown to dark brown. If the diarrhea is slight and your dog has no other symptoms, it may be nothing more than minor gastric upset. Withholding food for 24 hours and then feeding a mixture of cooked white rice and boiled chicken or extra-lean

hamburger browned in a skillet with any excess grease removed may correct the problem. Canned pumpkin is known to help with diarrhea, as well as constipation. Medications such as bismuth subsalicylate or kaolin/pectin every four hours may also fix the problem. A veterinarian will be able to give you the correct dosage. Always check with your veterinarian before giving your dog any medications intended for humans. If you have a puppy or older dog with diarrhea or if the diarrhea is black or green or your dog is showing other signs of illness, call your veterinarian right away.

Poisoning

If you suspect that your Bulldog has come in contact with a poisonous substance, treat it as a medical emergency. Do not delay. Seek immediate veterinary attention. If you see your dog eating or drinking a poisonous substance, do not wait for symptoms to develop. Call the Poison Control Center or take your dog to the nearest veterinary clinic. Do not induce vomiting unless instructed to do so by a veterinarian.

Treatment varies depending on the type of poison ingested. Take with you, if possible, the remains of the toxic product, be it a half-eaten plant, a mangled snail bait package, a leaking herbicide bottle, or an empty box of chocolates. If your dog has vomited, scoop up the remains and take it with you. It can provide the veterinarian with important clues regarding the type of poison your dog ingested.

Training Tidbit

Dogs don't always know what's good for them. Teaching your Bulldog to "leave it" or "drop it" or "give up" dangerous items will help to reduce the odds of his eating or ingesting poisonous substances.

Vomiting

Dogs vomit occasionally, and unlike humans, they can do so with little discomfort. They vomit when they get excited, drink too much water too fast (especially after exercise), gulp their food, when they go for a ride in the car, or after they've eaten grass. If your dog appears to be healthy, a single vomiting incident should not send you rushing to the vet. It may be nothing more than a simple upset stomach. Keep him away from any food for a few hours. Allow him small amounts of water, but don't let him gulp water. Nothing makes a vomiting dog vomit more than a tummy full of water or food. If the problem persists, especially with puppies or old dogs, or if your dog has other symptoms, such as diarrhea, stomach bloating, listlessness, labored breathing or pain, or you see blood or abnormal material in the vomit, contact your veterinarian right away. And don't forget to take a sample of the vomit with you.

CHAPTER 9

BULLDOG TRAINING

As your Bulldog grows and matures, it is important to continue his obedience training. This helps keep him mentally and physically stimulated, and of course, continues to make life more enjoyable for you and your dog. This section will help you to expand upon his puppy training discussed in Chapter 4. However, if your adult Bulldog has little or no training, consider starting with the exercises previously mentioned, as they apply equally well to both untrained puppies and adult dogs. Otherwise, this chapter will help to build upon his current foundation of obedience training.

THE *HEEL*

There are several variations to walking on leash. The formal *heel* command is used by most obedience competitors who are sticklers for precision. They spend years teaching their dogs to walk with their head and body in a specific position. Most Bulldog owners are not going to require that much precision. They are quite happy if their dog is not dragging them down the street.

While the traditional *heel* position is on the handler's left side, there may be times when you do not care whether he is on your left side, right side, or walking out in front of you. That said, it is always easier to teach a dog to walk on leash by starting on the left side and sticking with it until he understands the exercise. Once he has mastered walking nicely on leash, you can allow him to walk on the right side or out in front of you.

The goal is to teach your Bulldog to walk nicely on leash—anywhere within the full extension of his leash, on either side of you, or in front of you—without pulling. He should also learn that a loose leash means that he goes forward, which he is sure to find highly rewarding. Pulling on the leash means that he stops—definitely nonrewarding. Puppies who learn not to pull on the leash grow into adult dogs who do not pull on the leash. They are a joy to own because it is fun to take them for walks, and they are more likely to be included in family outings.

Training Tidbit

How to Teach *Heel*

To begin:

1. Teach this exercise on a buckle collar, never on a choke chain.
2. With your Bulldog on leash, encourage him to stand close to your left leg by luring him into position with a tasty tidbit of food.
3. Praise and reward him with the tidbit when he gets there. "That's my boy!" (Teach a separate command for getting into position on your left side, such as *close* or *with me*. When he is in the position you want, for example, on your left side, reward him with a tidbit and praise, "That's your close" or "Good close!" Eventually, the dog will learn to associate the *close*—or whatever command you choose—with being in position on your left side.)
4. Show him a tidbit of food. When you have his attention, hold the food ever so slightly above his nose, just high enough that his head is up and he can nibble the food without jumping up. With the food in his face, say his name and give your command for walking on a loose leash (e.g., "Fido, let's go," or "Fido, heel") and then start walking forward.
5. Keep your right hand (the one holding the leash) close to your body. This will keep the leash length consistent. As you walk forward, watch the leash. If it begins to tighten, stop walking and stand still. Most likely your Bulldog will come to an abrupt halt and look back at you as if to say, "What the heck?!"
6. Stand still and encourage your Bulldog back into position with a tidbit of food. Try to avoid moving or turning in circles to reposition him. A dog cannot find your left side (i.e., *heel* position) if your left side is constantly moving.
7. When your dog is repositioned on your left side, repeat the abovementioned steps until he is walking beside you without pulling on the leash. When you have taken a few steps, stop and praise and reward him while he is beside you. If you reward him when he is not in the correct position, you will have inadvertently taught him the wrong association.

As your Bulldog grows and matures, it's important to continue his obedience training.

Tips for Walking Nicely

- Always begin training in a familiar, quiet, and nondistractive environment. Your back yard, living room, or family room is ideal.
- Use random rewards and tasty tidbits (e.g., boiled chicken, leftover steak, turkey hot dogs) to keep your Bulldog interested and motivated.
- When first teaching this exercise, be sure to have a tidbit of food in your hand before starting. If you fumble in your pocket for food after your dog has done an excellent job, he will be out of position and you will have lost the opportunity to reinforce the correct position. Remember, timing is everything when training dogs!
- Always dispense the food from your left hand. This will keep your Bulldog from crossing over in front of you—tripping you in the process—to get the tasty tidbit in your right hand.
- If you do your part when your Bulldog is younger and still receptive to learning, then pulling and tugging on the leash will not be a problem as he grows bigger and stronger.
- Teaching a puppy or adult dog to walk on leash takes time. Be patient. You will need to repeat these steps over and over before your dog gets the hang of it.

8. When your dog is walking beside you, tell him that he is smart and clever. Chat sweetly to him to encourage him to walk beside you. Over time, gradually increase the number of steps he is walking on a loose leash, but try not to go so far that he gets out of position and begins pulling on the leash. The goal is to gradually increase the length of time between "Let's go" and rewarding with the treat.

In the beginning, treats are used to lure the dog into the correct position and show him what you want him to do. Once he understands walking nicely on leash, you can begin keeping the treats in your pocket and rewarding him less often.

THE *STAY*

The goal of the *stay* command is to teach your dog to remain in a specific position, such as in a *sit* or *down* until you say that it is okay to move. It is useful in a variety of situations, such as when you want to answer or open the door without your Bulldog bolting through it. It's also useful for when your dog needs to stand for a veterinary examination or stand while being bathed or groomed.

Some trainers teach the *stay* command as a separate command, while others prefer to use the *sit*, *down*, or *stand* command as their *stay* command. The theory is that that when you tell a dog to sit and then stay, you are not asking him to do anything new. Some theorize that this is confusing to the dog. If nothing else, it is somewhat redundant because the theory behind the *sit*, *down*, or *stand* command is that when you tell a dog to sit (or down or stand), he should remain in that position until you ask him to do something. In that sense, your *sit* command is also your *stay* command.

How you decide to teach *stay* will depend on your personal preference. In the grand scheme

Walking nicely on leash is something every Bulldog should learn.

of things, it won't make too much difference. However, consistency is the key. Pick one method and stick with it so as not to confuse your dog.

Sit, Down, or Stand: They All Mean Stay

If you want *sit* (or *down* or *stand*) to also mean *stay*, then from day one teach your adult dog, as well as your puppy, that he is never allowed to release himself from a command until you give him a release word, such as "Okay." Basically, this is teaching him to stay until he gets more information from you.

Always work within your dog's mental and physical capabilities so that you set him up to succeed. You never want to be nagging or correcting a dog during the *stay* exercise. A dog

should not be put in the position of getting corrected for breaking *stays*. He should be taught what *stay* means, as well as the position you want when you give the command. Most dogs do not realize that they are breaking a *stay* when they are just getting comfortable—

By the Numbers

Dogs younger than six or seven months of age are generally not mature enough to comprehend the *stay* command.

especially if they stay in the same spot. Make it clear to your dog if you want a *sit*, *down*, or *stand*. They all mean hold that position until I tell you otherwise.

How to Teach the *Sit-Stay*

If you decide to incorporate a *stay* command, here's how to do it:

1. Start with your dog on a loose leash, sitting beside you.
2. Tell your dog to sit and to stay. You can include a hand signal by holding the open palm of your hand in front of your dog's face about 2 inches (5 cm) from his nose as you say "Stay."
3. Watch your dog closely for the slightest movement that may indicate that he is about to stand up or lie down. Try to be proactive in your training by reminding your dog to stay before he moves. Once he has remained in position for a few seconds, praise calmly and warmly with "Good stay" and a treat. Include calm, physical praise, such as gentle stroking—but not so enthusiastically that he gets excited and forgets the task at hand.

The *stay* teaches your dog to remain in a specific position until you say that it's okay to move.

4. As soon as you see any movement, repeat your *stay* command firmly but not harshly.

5. If your dog stands up, use your leash to prevent him from moving away, and then get him into the *sit* position again. If he lies down, gently reposition him and remind him to stay.

6. Reward him with a treat first and then release him with an "Okay" or "Free" command. (If you release your dog first and then reward him, you will teach him the wrong association. He will think that he is being rewarded for moving. This can teach a dog to anticipate the reward, thereby encouraging him to break the *stay* command.)

7. As your dog becomes more confident and can remain sitting beside you for two or three minutes without moving, you can progress by giving the *stay* command and then stepping directly in front of his nose. Gradually begin increasing the distance between you and your dog.

8. Once you have a reliable *sit-stay* in a nondistractive situation, you can begin incorporating mild distractions, such as toys lying nearby on the floor. As your dog becomes reliable with mild distractions, begin escalating the distractions. Try training while other people or dogs play nearby. If your dog has a difficult time focusing on the task at hand, perhaps the increase in distractions was too soon or too severe.

Want to Know More?

For a refresher course in basic obedience training, see Chapter 4: Training Your Bulldog Puppy.

Multi-Dog Tip

Working multiple dogs together is a recipe for disaster. Spend 10 or 15 minutes daily with each dog. The dogs will learn quicker because they won't be distracted by or competing with your other dogs, and the time spent individually will help enhance the human/canine bond.

How to Teach the *Down-Stay*

To teach the *down-stay*, begin with your dog in the *down* position and tell him "Stay." Then follow the remaining instructions for the *sit-stay*. Ideally, avoid training these exercises back to back. For young or inexperienced dogs, doing a *sit-stay* and then a *down-stay* can be confusing. Try doing one, then the other later in the day or the next day.

THE *STAND*

The *stand* is another rudimentary behavior that all dogs should learn. Your dog will need to stand (and stay) for bathing and grooming, when you want to wipe his dirty feet, and for examinations at the vet's office. It is quite an easy command to teach, and there are several ways of doing so. It can also be taught to young puppies, and by the time a puppy is about five months old he should understand the *stand* and be doing it on command.

How to Teach Stand

1. With a young puppy or dog, get on the ground with him or pop him onto a grooming table so that you are not towering over him.

The *stand* is another rudimentary behavior that all dogs should learn.

2. Standing is a natural position for dogs, so if you see that your dog is already standing, praise with "Good stand." If your dog is sitting, use a treat in front of his nose to lure him into the *stand* position. Ideally, you want him to plant his front feet and pop his hind legs backward into a *stand*.

3. Praise with "Good stand," and reward with a tasty tidbit. For an older dog, you may need to use your hand under his tummy to help him into the stand.

An alternative method is have your dog standing on your left side. With your left hand in his collar (the back of your hand against his fur and the palm of your hand toward your left leg, which keeps his front feet stationary), gently touch his hind foot with your foot while simultaneously asking him to stand. This causes a dog to kick his hind legs back into a nice stand. You are gently touching the dog's foot. Do not step on his foot or heel him in the flank. Be gentle.

CHAPTER 10

BULLDOG PROBLEM BEHAVIORS

Problem behaviors are problematic for a number of reasons. Some are simply annoying, while others are potentially dangerous and life threatening—not to mention expensive in terms of property damage, unexpected veterinary bills, and fines imposed by animal control authorities. In a perfect world, your Bulldog would never get into trouble. In the real world, however, life is not so trouble-free. It is unrealistic to expect your Bulldog to go through his entire life without getting into some sort of mischief or developing an annoying habit or two.

A key component of preventing behavioral problems and building a strong human/canine relationship is seeing the world through your dog's eyes. When you understand the root cause of the problem—why your dog is chewing or barking or digging—you can reliably and accurately correct the problem. For instance, annoying or offensive behaviors do not suddenly appear—they are learned. Dogs do not do anything you do not allow to happen. Puppies and adult dogs do not pee from one end of the house to the other just to annoy you. Nor do they lie around the house conjuring up ways to make your life more difficult. Their brains are not hardwired

to be vindictive. If your dog is urinating in the house, it is because he is not housetrained and is not being supervised. When left to their own devices, dogs—your Bulldog included—will do exactly what they feel like at any given moment, which isn't always compatible with their owners' expectations.

PREVENTION IS KEY

It is much easier to prevent problem behaviors from developing by managing your dog's environment so that he is not put in a position where he can get himself into trouble than it is to put the proverbial genie back in the bottle. That said, if your Bulldog has already developed an annoying habit, a bit of detective work may be in order.

In the simplest of terms, most dog actions, big or small, can be grouped into two categories: behavioral and medical. Medical problems can include painful urinary tract infections, diabetes, or renal disease, which can make getting outside to potty a problem for some dogs. Any number of health issues, from allergies to hormonal imbalances to life-threatening diseases, could also be to blame. Pain, such as a broken tooth, broken bone, torn ligament, pinched nerve, sore muscles, etc., can cause a dog of sound temperament to growl, bite, or snap. Teething, while not a medical problem per se, causes puppies and junior dogs to chew and chew and chew, oftentimes on inappropriate items, to relieve the discomfort associated with teething.

If your dog receives a clean bill of health, the problem may be behavioral, which means that it's time for a bit of detective work because the root cause of naughty canine behaviors can be caused by one or more factors—some of which you could inadvertently be the cause of. The primary behavioral reasons dogs develop naughty behaviors include boredom, stress, and lack of training.

Boredom

Bulldogs are not high-drive, high-energy dogs, but they still need physical and mental stimulation. Without appropriate stimulation, they will find all sorts of ways to release excess energy, such as digging, chewing, or barking.

Lack of Training

Lack of training is a top reason why many dogs develop unwanted behaviors. Dogs can't read our minds, and they won't learn to come when called, potty outdoors, or stop barking unless they are trained to do so. Your dog will not magically stop peeing from one end of the house to the other unless you instill good housetraining practices from day one. Nor will he miraculously start coming when called just because you holler the command louder and more frantically each time. As a responsible owner, it is your job to teach your dog in a fun and humane manner which behaviors are acceptable and which should be dropped—and immediately.

Stress

Like humans, dogs become stressed for a variety of reasons, including boredom, lack of socialization, unfamiliar surroundings, isolation, strange or loud noises, other

A key component of preventing behavioral problems is seeing the world through your dog's eyes.

dogs and animals, unfamiliar people, and rambunctious toddlers running about. The constant stimulation of being in a crowd of people can stress even the sweetest, most lovable Bulldog, provoking him to bolt, growl, or snap. Pushing a puppy or adult dog beyond his mental or physical capabilities can trigger stress, impeding his ability to learn. Many seemingly innocuous events, such as another dog approaching or passing by too closely, tension among canine siblings, a change in your dog's schedule, or a change in your work schedule can stress some dogs. Injured dogs frequently become fearful and highly stressed, which can lead to aggression. Dysfunctional households, including those housing hyperactive children who can't sit still or families who frequently fight or yell, can cause many dogs stress too.

Although Bulldogs are not high-energy dogs, they still need physical and mental stimulation.

COMMON CANINE (MIS)BEHAVIORS

Depending on your Bulldog's temperament and personality, his early rearing, socialization (or lack of socialization), and his current living environment, you may be dealing with one or more of the following undesired behaviors. Depending on how long the problem (or problems) has been allowed to go on, it may take a while to restore order, but in most cases problem behaviors, with the possible exception of aggression, are entirely fixable. In many instances, behaviors are not fixed or cured but rather managed. Equally important, many of these canine "problems" are only problematic for humans. Barking, chewing, and digging are all normal behaviors for dogs. To an extent, so too is dog-to-dog aggression, although aggression in today's society is unacceptable. The significance of any behavioral problem is measured by how it affects the dog's owner and how it impacts a dog's life. Dogs, for instance,

see no problem with digging in your garden. Nor do they see a problem with howling or barking all night. How you react to and deal with many of these situations will directly affect your dog's welfare and quality of life—in either a positive or negative manner.

Aggression

The good news is that Bulldogs, for the most part, are not known for being aggressive. Breeders have done a good job of breeding out their once fierce and aggressive tendencies needed for their previous job of bullbaiting, although in some instances Bulldogs can still be dog-to-dog aggressive. The not-so-good-news is that aggression is a tricky topic because many types of aggression exist, with entire books written on this one topic. Fear aggression, for instance, is a defensive type of aggression. Dominance-related aggression is a reaction to a social situation. There is also possession-related aggression or what is often called territorial aggression, or guarding or resource-guarding aggression. There is also maternal aggression, protective aggression, pain-related aggression, predatory aggression, and redirected aggression, to name a few.

Further complicating the topic is the not-so-simple act of categorizing aggression. While some people tend to lump dogs into a specific category, dogs aren't machines, so it is not quite as simple as labeling a behavior as a particular type of aggression. For instance, a dog may be fearful and angry at the same time and may send conflicting signals. A dog's temperament and upbringing influence how he reacts in a particular situation too.

Like humans, dogs have different triggers that cause an aggressive state. Some dogs are mellow and nonconfrontational. Others short circuit with little provocation—or little provocation in the minds of humans. Intact male dogs frequently posture and challenge each other for the right to mate with a female. If neither male is prepared to back down, fighting that results in serious injury is highly likely.

It is worth noting that aggression typically does not happen overnight. Granted, some dogs are born with sour temperaments or a skewed view of the world. Generally speaking, however, most dogs are permitted by their owners to develop improper behaviors and subsequently follow a designated path to

If your dog has a problem behavior that you can't handle yourself, such as aggression, seek the help of a professional.

aggression. More often than not, these behaviors go unchecked by owners until someone, be it a child, adult, or another dog, gets bitten.

Want to Know More?

For a refresher course on puppy socialization, see Chapter 4: Training Your Bulldog Puppy.

Signs of Aggression

Some aggression signals can be subtle but important to recognize nevertheless. Look for these cues that your Bulldog may be headed down the wrong path:

- Object guarding, be it food, toys, or furniture. Signals include a puppy or adult dog who snarls, growls, snaps, or displays other guarding behaviors toward objects when people or other animals approach. Don't ignore the first signs, which can be as subtle as a dog lowering his head or crouching over an object, flicking his eyes, glaring, or turning his head in the direction of another animal.
- Growling at or biting you or other animals.
- Pushy, bossy behaviors, such as pawing, nudging, whining, and demanding attention.
- Ignoring learned obedience commands.

  Ignoring obedience commands or pestering you for affection does not mean that your dog is headed down a path of no return. However, obeying obedience commands means that your dog accepts you as a leader and is less likely to challenge your authority.

How to Manage It

The earlier you recognize these signs, the sooner you can put a stop to them, thereby making your life and your dog's life safer and more enjoyable. That said, aggression and aggression-type behaviors are a serious problem. Most dog owners—experienced ones included—are not adequately skilled or qualified to handle aggression-based behaviors. If you suspect that your dog has aggressive tendencies, seek professional advice at the first signs of trouble. Do not wait until they escalate into bigger problems. Choose a trainer who is knowledgeable about aggression as well as about the Bulldog breed.

Barking (Excessive)

The Bulldog was originally bred as a fighting dog—never a guard or watchdog. Therefore, Bulldogs are not known to be a noisy breed, and excessive or chronic barking is generally not a problem. However, if your Bulldog likes to vocalize and backchat, he needs to be taught to stop barking on command.

Understanding why your dog is barking is key to resolving the issue. It is natural for dogs to bark or otherwise vocalize, and they do so for a variety of reasons. It is highly unlikely that your dog is barking for no reason. You may not always be able to identify what triggers the barking, but you can usually learn why your dog does it.

The primary reasons dogs bark include:
- when they get excited
- when they are playing with other dogs
- when the doorbell rings and to greet you when you arrive home
- when they see other animals, such as a squirrel in a tree, a cat sitting on the fence, or a neighbor's dog
- when they are bored, such as being left unattended too often
- when they see other people, including solicitors, letter carriers, UPS drivers,

neighbors, and kids passing by

• when they experience separation anxiety or are left for extended periods

How to Manage It

If your Bulldog was properly socialized, he should not regard every little noise as an endless opportunity to bark. His barking is reasonable and appropriate if he is alerting you to suspicious intruders or unexpected visitors. If you can quiet him with a single command, you probably do not have much to worry about. Problems arise when your dog is too hyped up to stop barking. For this reason, it is best to curtail any problems immediately. This includes never encouraging your Bulldog to bark. For instance, when the doorbell rings, avoid asking your dog, "Who's there?" or "Let's

go see!" This can excite your Bulldog and encourage him to bark. It may seem like a fun game when he is 10 or 12 weeks old, but it is a difficult and annoying behavior to stop once it becomes ingrained.

If your dog is barking as an attention-seeking behavior, it is best to ignore him until he quiets. Then calmly praise, "Good quiet!" or "Good boy!" Resist the urge to verbally or physically acknowledge your dog's barking by shouting "No!" or "Shut up!" This will only encourage the unwanted behavior because, in a dog's mind, negative attention is better than no attention at all. By verbally responding to your dog, you are inadvertently giving him what he wants, which is attention.

Avoid soothing or otherwise coddling your Bulldog when he is barking. This too

The best prevention against future barking problems is smart dog management.

Training Tidbit

If your barking Bulldog is well on his way to wearing out his welcome, these tips will help enhance your chances of success:

- Consistency and timing are keys to success. Be consistent each time your dog barks until you can train him to respond to your quiet or no bark command.
- Positive reinforcement is much more productive than negative reinforcement. Verbally praise and reward the behavior you want, which is your dog's not barking.
- Dogs learn an appropriate alternative to barking when you are there to teach them. If you are seldom home, you cannot expect them to learn on their own.
- Dogs are individuals. They learn at different rates. You may see improvement within a few days—or it may take many weeks. Remember, Rome wasn't built in a day!

will inadvertently encourage the unwanted behavior. If your dog is barking and you are telling him, "It's okay, honey. Mommy loves you," the dog will think that he is being rewarded for barking. In the dog's mind, he is thinking, "When I bark, my mom tells me it's okay. So I should keep barking."

The best prevention against future barking problems is smart dog management. Never allow your puppy or adult Bulldog to be put in a situation where he is allowed to develop bad habits, such as leaving him unsupervised all day in the backyard where he is inspired to bark at constant stimuli, including other dogs barking, a cat on a fence, a bird overhead, leaves falling, neighbors coming and going, and life in general. Barking at environmental stimulation is often self-rewarding for the dog. A dog barks at the postman and when the postman leaves, the dog thinks, "Look how clever I am! My barking made that man leave!"

A Bulldog housed indoors can also develop barking habits. If he sits on the furniture and stares out the living room window, he may

be encouraged to bark at stimuli, such as neighbors, other dogs going for a walk, kids on bicycles, or the mailman. In these instances, you may need to keep the blinds or curtains closed so that he is not encouraged to gaze out the window in anticipation. Or consider using baby gates to corral him in the kitchen or family room while you are gone. Provide him with a food-dispensing toy or chew toy, such as those made by Nylabone, to stimulate his mind and take his attention off any excitement that might be going on outdoors.

If your dog barks while in the excitement of play, stop the game immediately. When your dog stops barking, praise: "Good quiet!" or "Good boy!" Once you have regained control of the situation, begin playing again.

Chewing

Chewing is a natural behavior for dogs. All dogs need to chew, and they do so for a variety of reasons. Puppies, for example, are going to chew while teething. It's a fact of life. Teething stimulates an uncontrollable urge to chew as a means of relieving some of the discomfort and as a way to facilitate the removal of their baby teeth. Few owners escape puppy rearing without losing a pair of shoes, a few magazines, or a potted plant.

How to Manage It

The key to minimizing destruction and preventing bad habits is management. To foster good habits and minimize destructive behaviors, follow these simple guidelines:

- Before bringing your new dog home, plan ahead. Have an exercise pen or play pen and a crate ready. Do not wait until you decide you need them. If you have a Bulldog, you will need them.
- When you cannot keep a constant watch on your dog, keep him confined in an exercise pen, playpen, crate, or pet-proofed area with his favorite chew toy. This includes when you need to jump into the shower for five minutes, while you are making dinner, or when you dash outside for two seconds to move the sprinkler.
- Once your dog arrives at your home, know where he is and what he is doing at all times. You would not dream of taking your eyes off a toddler, and you should never take your eyes off a new dog when he is not safely confined.
- Pet-proof your home. Dogs are ingenious when it comes to finding items on which to chew. Pick up anything and everything your Bulldog is likely to put in his mouth including shoes, purses, jackets, schoolbooks, candles, rugs, electrical cords, dolls, and so forth. Make sure that he receives plenty of exercise each day.

Pet-proof your home to keep your Bulldog from chewing things he shouldn't.

Provide Plenty of Chew Toys

A variety of chew toys available in all sizes and shapes will entertain your Bulldog for an hour or two. Chew toys will satisfy a puppy or adult dog's need to gnaw on something while diverting him from chewing on inappropriate items. While some chew toys are better than others, there is no scientific formula for finding the right chew toy. Most times it is a matter of trial and error. Avoid toys or bones that are too hard and may crack your dog's teeth, as well as ones that are too small or break apart and present choking hazards.

Both puppies and adult dogs require daily physical and mental stimulation. Lacking appropriate and adequate exercise, they will frequently release excess energy by chewing.

- Until your dog is reliably trained, never give him free run of the house. Some dogs have a stronger desire to chew than others. Much will depend on how conscientious and committed you are to managing your Bulldog's environment, instilling good behaviors, and discouraging unwanted behaviors.
- It is important to continue giving your dog safe and healthy bones and chew toys, like the ones made by Nylabone, throughout his life to exercise his jaws, keep his teeth clean, and entertain him for a few hours.

Destructive Chewing

Adult dogs also need and like to chew because sometimes it just feels good to gnaw on something. So chewing is not a behavior you want to eliminate. Problems arise with destructive chewing, which is typically a result of boredom, loneliness, or anxiety. Dogs can destroy drywall, carpet, drapes, and linoleum. They can turn your favorite pillows into confetti, shred your bedspread, and destroy electrical cords and potted plants. They will gleefully shred magazines and books and anything else they can get their teeth on. They will destroy outdoor gardens and planters,

fences, patio furniture, spa covers, electrical wiring, and even the siding on your house.

How to Manage It

The key to stopping destructive chewing is managing your dog's environment and putting an end to his boredom. Provide your Bulldog with plenty of mental and physical stimulation. For example, teach or reinforce obedience commands on a daily basis in a fun and positive manner. Teach him fun tricks, such as waving, speaking, spinning, twisting, walking backward, picking up his toys, and so forth. Give him a food-dispensing toy to stimulate his mind. Take him for walks or play a game of fetch. That said, always provide him with appropriate chew toys to satisfy his natural desire to chew.

Digging

Digging is another natural behavior for dogs. Some dogs love digging, and some breeds dig more than others. Generally speaking, Bulldogs are not tenacious diggers when compared to, say, terriers. They are, however, quite capable of wreaking havoc in your garden or yard given the right incentive, including boredom, gophers, or a stinky manure pile.

How to Manage It

Dogs dig for a variety of reasons. Some dogs dig holes to bury their favorite toys or bones.

If your dog is digging outdoors, consider setting aside a part of the yard where he can dig to his heart's content.

Many dogs dig out of frustration or boredom. Others will dig in order to find a cool spot to escape the heat.

Don't punish your dog for digging. Chances are he won't understand why you are upset, and you may end up exacerbating the problem. Instead, find out why he is digging and then manage his environment by not putting him in a situation where he can get himself into trouble.

If your Bulldog is digging to find escape from the heat, his digging may be the least of your problems. As previously mentioned, Bulldogs are predisposed to heat-related illnesses and do not tolerate hot weather. You need to get him out of the heat and provide him with a cool spot, such as an air-conditioned room or a grassy area with plenty of shade. Consider providing your Bulldog with a child's-size heavy-duty plastic wading pool for cooling off, provided of course he is carefully supervised. Remember, Bulldogs are not good swimmers, and leaving your dog unattended near any body of water is never a good idea.

For digging issues related to boredom, find something that will stimulate his mind, burn energy, and tire him out. For example, take him for a walk or play a game of fetch. Or purchase a food-dispensing toy that allows him to exercise his brain as he tries to outsmart the toy. There are chew toys that can be stuffed with squeeze cheese or peanut butter and will provide your Bulldog with hours of entertainment. Or use

NYLABONE

Around four weeks of age, puppies begin to develop their baby teeth—also known as deciduous teeth or milk teeth. Teething is the process of growing baby teeth. The process ends when a dog's permanent teeth are in place, which occurs between four and six months of age. However, chewing satisfies a dog's natural urge to gnaw on things, so most continue to do so as adults.

your imagination to come up with fun games, such as "find it" games where you hide a tasty tidbit of food under a small box or bucket and encourage him to find it. Or engage in fun hide-and-seek games in which you encourage him to find you.

The best solution for digging in gardens is prevention. Do not allow your Bulldog free access to the garden areas where he can dig and wreak havoc. An alternative is to install a small fence around the garden, or put chicken wire under the soil so that digging becomes less productive and rewarding for your dog. Or fence off a section of the yard just for him where he can dig and dig to his heart's content.

Jumping Up

Bulldogs, for the most part, do not jump on people. Bouncy and springy are not the first words that come to mind when describing a Bulldog's personality or physical structure. That said, some Bulldogs do jump up. It is their way of getting close to your face and saying "Hi!" Licking faces is a natural behavior for dogs when they greet each other,

and they don't understand that humans frequently take offense. If your Bulldog jumps on you and you don't mind the behavior, then you have nothing to worry about. Unfortunately, what appears to be cute, harmless puppy behavior is far from amusing when your Bulldog weighs 50 pounds (22.5 kg) and has four muddy feet. Bulldogs are solid, heavy dogs and can easily knock over a child or older adult and cause injury.

How to Manage It

The key is to discourage all occasions of jumping up. If you do not want your adult dog to jump on you, do not allow the behavior when he is puppy. It is equally unfair to allow him to jump on you but correct him for jumping on visitors, or to allow him to jump on you today but not tomorrow when you are wearing white pants. Your Bulldog will be confused if you correct him for jumping but your children or spouse allows it. Be sure that everyone follows the same rules.

For young puppies, try crouching down as your Bulldog comes to greet you. As you do this, slip your thumb in his collar under his chin (your thumb should be pointing down toward the ground) and apply very gentle pressure so that he cannot jump up. Give him praise only when all four feet are on the ground. Your praise should be sincere but not overly enthusiastic. Otherwise, you are likely to wind him up even more.

Also, teach him not to jump by ignoring him. Turn sideways or turn your back on him—totally ignoring him. When he stops jumping, use calm verbal praise. "That's my good boy." Eventually, he will figure out that jumping is not getting him the attention he wants.

You can also teach him not to jump by making him sit for a kiss or treat. Bulldogs are smart, but even the smartest one hasn't figured out how to simultaneously jump and sit for a treat.

To prevent your puppy or adult dog from jumping on visitors, put on his leash before you open the door. This allows you to control his behavior without grabbing at him or his collar. When he sits nicely without pawing or mauling your guests, calmly praise and reward him with a tasty tidbit. "That's my good boy!" or "What a good sit!"

Small children like to run, flail their arms, and make loud squealing noises. This type of behavior is especially attractive to young puppies. Most young children cannot control a jumping puppy, let alone a 50-pound (22.5-kg) Bulldog. Always supervise children and manage your dog so that he is not put in a position where he can develop bad habits or inadvertently get himself into trouble.

Running Off or Not Coming When Called

Bulldogs who run away from their owners or refuse to come when called can create an enormous amount of frustration and angst for them. The good news is that this is one of the easiest problems to solve.

How to Manage It

The key is to never allow your puppy or adult dog to be put in a situation where he is allowed to develop the bad habit of running off. Each and every time you go outside, your Bulldog should be on leash. If you want

Never allow your dog to be put in a situation where he is allowed to develop the bad habit of running off.

Multi-Dog Tip

Dogs are first and foremost individuals with their own personalities, quirks, and idiosyncrasies. No one training method works for all dogs. What works for your Bulldog may not work for your other dogs. What works for your puppy may not work for your adult dog. Rather than imposing the same training method for each dog, find training methods, tricks, and games that produce results for each individual dog.

your Bulldog to run around and explore his surroundings, he should be dragging his leash or a lightweight long-line. If your Bulldog starts to wander off, simply step on the long-line and reel him back in.

If your adult dog has already developed the annoying habit of running off or ignoring your *come* command, a leash or long-line will prevent him from continuing to do so. Then go back and reteach him to come with fun games and interactive play. You also should never get in the habit of chasing your dog or allowing your kids to chase him. Dogs think that this is a fun game, but it teaches them to run away from you, which is not only annoying but also dangerous. A puppy or adult dog who runs away from his owner can easily dart into traffic and cause serious injury to himself.

SEEKING PROFESSIONAL HELP

Despite your best efforts to raise a well-behaved Bulldog, times will arise when things go terribly, terribly wrong, and you may need to call in an expert. Some problems, such as aggression and separation anxiety, are difficult and complicated areas of canine behavior that require expert guidance. These behaviors are multifaceted and often have overlapping causes. For instance, genetics, lack of socialization, sexual maturity/frustration, lack of obedience training, inappropriate corrections, and pain are a few of the reasons why dogs might display aggression. Dogs with true separation anxiety issues can work themselves into a frenzy. They salivate, pace, whine, bark, and literally work themselves into an uncontrollable state of panic, destroying anything and everything they can get their teeth and paws on, including couches, walls, doors, rugs, and plants. If you feel that you and your dog need expert advice, don't hesitate to seek it. There is no shame in asking people who make their bread and butter training dogs for guidance. You and your dog will be much happier in the long run!

CHAPTER 11

BULLDOG SPORTS AND ACTIVITIES

Bulldogs probably aren't the first breed that comes to mind when contemplating canine activities and sports, especially some of the high-octane sports. Yet Bulldogs can and do compete in multiple venues, such as agility, conformation, obedience, and rally. Training and competing with your Bulldog is a great way to build a strong and mutually respectful relationship and have a great deal of fun in the process. And there are plenty of activities you can engage in that will stimulate your Bulldog's mind and allow him to display his intelligence and unique athleticism.

ACTIVITIES WITH YOUR BULLDOG

Bulldogs are people dogs, and many want nothing more than to hang out on the couch with their owners, but they also need physical and mental stimulation. Regardless of the activity (or activities!) you choose, positive interaction with your dog on a daily basis will help build a strong human/canine relationship, and that's what living with a Bulldog is all about.

Camping

Camping is a great way to incorporate family vacations with your precious pooch. No doubt you will both enjoy new sights and smells, as well as quality time spent together.

Remember, Bulldogs are predisposed to heat-induced illnesses, so you will want to choose your dates and locations carefully. Camping in the Mojave Desert in mid-July isn't the best choice. Likewise, you need to be careful about frostbite, which makes winter camping in the high sierras equally dicey.

If hiking, let your Bulldog walk at his own pace and within his own physical and mental capabilities. Keep him leashed so that he doesn't get lost or annoy other campers and animals. Remember to always pick up after your dog, which goes a long way in increasing good will for canines and allowing continued access to public parks and beaches.

Canine Good Citizen® Program

Training and interacting with your Bulldog is always fun, but if organized competitions are not your cup of tea, the American Kennel Club's

The Canine Good Citizen test requires a dog to perform some basic obedience cues, like lying down on command.

Canine Good Citizen® (CGC) Program might be the perfect alternative. Implemented in 1989, the CGC Program is a public education and certification program designed to promote good dogs and good owners, as well as demonstrate that the dog, as a companion, can be a respected member of the community. The CGC Program encourages owners to develop a positive and worthwhile relationship with their dogs by rewarding responsible dog ownership and good pet manners. It is designed to encourage owners to get involved with and obedience train their dogs.

The program does not involve the formality or precision of competitive obedience, but it does lay the foundation for good pet manners and is often used as a stepping-stone for other canine activities, such as obedience, rally obedience, and agility.

The CGC program is a noncompetitive, ten-part test that evaluates your dog's behavior in practical situations at home, in public, and in the presence of unfamiliar people and other dogs. The pass or fail test is designed to test a dog's reaction to distractions, friendly strangers, and supervised isolation. Additionally, a dog must sit politely while being petted, walk on a loose leash, walk through a crowd, and respond to basic obedience commands including *sit, down, stay,* and *come.* The evaluator also inspects the dog to determine whether he is clean and groomed. A dog who successfully completes the test receives a certificate stating that he is a Canine

Good Citizen and is entitled to use the initials "CGC" behind his name.

CGC tests are offered by local dog-training clubs and are often given in conjunction with dog shows or matches. Humane societies occasionally sponsor CGC tests too. While there is no age limit, dogs must be old enough to have received their immunizations.

Fetching and Retrieving

Bulldogs can fetch, and many of them love to do so. Others are more reluctant. Some like to fetch but aren't so enthusiastic about bringing the ball or toy back. Some bring it back but don't like to give it up. If your Bulldog is reluctant to fetch, help and encourage him by racing (or pretending to race!) after the toy with him and snatching it away just before he gets it. Tell him, "I got it! You're too slow!" Dogs always want what they can't have. Repeat this several times, encouraging him to "beat" you to the toy. When he does so, reward with plenty of praise. Retrieve games are an easy way to exercise your dog, and they are the foundation of many other games you can play with him. So it behooves you to encourage and build a fun and reliable *retrieve* command.

Swimming

Bulldogs, in general, are not good swimmers. Someone once said that they "swim like a rock." But that's not to say your water-loving Bulldog can't cool off in a kiddie or wading pool—provided you never leave him unattended, as it takes only a minute for a dog to drown. If you have a larger pool, get

Like all dogs, Bulldogs need to be mentally and physically stimulated.

in the water with him so that he is safe and comfortable, and practice showing him where the steps (or ramp) are so that he can get out on his own in an emergency.

Walking on the beach is great fun, but riptides and undercurrents are unpredictable, and your Bulldog can quickly wade into trouble. Dangers exist also in lakes, ponds, rivers, and other bodies of water. Be certain that your Bulldog is safely confined or controlled so that he doesn't accidentally wander into a dangerous situation.

Therapy Work

Bulldogs are charming and completely irresistible, which is perhaps Mother Nature's way of compensating for their lack of competitive and sporting prowess. If canine sports are not your Bulldog's forte, consider spreading the love with some therapy work.

Assistance Dogs/Service Dogs

The terms "therapy dog" and "service dog" are often used interchangeably. However, there is a significant difference. The Americans with Disabilities Act (ADA) uses the term "service dog" to define a dog who has been "individually trained to work or perform tasks for the benefit of a person with a disability." Professionals within the industry often refer to them as assistance dogs rather than service dogs. Therapy dogs provide companionship and emotional support but do not perform tasks, and federal law does not legally define them.

Under the umbrella of assistance dogs there are four categories: therapy dogs, guide dogs, service dogs, and hearing dogs. Most organizations tend to employ Golden Retrievers, Labrador Retrievers, or German Shepherds as guide dogs for the blind, hearing-alert dogs for the hearing impaired, and service dogs for the disabled. You are most likely to see Bulldogs doing therapy work.

Therapy Dogs

Therapy is an important area in which Bulldogs can help enhance the human/canine bond by providing unconditional love, companionship, and emotional support to nursing homes, hospitals, assisted living facilities, and mental health residences. Owners volunteering with their Bulldogs make regularly scheduled visits and brighten the lives of residents by providing stimulation, company, and a vehicle for conversation and interaction. Only Bulldogs who are well mannered and have a sound temperament should undertake this work. Your dog does 90 percent of the work, and he must have the physical and mental fortitude to cope with strange noises and smells, distractions,

By the Numbers

Most organizations have age limits in place to prevent dogs from competing in sanctioned events before they are physically and mentally mature. Here are a few of the AKC age requirements for competition:

- agility: 15 months
- Canine Good Citizen: no age limit, but dogs must be old enough to have received their immunizations
- conformation: 6 months
- obedience: 6 months
- rally obedience: 6 months
- tracking: 6 months

Bulldogs make wonderful therapy dogs.

and oftentimes erratic behaviors. Additionally, your Bulldog must be willing to accept a considerable amount of attention, petting, and touching from strangers. He should be bathed and groomed, have his nails trimmed, and be flea-free. It helps if he has a foundation of basic obedience training or his Canine Good Citizen certificate.

While the AKC does offer Canine Good Citizen certifications, they do not certify therapy dogs. There are independent organizations that certify therapy dogs. For additional information, contact therapy dog clubs in your area or the following national organizations, which perform a number of functions, including evaluating, educating,

training, registering and/or certifying therapy dogs: Delta Society; Therapy Dogs Inc.; Therapy Dogs International (TDI); and Love on a Leash.

Trick Training

Trick training is a great way to enhance the human/canine bond—and impress your friends and family in the process. Who hasn't seen the hilarious skateboarding and snowboarding Bulldogs? Or the Bulldog riding the rocking horse? Tricks are simply an extension of obedience training, and the tricks you choose to teach will vary depending on your dog's physical and mental capabilities, as well as your commitment. Bulldogs can learn everything from sit up (aka begging for food), play dead, spin, twist, and high-five, to name a few impressive stunts.

Trick training stimulates your dog's brain, which in turn helps prevent behavioral problems associated with boredom, such as barking, chewing, digging, and so forth. Obviously you won't get results and benefits unless you invest the time needed for training your dog. Surprisingly, five minutes several times a day—and a few longer sessions when you can squeeze them in—will be enough to see results.

Tug-of-War

Tugging has fallen out of favor with some trainers because they consider it a test of strength, and they fear that it will make dogs aggressive and dominant. Granted, tugging can stimulate or create arousal in some dogs, but if you follow some simple rules, tugging games need not be eliminated from your dog's list of fun things to do. First, you must win as often as your puppy or adult dog wins. Second, you must control all of the games—including the tugging. You determine when the two of you will tug, how hard, and how often each of you will tug.

That said, tugging is a great interactive game that allows you to incorporate specific

Training Tidbit

Be sure to teach your Bulldog a tug and release command. For instance, while he is tugging, tell him "Good tug!" or "Pull." This will teach him to associate the behavior with the command. By teaching him to tug, you can teach him to stop tugging with "Give" or "Out" or "Drop it" or whatever command you choose.

obedience commands. For instance, tug, tug, tug and then pop him through your legs with the command "Go through." Spin around and tug some more. Or, while he is tugging, pivot yourself into the heel position and take two or three steps while he is still tugging.

Use your imagination to come up with fun and creative games that will help instill confidence, expend mental and physical energy, and build a strong human/canine relationship.

Walking and Jogging

Bulldogs aren't known for their speed, so if you plan to walk or jog faster than your Bulldog's normal waddle, you should seriously consider

Tugging is a great interactive game that allows you to incorporate specific obedience commands.

Nylabone

a different four-legged jogging companion. That said, Bulldogs need daily exercise to keep physically and mentally fit, and walks in the park or around the block are ideal. As previously mentioned, Bulldogs are prone to heat-induced illnesses, so always walk at a speed comfortable for your dog and within his physical limitations. Always limit walking to cooler parts of the day, such as the early morning or evening. Equally important, hot sidewalks and roads can burn a Bulldog's feet, causing an enormous amount of pain and discomfort. If the sidewalks and roadways are too hot for your bare feet, they are too hot for your Bulldog to be outside. How far your Bulldog can walk will depend on his age, physical condition, the terrain covered, and the weather. Always carry plenty of fluids for both you and your dog.

BULLDOG SPORTS

Despite their couch potato reputation, Bulldogs can and do successfully compete in a number of canine sports. Here are a few of the more popular AKC and non-AKC sports.

Agility

Agility is one of the fastest-growing dog sports, and for good reason. It's fun! And addictive! Obviously, Bulldogs are not as fast and agile as, say, Border Collies or Australian Shepherds, but Bulldogs can and do successfully compete in this fast-paced, fun-filled canine sport.

Similar to equestrian Grand Prix courses, agility is truly a team sport, with dogs demonstrating their agile nature and versatility by maneuvering through a timed obstacle course of jumps, tunnels, A-frames, weave poles, ramps, a teeter-totter, and a pause box. A perfect score in any class is 100, and competitors are faulted if they go over the allotted course time or receive a penalty for doing things like taking an obstacle out of sequence, missing a contact zone, and so forth.

Canine Freestyle

Bulldogs may not be able to literally kick up their heels, but creative owners can come up with plenty of safe yet fun routines suitable to the breed's unique physical characteristics. Canine freestyle is a choreographed performance between a dog and handler set to music, which usually has a catchy melody and a good dance beat. Dog and owner wear matching costumes or accessories, which also

Bulldogs can—and do—successfully compete in fast-paced canine sports like agility.

complement the performance.

Don't let the catchy name fool you, though. Canine freestyle is more than dogs heeling to music. The sport is patterned after Olympic skating, with dogs and handlers performing twists, turns, leg kicks, pivots, and other cool and creative maneuvers. These maneuvers are entwined with basic obedience commands, such as heels, sits, downs, and fronts. Many advanced competitors teach their dogs to crawl, back up, wave, bow, bounce, roll over, spin, and play dead. Freestyle routines vary dramatically and are creatively choreographed with an emphasis on the human/canine bond.

Conformation (Dog Shows)

Conformation shows (dog shows) are the signature events of the competitive dog world.

The conformation ring, commonly referred to as the breed ring, provides a forum for breeders and handlers to showcase the best in breeding stock. These animals are evaluated as potential breeding stock and are usually incorporated into future breeding programs in an effort to improve the breed. For this reason, dogs competing in conformation may not be spayed or neutered.

How Dog Shows Work

The best way to understand the conformation ring is to think of it in terms of an elimination process. Each Bulldog enters a regular class and is evaluated against the Bulldog breed standard. For the newcomer, it often appears as if the dogs are competing against one another. And in a sense they are. However,

Conformation events evaluate a dog on how closely he conforms to the breed standard.

the judge is not comparing the quality of one Bulldog against the quality of another Bulldog. The judge is evaluating each Bulldog against the breed standard and seeing how closely each dog measures up to the ideal Bulldog as outlined in the breed standard.

The regular classes are divided by sex, with the male and female dogs being judged separately. The male dogs are always judged first, and after being examined by the judge, they are placed first through fourth according to how well they measure up to the Bulldog breed standard in the judge's opinion. After the males have been judged, the females go through the same judging process.

After the regular classes have been judged, the first-place winners of each class are brought back to the ring to compete against one another in the Winners Class. The dog selected is the Winners Dog and is awarded championship points. A Reserve Winners Dog is also chosen but does not receive points unless the Winners Dog, for any reason, is disallowed or disqualified. The same process is then repeated with the female dogs, resulting in a Winners Bitch and Reserve Winners Bitch.

The Winners Dog and Winners Bitch go back into the ring with any Champions entered to compete for the Best of Breed award. If either the Winners Dog or Winners Bitch wins Best of Breed or Best of Winners, they may also win more points. The Best of Breed dog or bitch then goes on to the Group. The Group winners are then judged with Group placements—first through fourth place—being awarded in each

of the seven groups. The first place Group winners compete for the most coveted and most prestigious award: Best in Show.

Flyball

Like most other canine activities, flyball is not your typical Bulldog sport, as it is a high-octane relay race that attracts high-drive, high-energy tennis ball-loving breeds! That's not to say that you can't teach your tennis-ball loving Bulldog to have fun with flyball.

Flyball is a team sport, rather than an individual competition—the course consists of four hurdles (small jumps) spaced approximately 10 feet (3 m) apart. Fifteen feet (4.5 m) beyond the last hurdle is a spring-loaded box that contains a tennis ball. Just as in any relay race, the fastest team to successfully complete the game wins. The goal is for each dog to take a turn running the relay by leaping each of the four hurdles and then hitting a pedal or lever with his paw to trigger the box, which shoots a tennis ball up in the air. Once the dog catches the ball in his mouth, he races back over the four hurdles to the finish line, where the next dog is anxiously awaiting his turn.

The first team to have all four dogs run without errors wins the heat. If a dog misses a hurdle or fails to retrieve the ball, he must repeat his turn.

Obedience

Competitive obedience goes beyond rally or the CGC Program and tests a Bulldog's ability to perform a prescribed set of exercises in a formal environment. Some compare it to

---

Want to Know More?

If your Bulldog gets especially dirty participating in a sport or activity, he may need a full-on grooming session. See Chapter 6: Bulldog Grooming Needs for some pointers.

Even if you don't participate in an official event, spending time with your Bulldog is well worth it.

ballroom dancing because both dog and owner are extensions of each other—both working in sync. Others compare it to the formal and elegant equine dressage tests, with owners achieving a harmonious relationship with their dogs, all the while observing meticulous attention to minute details.

In addition to enriching the bond and relationship between a dog and handler, obedience training is designed to emphasize "the usefulness of purebred dogs as the ultimate companion and helpmate to man, and as a means of recognizing that dogs have been trained to behave in the home, in public places, and in the presence of other dogs."

Rules and regulations vary slightly between the multiple organizations that offer obedience. However, the primary requirements for earning titles are basically the same. There

are three levels of competitive obedience: Novice, Open, and Utility.

The best way to get involved in obedience is to sign up for a dog obedience class or join a local dog obedience club. If you are interested in competitive obedience, it is helpful to find a trainer who successfully competes in the sport and who teaches competitive obedience classes.

Rally Obedience

Rally obedience is the AKC's newest event, and it is generating a lot of interest from dog owners. The emphasis is less on speed and precision and more on how well dogs and handlers perform together as a team. Created with the average dog owner in mind and as a means to help promote a positive human/canine relationship, rally emphasizes fun and excitement while allowing owners to showcase their dog's obedience skills.

In rally obedience, the dog and handler move through a course that has been designed by the rally judge. The dog and handler proceed at their own pace through a course of designated stations—between 10 and 20 stations, depending on the level. Each of these stations has a sign providing instructions regarding the skill that is to be performed, such as halt & sit; halt, sit, & down; right turn; about right turn; or perform a 270-degree left turn while heeling.

Unlike traditional obedience competitions, handlers are permitted to talk to their dogs, use praise, clap their hands, pat their legs, or use any verbal means of communication and body language throughout the performance. Handlers may not touch their dogs or make physical corrections. Any dog who is eligible for AKC registration can enter rally obedience.

Tracking

Tracking is a popular sport that tests a dog's ability to recognize and track a human scent over varying terrains and climatic changes. It is designed to showcase a dog's intelligence and extremely high level of scent capability, which could be challenging for Bulldogs. Nonetheless, some Bulldogs might enjoy tracking—especially if they are "tracking" treats or a favorite toy around the house or in the yard. Teach your Bulldog to track for fun, such as finding his toys or a treat you've hidden in the house or around the yard. Teach him to "Go find the kids" or find a wayward senior dog.

TRAVELING WITH YOUR BULLDOG

What's the fun in going away if you can't take your precious Bulldog with you? Traveling with your Bulldog can be great fun—provided you plan ahead. Ideally, you should accustom your Bulldog to traveling while he is young and more receptive to new adventures. If you have an older Bulldog, don't despair. Dogs are resilient, and many adult dogs learn to love traveling.

By Car

One of the best ways to accustom your new puppy to traveling is to put him in his crate and take him everywhere (weather providing, of course). Take him for rides to the post office, bank, and grocery store and to visit your friends and family. Make the experiences fun by giving him treats and telling him he's great!

Bulldogs who have never been in a car or who have developed phobias are often anxious or apprehensive about car rides. Some dogs drool, shake, and even vomit. For dogs who have true motion sickness, which is normally associated with an inner ear problem, medications are available and can be used with the supervision of a veterinarian. Carsickness, on the other hand, is usually associated with fear or an apprehension of the car noise and movement, a response to the dog's inability to control his circumstances, or a traumatic experience in a car or at the journey's end, such as an unpleasant experience at a vet's office or obedience class.

If your Bulldog doesn't enjoy riding in the car, recondition him slowly, rewarding progress with treats.

Travel Safety Tips

Now that you're ready to head out on a fun adventure with your Bulldog, keep these safety tips in mind:

- Pack enough of your dog's regular food and water to last the duration of the trip—and perhaps a day or two longer in case of unexpected delays. A sudden change in food or water can cause your dog to suffer from an upset stomach or diarrhea. Purchase bottled water if necessary.
- Unless your Bulldog is a seasoned traveler, it is best to limit his food intake two hours before traveling. Feed the bulk of his food after you have stopped for the day.
- Never allow you Bulldog to travel in the open bed of a pickup or with his head hanging out an open window. Dust, debris, and bugs are an ever-present danger and can damage his eyes and nostrils. A sudden unexpected stop could throw him from the car, causing serious injury or death.
- Be careful that your Bulldog does not overheat. Use a window shield to keep the sun from beating through the window on him, and never leave him in the car unattended.
- Walk your Bulldog in areas designated for pets. Pick up after your dog, and deposit his waste in the nearest trash bin.
- Do not permit your Bulldog to run free, bark incessantly, or disturb other travelers.

If your Bulldog has problems riding in the car, you can begin reconditioning him by simply sitting in the car without the motor running while you verbally praise him for being brave and reward him with tasty treats. Progress to sitting in the car with the motor running. Again, verbally praise and reward him with yummy tidbits. Next, try short fun trips around the block, to the post office, bank, and so forth. Each time gradually increase the distance, always making the experience fun and positive. Put a favorite blanket, toy, or treat in his crate to keep him comfy and occupied.

Over-the-counter products are available to help calm your Bulldog. In severe cases, your veterinarian can prescribe a stronger anti-anxiety medication. Always consult a veterinarian before giving your Bulldog

tranquilizers, aspirins, or medications prescribed for humans.

Remember, traveling with a Bulldog is similar to traveling with toddlers and small children. Make frequent pit stops a priority so that your dog can relieve himself, stretch his legs, and burn off some pent-up energy.

By Air

Dogs traveling by air are protected by U.S. Department of Agriculture (USDA) regulations. That in itself does not guarantee that your pet will be safe flying the friendly skies. Unless you are flying with a puppy, your Bulldog will need to fly in cargo, which is not advisable. This can be extremely stressful for some Bulldogs. As previously mentioned, stress can exacerbate problems associated with their restricted airways, putting them in a dangerous and life-threatening situation. Get advice and a clean bill of health from your veterinarian before scheduling a flight.

Lodging

If you plan to stay at a hotel or motel, call ahead to be sure that they accept dogs. Not all hotels and motels accept pets—even charming, well-behaved Bulldogs. Some facilities allow dogs in the rooms but may require the dog be crated. Some larger hotels provide kennel facilities. Many require a refundable pet deposit or a nonrefundable pet fee.

Be a good ambassador for the Bulldog breed—as well as all other dogs—by following hotel and motel rules, including never leaving an unattended dog in the room. An otherwise calm Bulldog may become anxious in unfamiliar surroundings. He may chew furniture, shred pillows, urinate, defecate, or annoy other visitors with his barking and whining. Without exception, always clean up after your dog and deposit any messes in designated trash bins.

The Automobile Club of America (AAA) publishes a guide called *Traveling With Your Pet*, which lists thousands of pet-friendly places to stay. If your favorite haunt is not in the book, call ahead and ask about its pet policy.

When You Can't Take Your Bulldog With You

A summer holiday in the Southwest, a backpacking trip in the Rockies, or honeymooning in the Caribbean may exclude your Bulldog from your travel plans. So too might family emergencies and unexpected business trips. Whatever the reason, occasions may arise when you need to leave your Bulldog for a few days or a few weeks. Yes, it's heartbreaking, but there are a few options that may give you some peace of mind.

Multi-Dog Tip

When boarding your dogs, double-check to be sure that you can board them together in the same kennel and what, if any, fees (or discounts!) this might incur.

Boarding Facilities

Boarding facilities have come a long way in the last 10 or 15 years. Many are now designed with the discriminating pet owner in mind, providing a variety of services in addition to boarding, including training, daily exercise, and grooming. Some facilities provide video cameras that allow you to view your Bulldog via a laptop or PC.

Your Bulldog's physical safety and emotional well-being are paramount. Here are some tips for reducing your dog's stress, as well as your own, by choosing the best facility:

- Visit and tour the entire facility. A clean and inviting reception area does not guarantee clean kennel runs. If the proprietors do not want you touring the facility, hightail it to the nearest exit.
- Does the kennel or exercise area smell? Check the cleanliness of the kennels, runs, and exercise areas. Make sure that they are free of debris and excrement and cleaned and disinfected between boarders.
- Do the dogs have fresh water and clean food bowls?
- What type of food and how often do they feed (i.e., once or twice a day)? Can you supply your own food? This is doubly important if your Bulldog is on a special diet or you don't want his diet changed.
- Check the security of the facility. It should be completely fenced; the kennels and exercise

yards should have good latches; and the fences should be sturdy and at least six feet (2 m) high.

- Find out whether your Bulldog will be boarded indoors or out (or a combination of the two). The indoor facilities should be heated and the outdoor facilities protected from the weather.
- What will your Bulldog be sleeping on? Most importantly, are you allowed to bring his favorite bed or blanket?
- Find out how frequently and for how long your Bullodg will be walked or exercised. Be sure that whoever does the walking is familiar with the requirements of brachycephalic breeds. A good boarding facility will have someone interact or play with your Bulldog and not just leave him unattended in an exercise yard.
- Housing your Bulldog with unfamiliar dogs can be dangerous and stressful. If you don't want a kennelmate for your dog, speak up.
- Ask about the facility's veterinarian and whether there is a 24-hour emergency clinic nearby. Is the veterinarian familiar with Bulldogs and their respiratory issues?
- Find out the facility's admission and pick-up hours and what happens if your return is delayed.
- Get a list of required vaccinations.

If you can't take your Bulldog with you while you're away, a kennel or pet sitter may be a good option.

Once you have decided on a facility, remember to book early. Many facilities are booked months in advance, especially during the holidays. Always leave special pet-care instructions, your itinerary, and numbers to contact you, your veterinarian, or a trusted friend or relative in the event of an emergency.

Pet Sitters

Boarding your Bulldog may be out of the question, and that's okay because other options are available, such as a pet sitter. Being at home—sleeping in his bed, surrounded with his prized possessions—may be less stressful than a boarding facility. You may be lucky enough to have a responsible neighbor, trusted friend, or relative you can rely on to stop by several times a day, but if not, you might want to seek out the services of a professional pet sitter.

Pet sitters either stay at your home while you are gone or stop in during the day to feed, exercise, and check on your dog. Ask your dog-owning friends, local veterinarians, trainers, or groomers for a referral.

If you choose the pet-sitting route, have the pet sitter come to your home for an interview:

- Is she professional? Did she show up on time?
- How does she relate to your Bulldog?
- How much experience does she have?
- Is she familiar with Bulldogs? Will she be able to recognize whether your dog is sick or having a problem?
- If she is not staying at your house, how often will she come by?

- Will she play with your Bulldog? Talk to him? Kiss him? Love him? Whisper sweet nothings in his ear?
- Is she licensed? Bonded? Insured?
- Also, dogs react differently to "strangers" wandering around their house while you are not home. Be sure that your Bulldog recognizes the pet sitter as a friend. Accomplish this by having the pet sitter come by several times while you are home.

Doggy Day Care

Doggy day cares are similar to day care centers for human babies and toddlers but with a twist. They are for dogs! If you want your Bulldog to play and interact with other dogs while you slave away at work, then doggy day care may be your cup of tea.

Day care centers vary in their appearance, amenities, and cost. Some resemble park-like atmospheres, with trees, park benches, kiddie pools, and playground equipment. Some facilities provide spa-like amenities and lavish attention on the dogs, including hydro-baths, nail trims, and massages.

To find the right day care facility for your Bulldog, consider the same points as you would for a boarding facility.

PART III

SENIOR YEARS

CHAPTER 12

FINDING YOUR BULLDOG SENIOR

Few things are sweeter or more charming than a senior Bulldog. Noble and honorable, with a vital strength of character, aging Bulldogs are to be cherished. Their main priority in life is that they are close to the ones they love and those who love them back. Senior Bulldogs can and do make excellent companions. Their legendary patience with children and elderly people means that acquiring one may well suit your lifestyle—for a number of reasons.

THE BENEFITS OF ADOPTING A SENIOR

Senior Bulldogs lose their homes for many of the same reasons discussed in Chapter 5: Finding Your Adult. And as with junior and adult Bulldogs, many expensive, well-bred senior Bulldogs find their way into shelters and rescue organizations. These dogs, through no fault of their own, are alone.

An enormous misconception is that senior dogs—say, six, seven, or eight years old—have outlived their usefulness. Not so! Canine companionship is about the quality of time more than the quantity or length of years. Senior Bulldogs have the rest of their lives

By the Numbers

Bulldogs, for the most part, are considered "senior" around six or seven years of age. Dogs are individuals, and some Bulldogs may be physically old sooner or later than others.

in front of them, and you can shower them with love and affection and give them the best years of their life. In return, they will provide unconditional love and companionship.

Senior Bulldogs are instant companions, as most of them are ready for walking, riding in the car, or snuggling on the couch. Most do not need 24-hour supervision, as do puppies, and they generally don't require as much of your energy. Most senior dogs are willing to patiently wait for you to finish your coffee and newspaper, and they are seldom demanding of your attention. They can be easier to train too. Many have basic obedience skills and simply need a refresher course. In most instances,

A senior Bulldog will provide unconditional love, affection, and companionship.

those lacking obedience skills are easier to train because they are older, wiser, and calmer, with longer attention spans than puppies. Many are eager to please and will try hard to win your affection and approval.

Studies indicate that the older the dog, the less chance he has of being adopted. At animal shelters, an older dog is more likely to be passed up in favor of a puppy or junior dog, which means that he's more likely to be euthanized. Adopting an older dog makes a statement about compassion and the value of a dog's life regardless of his age. It also helps reduce the number of homeless dogs euthanized yearly at shelters.

SENIOR BULLDOGS FOR SENIOR CITIZENS

Senior dogs can make excellent companions for senior citizens. Senior citizens and senior dogs face many of the same challenges, including loneliness. In many instances, both the senior citizen and the senior dog are looking for the same thing: companionship. Studies indicate that canine companionship provides not only friendship but social and psychological benefits too. Being in the presence of dogs can lower a person's blood pressure and stress level and can help increase a senior citizen's daily exercise because people are more likely to get outside for a walk if their

Want to Know More?

If you'd rather adopt a younger adult dog, see Chapter 5: Finding Your Bulldog Adult for some pointers.

dog needs walking. Once outside, dogs also provide opportunities for social interaction because people tend to engage in conversations about their dog. Studies also indicate that people who have access to pets recover faster from illness or surgery.

Older Bulldogs are slower-moving and calmer than their puppy counterparts. They aren't constantly underfoot, as are puppies, so there is less chance of someone tripping over them. Senior citizens' homes are generally quieter, which, depending on the dog, can make the rehoming process much easier. Senior citizens tend to be home more often, so they are able to spend more time getting acquainted and lavishing affection on their new Bulldog.

SENIOR BULLDOGS FOR FAMILIES

Senior Bulldogs are a good choice for families with small children, too, because an older dog's personality is already in place. Unlike as with a puppy, you are able to assess his temperament and good and bad habits, and pick a dog who is suitable for your family's lifestyle. Juggling small kids *and* a puppy is time consuming and requires a good deal of energy and organization. Senior Bulldogs do not make the same demands on your

Extremely patient and calm, senior Bulldogs are a good choice for families with children.

time as do young puppies. They are well past the teething stage, which means that the likelihood of losing a purse, shoe, potted plant, or treasured rug is greatly reduced, although older Bulldogs can chew out of boredom or frustration. Older dogs tend to sleep longer, which means that you are more likely to get a nap in the afternoon or a good night's sleep. Puppies, on the other hand, want to play and pee and whine and cry when you want to sleep.

WHAT TO LOOK FOR

Finding the perfect senior dog is a lot like finding the perfect puppy. Start by asking questions and finding out as much information about the dog as possible. However, depending on why and how the dog ended up in a shelter or rescue organization, the information may be limited or nonexistent. For instance, an older Bulldog abandoned at a shelter or a

Training Tidbit

All dogs, including senior Bulldogs, are individuals and must be treated as such. Your dog's physical and mental limitations will dictate how long and how much he can train. Always work within his limitations and always quit while he's still enjoying the "game" of training and playing.

lost Bulldog picked up by animal control will arrive at a shelter with little information other than obvious health and physical observations. His history, breeding, and quirky behaviors will no doubt remain an unsolved

Most senior Bulldogs can adapt to their new homes easily.

mystery. An older Bulldog surrendered by his owners may come with limited information, such as his name, medical history, training, breeding, and so forth.

Shelter and rescue workers generally evaluate a dog's temperament, personality, and suitability for adoption via temperament testing, observation, and interaction before placing him in a permanent or foster home. They tend to be knowledgeable dog people and can provide a good assessment of the dog's personality quirks, behaviors, and adoption requirements. For instance, some senior Bulldogs may not be suitable for placement in homes with kids or other animals. They may have limited sight or hearing or serious medical issues. Again, this does not make them unadoptable, but finding the perfect home means finding the perfect owner.

Senior Bulldogs are often advertised for sale or free via newspaper ads or online. The person placing the dog may or may not be a good source of information. If possible, take a knowledgeable dog person—ideally a Bulldog person—with you when looking at the dog, as that person can provide a general assessment and will ask a number of good questions.

SENIOR BULLDOG NEEDS

When given love, patience, and guidance, most senior Bulldogs adapt to their new homes quite easily with few problems. Some dogs may have physical or behavioral issues and may take longer to adjust. Some senior dogs, regardless of the breed, are set in their ways. They may not be as eager to change their ways or learn new routines. That doesn't mean that they can't learn, but it may take time, patience, love, and plenty of yummy rewards. No doubt a senior dog is used to someone else's lifestyle and routine. He may take time to adjust to your routine, just as you will need time to adjust to his quirks and idiosyncrasies.

Older dogs usually have simple, uncomplicated lives. They like routine and simplicity. Old dogs can learn new tricks, but insisting that an older dog learn beyond his physical and mental capabilities will cause him undue stress.

Senior Bulldogs, for the most part, require the same things as their younger counterparts: good nutrition, regular grooming and veterinary care, age-appropriate physical and mental stimulation, a bed of their own, and plenty of love and companionship.

Multi-Dog Tip

Bulldogs generally get along well with most other dogs. However, they can be dog-to-dog aggressive if they lack proper and adequate socialization, which is often the case with rescued dogs. When adding a senior Bulldog to your household, be sure that he will get along with your existing pets. Some organizations will want to meet your other pets prior to releasing a Bulldog to you.

CHAPTER 13

CARE OF YOUR BULLDOG SENIOR

Bulldogs age just as people do, and older Bulldogs are still excellent companions. Time invested in nurturing the human/canine bond—a bond based on mutual love, respect, and consistency—will continue to serve you in good stead through your dog's senior years.

Bulldogs live on average about eight to ten years. The old adage of seven dog years for each human year was developed years ago, but many experts say that the conversion is about four human years for each adult dog year. That said, no universally accepted definition of "old age" exists. Most Bulldogs are considered "senior" around six or seven years of age, but dogs, like humans, age differently depending on their size and physical and nutritional habits. Research supported by the National Institute on Aging (NIA) indicates that regular physical activity, mental stimulation, and a diet rich in antioxidants can help keep aging dog brains in tip-top shape.

As your Bulldog ages, you must consider his medical, physical, and emotional needs. You will need to make it a point not to take him for granted or ignore him in favor of a new or younger dog. Do not ask him to participate in activities that are beyond his physical or mental capabilities. Yet continue his regular daily routine, if possible. Shorter and slower walks may be necessary, but they will give you and your Bulldog pleasure and continue to enhance your relationship. No doubt he will continue to enjoy gentle grooming, and his continued good looks will keep him in high spirits.

Caring for an older Bulldog can take a good deal of time and energy, but many owners say that this time of their dog's life is the most enjoyable—a time to care for and prolong an already enjoyable life.

THE AGING PROCESS

Aging is not a disease. Experts define it as "a complex biologic process resulting in progressive reduction of an individual's ability to maintain homeostasis under physiologic and external environmental stresses, thereby decreasing the individual's viability and increasing its vulnerability to disease, and eventually causing death."

Like humans, as dogs age they tend to slow down. Even in his prime, the Bulldog is not a high-drive, high-energy dog, but you may notice subtle changes in the way he moves. Older dogs do not have the ability to exchange

As your Bulldog ages, you must consider his medical, physical, and emotional needs.

discomfort of arthritis. Stiffness or lameness can also be indicative of injury or neurological problems. Another potential cause of slowing down is hypothyroidism, which is common in dogs and easily diagnosed and treated.

As dogs age, they generally require more sleep, and their metabolism slows. Again, Bulldogs are not turbo-charged dogs by any stretch of the imagination, but with age and decreased physical activity comes a slower metabolism, which means that all of the chemical reactions that combine to keep your Bulldog alive and working are slowed down. His body produces fewer of the hormones that help maintain normal body temperature, and glucose is in less demand for fuel. As a dog's metabolism slows, the body's entire machinery slows. A slower metabolism, coupled with reduced activity and increased caloric intake, can lead to weight gain and obesity in older dogs. As a result, older dogs need about 20 percent fewer calories than do middle-aged dogs. A little weight gain in older dogs is not unusual, but too much weight gain can contribute to health problems or exacerbate existing medical conditions.

and deliver oxygenated blood as efficiently as their younger counterparts, which is one reason why the frequency and intensity of exercise decreases. Also, muscles atrophy—especially the hind legs—and a dog's joints may become stiff. One of the more common causes of lameness in dogs is osteoarthritis (OA)—the wear-and-tear-type arthritis—and it is estimated to affect 20 percent of dogs one year of age and older. A progressive degenerative disease of the synovial joints, it is characterized by pain, disability, and the destruction of articular cartilage. As a result, your dog may move slower than normal or have difficulty getting up, lying down, or ascending or descending stairs. Different medications are available that can help ease the

PREVENTIVE CARE AND CHECKUPS

Scheduling (and keeping!) bi-annual veterinary examinations is a must for older dogs. It's easy to overlook regular checkups when your Bulldog is happy and healthy. However, diseases such as diabetes, kidney failure, arthritis, dental disease, and cancer become more prevalent as dogs age. Biannual examinations can catch and delay the onset or progression of diseases. Remember, dogs age about four to seven human years for each dog year, so a veterinary examination every six months is equivalent to a human going to the doctor every two to three and a half years.

Want to Know More?

As previously mentioned in Chapter 3: Care of Your Bulldog Puppy, extra weight predisposes a dog to heart and lung disease, gastrointestinal disorders, and bone, joint, and muscle problems.

Similar to a puppy checkup or yearly wellness examination, your veterinarian will want to know about changes in your dog's appetite, water consumption, energy, exercise, sleep habits, and whether or not he is urinating and defecating regularly. In addition to a full body examination, which includes checking his pulse, heart, lungs, etc., she may run a blood-chemistry panel to measure electrolytes, enzymes, and chemical elements, such as calcium and phosphorus. This helps a veterinarian determine how a dog's kidneys, pancreas, and liver are functioning. She may recommend a complete blood count (CBC) test, which measures the number of red blood cells, white blood cells, and platelets in a given sample of blood. This information is helpful in diagnosing anemia and infections. A urinalysis will detect the presence of specific substances that normally do not appear in urine, such as protein, sugar, white blood cells, or blood. It also measures the dilution or concentration of urine and helps diagnose diseases, urinary tract infections, diabetes, dehydration, kidney problems, and many other conditions.

HEALTH CARE

As dogs get older, they become more susceptible to age-related disorders. The more common include congestive heart failure, Cushing's disease, renal failure, and canine cognitive dysfunction syndrome (CCDS).

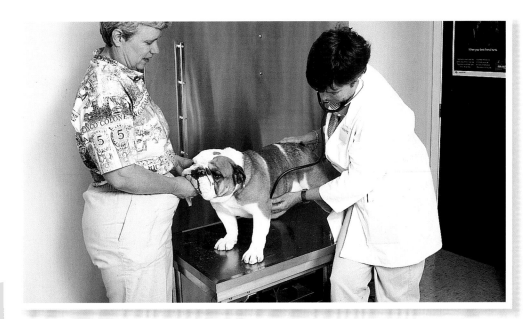

Bi-annual checkups are necessary to ensure your older dog's optimal health.

Congestive Heart Failure (CHF)

Dogs do not suffer heart attacks as people do. More commonly, they experience what is called congestive heart failure (CHF), which is also suffered by people. A progressive and nonreversible disease, CHF occurs when the heart can't pump enough blood to the body's other organs. The failing heart keeps working but not as efficiently as it should. As the condition develops, it affects all of other organs that rely on the efficient supply of nutrient-rich blood. The two most common causes of CHF in dogs are degenerative valvular disease (DVD) and dilated cardiomyopathy (DCM). Symptoms include exercise intolerance, sleepiness, coughing, wheezing or gurgling sounds, decreased appetite, syncope (fainting), and ascites (fluid in the abdomen).

Treatment generally includes medications that increase the body's urine output, dilate the blood vessels, strengthen the heart's beat, and suppress coughing. A reduced-sodium diet may also be recommended. Prognosis depends on the cause, severity, and the dog's response to treatment.

Cushing's Disease

Cushing's disease (hyperadrenocorticism) is considered a disease of middle age and older dogs and is a condition that results from the chronic overproduction of too much glucocorticoid in the body. Symptoms include increased water consumption and urination, increased appetite, abdominal enlargement, hair loss, and thin skin, which are often mistaken by owners as normal symptoms

Typical signs of canine cognitive dysfunction syndrome include disorientation and forgetfulness.

of aging. Several tests, including a urine cortisol:creatinine ratio test and an ACTH test, can generally provide a diagnosis. Treatment generally involves medications and/or surgery.

Cushing's disease has two forms:

Pituitary Dependent Hyperadrenocorticism (PDH)

PDH involves the oversecretion of a hormone called ACTH by the pituitary gland. ACTH in turn stimulates the adrenal gland to produce glucocorticoids. PDH is responsible for about 80 percent of the cases of Cushing's disease.

Adrenal-Based Hyperadrenocorticism

This form of the disease is usually a result of an adrenal tumor that causes an oversecretion of glucocorticoids. It is responsible for about 20 percent of the cases of Cushing's disease.

Chronic Kidney Failure

In a healthy dog, toxins circulate to the kidneys where, dissolved in water, they are filtered out and urinated away. An efficient kidney can produce enough of a highly concentrated urine that a large amount of toxin can be excreted in a relatively small amount of water. Kidney failure, which is common in older Bulldogs and dogs in general, occurs when the kidneys lose their ability to concentrate urine and more water is required to excrete the same amount of toxin. A classic symptom is increased water consumption, which is the dog's body trying to provide enough water to the failing kidneys. Ultimately, the dog cannot drink enough water and the toxin levels begin to rise. As the disease progresses, symptoms include weight loss, listlessness, nausea, constipation, and poor appetite. A blood panel will help your veterinarian assess the situation and determine a course of treatment. Special diets, as well as subcutaneous fluids and medications, can help.

Multi-Dog Tip

Senior Bulldogs need more sleep than their younger counterparts, and many do not have the patience they once had. Therefore, be sure that your senior has a bed or crate or special place of his own to escape his rambunctious counterparts. Take care that your younger dogs do not antagonize, annoy, pester, or harass him.

Currently, however, there is no cure for kidney failure.

Canine Cognitive Dysfunction Syndrome (CCDS)

Experts believe canine cognitive dysfunction syndrome (CCDS) may be a progressive degenerative brain disorder that is frequently associated with aging, especially in dogs over the age of eight. Sixty-two percent of dogs between 11 and 16 years of age show at least one symptom of CCDS, according to a study at the University of California-Davis.

While the cause of CCDS is unknown, it is frequently compared to Alzheimer's disease in humans because, like people, older dogs frequently experience forgetfulness and confusion and occasionally fail to recognize family members. However, dogs do not develop Alzheimer's disease because they lack neurofibrillary tangles, one of the classic markers of the disease. Yet similarities include an accumulation of B-amyloid protein in the form of senile plaques in similar cortical areas of the brain, with cognitive decline in older dogs strongly associated with the accumulation of B-amyloid.

Typical symptoms vary but generally include disorientation in their surroundings; dogs may "space out" and get stuck in corners or behind chairs or stand at the hinge side of a door rather than the latch side. Dogs often sleep more soundly, may be confused when awakened, and may wander purposelessly at night when they should be sleeping. Dogs often whine, bark, or otherwise vocalize for seemingly no reason. Frequent accidents—especially urinating—in the house even though they were reliably trained as youngsters is yet another symptom. Interaction with family members may become less frequent and/or less intense. Some dogs may not recognize family members. A Bulldog with CCDS is also likely to forget previously learned behaviors, such as basic obedience commands or housetraining. Other symptoms can include intolerance to exercise, increased irritability, difficulty navigating up a flight of stairs, new fears, phobias, destruction during their owner's absence, and a "clinginess" when their owners are around.

Diagnosis is typically made via a physical examination, consideration of a detailed history of the behaviors, including when they started, their trend, etc., and by ruling out all other causes of cognitive impairment. Treatment can include placing baby gates around the house to prevent your dog from wandering too far and possibly hurting himself by falling down stairs, using a leash while outdoors or fencing your property and/or a section of the yard so that he can't wander off, and removing clutter in the house to ease the dog's mobility.

Vestibular disease interferes with a dog's balance system.

Never isolate or punish your dog. In CCDS dogs, it causes fear and anxiety and possibly injury. Medications that have recently been approved for use with CCDS may be recommended by your veterinarian.

Vestibular Disease

The vestibular system is responsible for a dog's ability to balance. It's what allows a dog to run, walk, and maneuver uneven ground without falling, and it allows a dog's eyes to follow moving objects without getting dizzy. Vestibular disease interferes with the balance system, causing sudden loss of balance, with many dogs being unable to stand up. Motion sickness, circling, nystagmus (oscillating movements of the eye—either back and forth or up and down), falling to one side, trouble with nerves controlling the head and face, and a head tilt, which is the cardinal sign of vestibular disease, are some other signs. Symptoms are commonly albeit incorrectly referred to as a stroke.

Vestibular disease can arise from two different locations: the peripheral location, which is located in the inner ear (outside the central nervous system) and the central location, which is located in the brain stem and cerebellum. Peripheral disease is much more common than the central disease, and the idiopathic form—meaning it happens for no known reason or cause—is the most common form of peripheral vestibular disease.

Symptoms are usually acute, with many dogs appearing fine right up until the moment that signs appear. Diagnosis of peripheral vestibular disease is made by a physical examination and observation of the symptoms, as well as a neurological exam, which will determine a peripheral or central location; ostoscopic (deep ear) exam; and sometimes radiographs, blood tests, cultures, and cytology (the medical and

scientific study of cells) may be performed to differentiate among possible causes. Diagnosis of central vestibular disease may include spinal fluid taps, MRI, CT scan, and blood tests.

Treatment depends on the location, with many peripheral cases being treated with antibiotics. Central cases are more complex in their treatment.

Prognosis for peripheral vestibular disease is good, with most dogs showing improvement within 72 hours and being "normal" within 7 to 14 days. The head tilt may persist for several months or may never resolve completely. Central vestibular disease carries a poor prognosis, as it indicates potential damage to the brainstem.

Other Age-Related Issues

Older dogs can have age-dependent changes in drug distribution as a result of a decrease in body water and an increase in the percentage of body fat. How they metabolize lipid-soluble drugs and water-soluble drugs can change with age. Liver and kidney disease can have a variable effect on how drugs are cleared from the body.

Visual and hearing senses also diminish as dogs age. Your Bulldog may be harder to wake up while sleeping. He may be easily startled because he didn't hear you approach. He may not hear your commands, such as *come* or *down*, so be patient with him. Protect him from hazards, including cars, bicycles, kids, and other animals that he may not hear. Not much can be done for age-related hearing loss, but a veterinarian can rule out any underlying medical problems, such as an infection or a foreign body in the ear.

As dogs age, their eyes often show a slight bluish or grayish haze in the pupil area. The medical term for this normal effect of aging that occurs in the lenses of older dogs

Caring for the Older Bulldog

Caring for an aging Bulldog can test your patience, disrupt your normal schedule, and break your heart. But your Bulldog needs you now more than ever, and the good news is that there are a number of things you can do to help him negotiate his senior years, including:

- Get him regular checkups.
- Encourage him to continue his regular routine or modified versions of playing or short walks. Exercise is important to a dog's brain functions.
- Avoid disrupting his regular schedule. Older dogs like consistency and routine.
- Never relegate him to the isolation of the back yard, laundry room, or garage.
- Never scold or punish him for accidents or ignoring an obedience command. Older dogs are often forgetful and hard of hearing.
- Keep his environment safe. Avoid leaving chairs, boxes, backpacks, etc., lying about, as he is likely to bump into them.
- Love your Bulldog, and be patient with him during this time.

is lenticular or nuclear sclerosis. Typically, it occurs in both eyes at the same time and occurs in most dogs six years and older. The loss of transparency occurs because of the compression in the linear fibers in the lens and does not appear to affect a dog's vision.

Lenticular sclerosis is often confused with cataracts, which are completely different. Cataracts, which are white and opaque, are opacities in the lens of the eye. Some cataracts are inherited; others are not. Some are congenital, meaning that they are present at birth. Some are trauma or disease related. Others are developmental, meaning that they develop early in life. Cataracts are classified by several factors, including age at the onset and the cause. No medication is available to prevent, reverse, or shrink cataracts. Surgery is the only known treatment. Vision can be affected with cataracts, and consultation with a veterinarian or canine ophthalmologist is recommended.

Older dogs are more likely to develop tooth and gum issues, including tartar buildup. Sore gums and loose or broken teeth can

be associated with pain and weight loss. An infected mouth can also send bacteria into the bloodstream, causing cardiac and renal problems.

FEEDING

Senior dogs who are healthy and eating an appropriate diet do not necessarily need to be changed to a senior food simply based on their age. Caloric and nutritional requirements of the aging Bulldog need to be determined on an individual basis. The diet must be balanced to meet his changing metabolic needs yet still have adequate protein, fat, and fiber. However, as previously mentioned, dogs tend to physically slow down as they age; they become less active, and their metabolism slows as well. To prevent your Bulldog from becoming overweight, you may need to decrease his daily caloric intake. Some dogs may be able to continue eating their normal adult food without any problems—or simply in smaller quantities. Or you may need to switch him to a specially formulated senior diet that fills the same nutritional requirements as most adult dog foods but with less fat, less protein, and more fiber.

Special Diets

Many food companies have special diets for the changing needs of older dogs. If your Bulldog is experiencing medical problems, he may benefit from a special diet formulated to help meet the nutritional needs associated with heart conditions, gastrointestinal conditions, kidney problems, obesity, and so on. Some foods have enhanced palatability to appeal to an aging dog's weakening sense of smell. Some foods include antioxidants to inhibit cellular deterioration. Others are designed specifically for the Bulldog's unique jaw structure. Others are formulated to reduce dental plaque and inhibit tartar.

Interestingly, studies have explored the use of nutrigenomics (the effect of nutrients on gene expression) to understand and modify metabolic pathways to optimize the nutritional and health status of companion animals. By understanding and further defining what impact specific nutrients have on gene expression, experts can then develop diets containing specific macro and micro nutrients, as well as biochemical consequences of aging.

Lack of Interest in Food

Some dogs become disinterested in food as they age. Underlying medical problems, such as liver or kidney disease or dental problems, can cause a dog to consume less food. So a

By the Numbers

To prevent your older Bulldog from becoming overweight, you may need to decrease his daily caloric intake. Reduced-fat diets usually translate to lower calories, with most commercially prepared senior foods containing about 10 to 12 percent fat and about 18 percent protein. As dogs age, they are more prone to developing constipation, so most senior diets contain higher fiber—about 3 to 5 percent—which helps maintain a healthy digestive system, as well as diluting calories and quelling hunger.

trip to the veterinarian may be necessary. If everything checks out, getting the senior dog to eat can be challenging. Consider a food designed specifically for the Bulldog's unique jaw structure. Smaller kibble moistened with water may be easier to chew. Adding small amounts of canned food, broth, or cooked or boiled eggs to the food may make it more appealing. Try warming canned or moistened dry food in the microwave to increase the aroma. Be sure to stir the food after warming to eliminate any hot pockets. Feeding smaller

Special diets and treats are available for the changing needs of older dogs.

NYLABONE

amounts of food several times a day may increase an aging dog's total daily intake. Homemade diets of boiled rice, potatoes, veggies, and chicken or hamburger may work, but always consult your veterinarian to be sure that you are providing adequate vitamin and mineral levels.

GROOMING

As your Bulldog ages, you will need to continue grooming him. If grooming has been an enjoyable experience throughout his life, chances are high he will continue to enjoy being pampered. Regular grooming will keep his coat in tip-top shape and allow you to check for tumors, lumps, cuts, broken nails, skin irritations, or other abnormalities.

Daily brushings—or at least three times a week—also help stimulate natural oils, improve circulation, and keep the coat in good condition.

Oral hygiene is doubly important as dogs age. As previously mentioned, an infected mouth can send bacteria into the bloodstream, causing cardiac and renal problems. Regular dental care allows you to check for tartar buildup as well as for loose, broken, or chipped teeth and mouth sores—all of which can be painful to the aging Bulldog.

Because of his predisposition to respiratory issues, be sure to keep your aging Bulldog warm and protected from drafts during the grooming process—especially during and after bathing—to prevent chilling.

As your Bulldog ages, you will need to continue grooming him.

Depending on how long you've had your senior, he may have forgotten some basic commands or picked up a few bad habits. Seniors can be set in their ways, so you will need to use your imagination to come up with fun games, such as "Find me!" to teach and/or reinforce obedience commands. Rewarding behaviors he performs on his own, such as sitting, coming, rolling over, etc., will help to reinforce desired behaviors and pump up his ego! Keep in mind that seniors generally aren't as energetic as their younger counterparts, so make sessions short and fun.

Older dogs tend to have stiff and sore joints, so extra precautions must be taken when lifting your Bulldog on and off a grooming table, as well as throughout the grooming process. Be sure to place a comfy towel or fleece mat on the floor or grooming table as well. This will help protect his joints and make the grooming process more enjoyable.

TRAINING

As long as your Bulldog enjoys training and working and he is physically capable of doing so, there is no reason why he can't continue to work into his senior years. Granted, most Bulldogs much prefer the couch to exercising or an obedience or agility ring, but physical exercise within your dog's capabilities will help to keep his body functions working. Never push your Bulldog beyond his physical and mental capabilities, and remember to keep training fun. Play plenty of games that let him win, which will boost his ego and make him feel good about himself. Let him strut around, savoring his mammoth victory. Follow play with plenty of physical and verbal rewards. And always stop before your Bulldog gets too tired. Remember, his eyesight and hearing may not be as sharp as they were, so make sure that he hears or sees your commands, and always be patient with him. Enjoy your Bulldog during this time of his life. Remember, he won't live forever. Treasure him while you can.

Clicker Training

Clicker training, which is based on the laws of learning and operant conditioning, is a great way to teach fun tricks and obedience commands to your senior Bulldog using positive motivation. A clicker is nothing more than an inexpensive plastic device that makes a clicking noise. It is a training tool that rewards or "marks" a behavior—a snapshot, so to speak, of a specific behavior you want to capture. The click tells the dog exactly which behavior you liked. It also tells him that a reward is on the way, be it a treat or a toy. The loudness of the "click" varies from clicker to clicker. If your senior Bulldog has diminished hearing, look for a clicker with a loud click.

Theoretically, you don't even need to use a clicker. A verbal cue or "marker word" such as a crisp "Yes!" or any perfectly timed one-syllable word like "yea!" works too.

A number of good books are available that delve into the intricacies of clicker training. Sometimes, however, books are not enough and you may need a trainer who can set you on the path to proper clicker training.

CHAPTER 14

END-OF-LIFE ISSUES

Someone once said, "A dog's only fault is that they don't live long enough." We love our dogs, and their lives *are* too short. No matter how well you care for and love your Bulldog, chances are he will live only eight to ten years. In those short years, a dog becomes a much-loved part of your family. Oftentimes, a dog is a bigger part of your life than your human friends. Sometimes a dog is your only family and friend. Losing him is traumatic.

Sadly, a day may come when your Bulldog is not able to enjoy life. As he ages, he may suffer from the pain and discomfort associated with aging or illness. Some owners hope that their dog goes quietly in his sleep to keep him from further suffering, but that isn't always the case. Thankfully, pet owners have the opportunity to end their dogs' suffering through euthanasia— the painless ending of a dog's life by a veterinarian. Deciding when that should happen is never easy, and it never should be. Feeling your heart break in a thousand tiny ways is

excruciating. However, euthanasia may also be the kindest and most compassionate decision you ever make for your dog. As your Bulldog's best friend, you owe him the blessing that only you can give. While in the comfort and security of your arms, and often in your own home, a veterinarian can help you let him go painlessly in seconds without further suffering.

MAKING THE DECISION

Making the decision to end your beloved Bulldog's life is an intensely personal and difficult one. Some owners don't want to think about making that decision until it's time, which is understandable. The thought of picking up the pieces and carrying on without your dog is too painful. Owners often have questions about how to tell when the time is right. They usually ask their veterinarian if it's time or what the vet would do. Few, if any, veterinarians will make that decision for pet owners. No doubt the vet's heart is breaking too, but the best he or she can do

---

Want to Know More?

If and when you're ready to add a new dog to your home, see Chapter 2: Finding and Prepping for Your Bulldog Puppy, or Chapter 5: Finding Your Bulldog Adult, for some pointers.

It's never easy to decide when your Bulldog is ready to go.

is offer medical advice and facts. Only you—your Bulldog's best friend—can decide it's time.

As your Bulldog's faithful friend, you will know when his bad days outnumber the good days. And when this happens—when the bad days outnumber the good days—it's probably time to say goodbye. No loving pet owners want their dog to suffer.

WHAT HAPPENS WHEN A PET IS EUTHANIZED

Veterinarians differ in their protocols, but generally speaking most vets administer a sedative tranquilizer prior to the euthanasia drug, which is given in the vein. The dog is then restful, and owners may decide to spend some quiet time saying goodbye. At this point, some owners opt to leave, while others prefer to stay until the end. There are no right or wrong decisions—it all depends on what you want to do. The euthanasia drug, which is administered through a needle and syringe or IV catheter, is an overdose of a barbiturate that stops the heart and breathing muscles. Although animals and situations differ, in most instances you will notice nothing other than your Bulldog's peaceful release from life.

The average life span of a Bulldog is 8 to10 years, with many living to 12 years of age.

GRIEF

Grief is natural. Grieving over the loss of your Bulldog is natural too. People grieve differently, and there are no simple answers about how long to grieve. Some owners decide to get another dog right away, but maybe a different breed. Others may need a good deal of time to adjust—to accept their loss. Some owners can't imagine replacing their beloved dog, but perhaps eventually, in time, they can let a new dog come into their lives. Children are often remarkably resilient and often cope exceedingly well. However, you know your children better than anyone, and you are the best person to assess their pain and sorrow and how much information they are capable of handling. And you are the only one who knows what is best for you. Don't let anyone talk you into another pet if you aren't ready. And don't let them talk you out of another dog if that's what you really want.

Some owners have an overwhelming sense of sadness or feelings of anger. Some owners second-guess their decision—questioning whether or not they exhausted all of their options. Some owners blame others or themselves. If the burden of grief is too

Only you will know when it's time to add another Bulldog to your family.

Training Tidbit

End-of-care training often involves training yourself more so than your dog. Your dog needs you now more than ever. To help him through end-of-life issues, consider learning the following:

- how to assess his quality of life
- how to minimize his pain
- how to assess his hydration and respiration and detect sepsis
- how to take his temperature
- how to administer subcutaneous fluids
- how to administer medications
- how to massage his sore muscles
- how to hand-feed him, if necessary

overwhelming, you may decide to seek counseling. Fortunately, many community support groups exist that can help you deal with the pain and sorrow that accompany this type of grief. Your local animal shelter or veterinarian may be able to recommend organizations that have specially trained individuals available to counsel pet owners.

REMEMBERING YOUR BULLDOG

Part of the grieving process is remembering all that was perfect and good about your Bulldog. Some owners choose to celebrate their years together by doing one or more of the following:

- Make a financial donation to an animal organization, such as the local humane society, in their dog's name.
- Plant a tree or shrub in their dog's memory.
- Make a memorial collage or shadow box that includes their dog's photo, leash, collar, or ID tag.
- Place a memorial on an online memorial site specifically for pets.
- Preserve the dog's ashes in a special urn, box, or glass pendant. A few glassblowers infuse a pinch of a beloved dog's ashes into a hand-

blown glass object, such as a paperweight or a glass necklace.

- Store ashes to be buried with them at a future date. (Some owners opt to store their pet's ashes so that they can be buried together.)
- Bury the dog's ashes on their property. (Always check the local regulations in your area before doing so.)

Multi-Dog Tip

Just as with people, dogs in a household grow attached to one another and know when another canine companion is missing. They feel the loss of their friends and may become depressed or show signs of grieving such as loss of appetite, disinterest in their favorite toys or activities, or sleeping more. Be patient, and treat your surviving dog just as you would any family member by giving him a lot of extra attention and love during this difficult time.

50 FUN FACTS EVERY BULLDOG OWNER SHOULD KNOW

1. The average life span of a Bulldog is 8 to 10 years, with many living up to 12 years of age.

2. Today's Bulldog is a descendant of the dogs used to bait bulls hundreds of years ago.

3. The Bulldog's ancient ancestors were known as "pugnaces," or war dogs, in Britain.

4. During the period of Roman domination, the fighting dogs of Britain were known as "the broad-mouth dogs of Britain."

5. Bulldogs are mentioned in a number of literary works, including those by William Shakespeare.

6. Today's Bulldog is smaller than his ancestors, weighing in at 50 pounds (18 kg) for mature males and 40 pounds (22.5 kg) for mature females.

7. Bullbaiting was banned by the British Parliament in 1835.

8. Since the mid- to late 1800s, the Bulldog has been fashionable as a show dog and companion.

9. In 1864, the first breed club was formed in England. It lasted only three years.

10. The best Bulldog of the first show dogs in England was a dog named King Dick.

11. Bulldogs are believed to have been present in America as early as 1774.

12. The Bulldog was accepted into the American Kennel Club in 1886.

13. One of the first dogs to be shown in the United States was a male named Donald.

14. The first Bulldog to become an American Kennel Club (AKC) champion was a dog named Robinson Crusoe.

15. Sergeant Chesty XI is the official mascot of the Marine Barracks in Washington, DC.

16. Handsome Dan is the name of the Yale University Bulldog mascot.

17. The Bulldog has been the official corporate symbol of Mack Trucks since 1922.

18. Bulldogs are well known for their patience with children and senior citizens.

19. Bulldogs can and do compete in a number of competitive canine sports, including agility and obedience.

20. The Bulldog Club of America (BCA) is the AKC parent club of the Bulldog breed.

21. Bulldogs are known as a brachycephalic breed, which means they have short muzzles.

22. Bulldogs are inherently predisposed to heat-induced illnesses.

23. Nearly all Bulldogs are born via caesarean section.

24. Bulldogs are rarely bred naturally. Breedings occur through artificial insemination.

25. Bulldogs are famously stubborn.

26. The original breed standard was known as the "Philo-Kuon Standard."

27. Bulldog owners are known as Bulldoggers.

28. Bulldogs are prone to itchy skin, especially in hot weather.

29. Most Bulldogs are extremely adaptable.

30. Bulldogs are an example of genetic manipulation.

31. The perfect Bulldog is of medium size, with a smooth coat.

32. The Bulldog's tail may be either straight or "screwed" but never curved or curly.

33. "Chops" is a term used in the British Bulldog standard to describe a dog's flews.

34. Bulldogs are predisposed to cystinuria.

35. Old-time breeders referred to a Bulldog's characteristic expression as a "sour" expression.

36. Bulldogs belong to the AKC's Non-Sporting Group.

37. Bulldogs are the second most popular breed in Las Vegas, Long Beach, and Los Angeles (2008).

38. Bulldogs are often referred to as "English" or "British" Bulldogs to distinguish them from other Bulldog-related breeds.

39. Bulldogs are indoor dogs.

40. Bulldogs shed.

41. Bulldogs do not drool very much.

42. Bulldogs are intelligent.

43. A Bulldog's tail is never docked.

44. Bulldogs whelp a higher than normal number of anasarca puppies.

45. Overweight Bulldogs have more health problems and generally do not live as long as their slimmer counterparts.

46. Jack is the name of the Georgetown University Bulldog Mascot.

47. The Bulldog was unofficially adopted as the Marine Corp mascot during WWI, when the German Army reportedly nicknamed the attacking Marines Teufel-hunden, meaning "Devil Dogs."

48. Former heavyweight boxing champion James J. "Gene" Tunney, who had fought with the Marines in France, donated his English Bulldog to the Marines as an official mascot.

49. President Calvin Coolidge owned a Bulldog named "Boston Beans."

50. President Warren Harding owned a Bulldog named "Oh Boy."

ASSOCIATIONS AND ORGANIZATIONS

Breed Clubs

American Kennel Club (AKC)
5580 Centerview Drive
Raleigh, NC 27606
Telephone: (919) 233-9767
Fax: (919) 233-3627
E-Mail: info@akc.org
www.akc.org

Bulldog Club of America
www.thebca.org

Bulldog Club of Central Canada
www.bulldogclubofcentralcanada.net

Canadian Kennel Club (CKC)
89 Skyway Avenue, Suite 100
Etobicoke, Ontario M9W 6R4
Canada
Telephone: (416) 675-5511
Fax: (416) 675-6506
E-Mail: information@ckc.ca
www.ckc.ca

Federation Cynologique Internationale (FCI)
Secretariat General de la FCI
Place Albert 1er, 13
B–6530 Thuin
Belqique
www.fci.be

The Bulldog Club, Inc.
www.bulldog-inc.com

The Kennel Club
1 Clarges Street
London W1J 8AB
England
Telephone: 0870 606 6750
Fax: 0207 518 1058
www.the-kennel-club.org.uk

United Kennel Club (UKC)
100 E. Kilgore Road
Kalamazoo, MI 49002-5584
Telephone: (269) 343-9020
Fax: (269) 343-7037
E-Mail: pbickell@ukcdogs.com
www.ukcdogs.com

Pet Sitters

National Association of Professional Pet Sitters
15000 Commerce Parkway,
Suite C
Mt. Laurel, NJ 08054
Telephone: (856) 439-0324
Fax: (856) 439-0525
E-Mail: napps@ahint.com
www.petsitters.org

Pet Sitters International
201 East King Street
King, NC 27021-9161
Telephone: (336) 983-9222
Fax: (336) 983-5266
E-Mail: info@petsit.com
www.petsit.com

Rescue Organizations and Animal Welfare Groups

American Humane Association (AHA)
63 Inverness Drive East
Englewood, CO 80112
Telephone: (303) 792-9900
Fax: 792-5333
www.americanhumane.org

American Society for the Prevention of Cruelty to Animals (ASPCA)
424 E. 92nd Street
New York, NY 10128-6804
Telephone: (212) 876-7700
www.aspca.org

The Humane Society of the United States (HSUS)
2100 L Street, NW
Washington, DC 20037
Telephone: (202) 452-1100
www.hsus.org

Royal Society for the Prevention of Cruelty to Animals (RSPCA)
RSPCA Enquiries Service
Wilberforce Way, Southwater,
Horsham, West Sussex RH13 9RS
United Kingdom
Telephone: 0870 3335 999
Fax: 0870 7530 284
www.rspca.org.uk

Sports

International Agility Link (IAL)
Global Administrator: Steve Drinkwater
E-Mail: yunde@powerup.au
www.agilityclick.com/~ial

The World Canine Freestyle Organization, Inc.
P.O. Box 350122
Brooklyn, NY 11235
Telephone: (718) 332-8336
Fax: (718) 646-2686
E-Mail: WCFODOGS@aol.com
www.worldcaninefreestyle.org

Therapy

Delta Society
875 124th Ave, NE, Suite 101
Bellevue, WA 98005
Telephone: (425) 679-5500
Fax: (425) 679-5539
E-Mail: info@DeltaSociety.org
www.deltasociety.org

Therapy Dogs, Inc.
P.O. Box 20227
Cheyenne, WY 82003
Telephone: (877) 843-7364
Fax: (307) 638-2079
E-Mail: therapydogsinc@qwestoffice.net
www.therapydogs.com

Therapy Dogs International (TDI)
88 Bartley Road
Flanders, NJ 07836
Telephone: (973) 252-9800
Fax: (973) 252-7171
E-Mail: tdi@gti.net
www.tdi-dog.org

Training

Association of Pet Dog Trainers (APDT)
150 Executive Center Drive, Box 35
Greenville, SC 29615
Telephone: (800) PET-DOGS
Fax: (864) 331-0767
E-Mail: information@apdt.com
www.apdt.com

International Association of Animal Behavior Consultants (IAABC)
565 Callery Road
Cranberry Township, PA 16066
E-Mail: info@iaabc.org
www.iaabc.org

National Association of Dog
Obedience Instructors (NADOI)
PMB 369
729 Grapevine Hwy.
Hurst, TX 76054-2085
www.nadoi.org

Veterinary and Health Resources

Academy of Veterinary Homeopathy (AVH)
P.O. Box 9280
Wilmington, DE 19809
Telephone: (866) 652-1590
Fax: (866) 652-1590
www.theavh.org

American Academy of Veterinary Acupuncture (AAVA)
P.O. Box 1058
Glastonbury, CT 06033
Telephone: (860) 632-9911
Fax: (860) 659-8772
www.aava.org

American Animal Hospital Association (AAHA)
12575 W. Bayaud Ave.
Lakewood, CO 80228
Telephone: (303) 986-2800
Fax: (303) 986-1700
E-Mail: info@aahanet.org
www.aahanet.org/index.cfm

American College of Veterinary Internal Medicine (ACVIM)
1997 Wadsworth Blvd., Suite A
Lakewood, CO 80214-5293
Telephone: (800) 245-9081
Fax: (303) 231-0880
E-Mail: ACVIM@ACVIM.org
www.acvim.org

American College of Veterinary Ophthalmologists (ACVO)
P.O. Box 1311
Meridian, ID 83860
Telephone: (208) 466-7624
Fax: (208) 466-7693
E-Mail: office09@acvo.com
www.acvo.com

American Holistic Veterinary Medical Association (AHVMA)
2218 Old Emmorton Road
Bel Air, MD 21015
Telephone: (410) 569-0795
Fax: (410) 569-2346
E-Mail: office@ahvma.org
www.ahvma.org

American Veterinary Medical Association (AVMA)
1931 North Meacham Road, Suite 100
Schaumburg, IL 60173-4360
Telephone: (847) 925-8070
Fax: (847) 925-1329
E-Mail: avmainfo@avma.org
www.avma.org

ASPCA Animal Poison Control Center
Telephone: (888) 426-4435
www.aspca.org

British Veterinary Association (BVA)
7 Mansfield Street
London W1G 9NQ
England
Telephone: 0207 636 6541
Fax: 0207 908 6349
E-Mail: bvahq@bva.co.uk
www.bva.co.uk

Canine Eye Registration Foundation (CERF)
VMDB/CERF
1717 Philo Rd.
P.O. Box 3007
Urbana, IL 61803-3007
Telephone: (217) 693-4800
Fax: (217) 693-4801
E-Mail: CERF@vmbd.org
www.vmdb.org

Orthopedic Foundation for Animals (OFA)
2300 NE Nifong Blvd.
Columbus, MO 65201-3856
Telephone: (573) 442-0418
Fax: (573) 875-5073
E-Mail: ofa@offa.org
www.offa.org

US Food and Drug Administration Center for Veterinary Medicine (CVM)
7519 Standish Place
HFV-12
Rockville, MD 20855-0001
Telephone: (240) 276-9300 or (888) INFO-FDA
http://www.fda.gov/cvm

PUBLICATIONS

Books
Anderson, Teoti. *The Super Simple Guide to Housetraining.* Neptune City: TFH Publications, 2004.

Anne, Jonna, with Mary Straus. *The Healthy Dog Cookbook: 50 Nutritious and Delicious Recipes Your Dog Will Love.* UK: Ivy Press Limited, 2008.

Dainty, Suellen. *50 Games to Play With Your Dog.* UK: Ivy Press Limited, 2007.

Gagne, Tammy. *Bulldogs.* Neptune City: TFH Publications, 2007.

Morgan, Diane. *Good Dogkeeping.* Neptune City: TFH Publications, 2005.

Morgan, Diane. *The Bulldog.* Neptune City: TFH Publications, 2005.

Magazines
AKC Family Dog
American Kennel Club
260 Madison Avenue
New York, NY 10016
Telephone: (800) 490-5675
E-Mail: familydog@akc.org
www.akc.org/pubs/familydog

AKC Gazette
American Kennel Club
260 Madison Avenue
New York, NY 10016
Telephone: (800) 533-7323
E-Mail: gazette@akc.org
www.akc.org/pubs/gazette

Dog & Kennel
Pet Publishing, Inc.
7-L Dundas Circle
Greensboro, NC 27407
Telephone: (336) 292-4272
Fax: (336) 292-4272
E-Mail: info@petpublishing.com
www.dogandkennel.com

Dogs Monthly
Ascot House
High Street, Ascot,
Berkshire SL5 7JG
United Kingdom
Telephone: 0870 730 8433
Fax: 0870 730 8431
E-Mail: admin@rtc-associates.freeserve.co.uk
www.corsini.co.uk/dogsmonthly

Websites
Nylabone
www.nylabone.com

TFH Publications, Inc.
www.tfh.com

INDEX

Note: Boldfaced numbers indicate illustrations.

A

accidents, housetraining, 66, 71–72
activities, 171–177. *See also* sports
  age requirements for, 174
  camping, 171
  Canine Good Citizen, 171–173, **172**, 175
  fetching and retrieving, 173, **173**
  swimming, 173–174
  therapy work, 174–175, **175**
  traveling, 181–185
  trick training, 175–176
  tug-of-war, 176, **176**
  walking and jogging, 176–177
acupuncture, 142–143, **143**
adenovirus, canine, 53
adrenal-based hyperadrenocorticism, 199
adult Bulldogs. *See also* activities; problem behaviors; sports
  advantages/disadvantages of, 81–82, **82**
  age of, 23, 81, 106
  annual vet exam for, 117, 118
  collars for, 38
  crates for, 39–40
  feeding, 103–115
  finding, 83–87
  grooming, 89–101
  health issues in, 117–147
  male vs. female, 82–83
  training, 85, 149–155
age
  adult, 23, 81, 106
  for competitive events, 174
  estimating, 81
  puppy, 23, 33, 36
  senior, 189, 195
aggression, 159–161
  new senior dog and, 193
  professional help for, 169
  sex and, 25, 28, 83
agility, 33, 174, 177, **177**
aging process, 195–196
air travel, 182–183
alaunts, 9–11
allergies, 103, 129, 129–130, 145
alternative therapies, 142–145, **143**, **144**
Alzheimer's disease, 199
America, Bulldogs in, 14–15

American Academy of Veterinary Acupuncture (AAVA), 143
American Bulldog, 21
American Kennel Club (AKC), 14
  breed standard of, 20
  Bulldog names of, 21
  buying tips from, 86
  Canine Good Citizen Program of, 171–173, 172, 175
  event age requirements of, 174
  finding breeders through, 34
Americans with Disabilities Act (ADA), 174
American Veterinary Chiropractic Association (AVCA), 143
American Veterinary Medical Association (AVMA), 52, 142, 143, 144
amino acids, 106, 130
anasarca, 57, 139
anesthesia, 139
animal welfare groups, 214
antibodies, 51–52
aortic stenosis, 139–140
arthritis, 138, 196
artificial insemination, 57
assistance dogs, 174
Association of Pet Dog Trainers (APDT), 61
associations, 214–215
atopic dermatitis (AD), 129, 129–130
attention span, 48, 62, 73
Automobile Club of America (AAA), 183

B

balance, loss of, 201
bandogs, 9–11
BARF diet, 111, 111–112, 112
barking, 159, 161–163
bathing
  adult, 90–93, **92**
  senior, 204
  supplies for, 49
bearbaiting, 9, 12
beds, 38
  in multi-dog home, 76
  for puppy, 43
  for senior, 199
bee and insect bites, 145
behaviors, 157. *See also* problem behaviors
  acceptable vs. unacceptable, 59–60, 73
  marking, 205

bites, 145
bladder control, 37, 68–69
bleeding, 97
blepharospasm, 132
bloat, 115
blow dryers, 92–93
boarding facilities, 183–185
body, 7, 23–24, **24**
body language, 29, 65, 71
body temperature, 136, **137**, 138
bones, 113–114
bones and raw food (BARF) diet, 111, 111–112, **112**
books, 215–216
bordetellosis, 53
boredom, 158, 165, 166–167
Borrelia burgdorferi, 53
Boston Terrier, 21
brachycephalic airway syndrome (BAS), 27, 136
brachycephalic dogs, 27, 135
breathing problems, 27, 46, 47, 135–136
breed clubs, 13, 34, 214
breeders
  adopting adults from, 84
  buying from reputable, 33–34
  documents and guarantees from, 35–36
  finding, 34
  interview with, 34–35
  socialization by, 63
breeding, 11, 21
  control of, 56–57
  cost of, 57
breed standard, 13, 14, 19–27
  breed type in, 20–21
  character and temperament in, 21–23
  conformation to, 26, 178, 178–179
  physical structure in, 23–27, **24**
breed type, 20–21
brindles, 27
brushes, 48, 90
brushing
  adult, 89–90, **90**
  puppy, 48
  senior, 204
  supplies for, 48–49
  tooth, 97, 98–100
bullbaiting, 7, 9, 11–12
  breed type for, 21
  physical traits for, 23–24, 25, 26
Bulldog Club, Inc., The, 13

soft palate, elongated, 136
spaying, 56–57, 141
special diets, 110, 113, 203
spider bites, 145
sports, 171, 177–181. *See also* activities
  age requirements for, 174
  agility, 177, 177
  capability for, 22
  conformation, 178, 178–179
  flyball, 179
  obedience, 179–180
  performance dog for, 33
  rally obedience, 180–181
  resources for, 214
  tracking, 181
squeaker toys, 41–42
stacking, 26
stand command, 151, 152–153,
  154–155, 155
stay command, 151–154, 153
  down and, 154
  other commands used as, 152–153
  sit and, 153–154
  stand and, 154
stenotic nares, 136
stifle, 141
stimulation, need for, 158, 165
stolen Bulldogs, 85, 86
stools, normal, 146
"stop," 25
strangers, exposure to, 64
stress, 158–159, 182
subaortic stenosis (SAS), 139–140
submissiveness, 72
supplements, 113
  fatty acid, 129, 130
  herbal and natural, 142, 143–144,
    144
supplies, 38–42, 39, 41, 42
  first-aid, 145
  grooming, 48–49
swimming, 173–174

T
tags, ID, 38, 40–41
tail pocket care, 101
tapeworms, 118, 122–123
tartar, 97, 202, 204
tearstains, 94–95
teeth
  age estimation based on, 81
  care of, 49, 97–100, 98, 204
  senior issues with, 202
teething, 158, 163–164, 167
Tellington-Jones, Linda, 144
temperament, 19, 21–23, 59
temperature, body, 136, 137, 138
territorial aggression, 160
textured protein, 108–109
therapy work, 174–175, 175, 214–215

third eyelid gland, prolapsed, 133
ticks, 54, 118, 127–128
toothaches, 97
toothbrush and toothpaste, 49, 99
toys, 41, 41–42, 42
  chew, 113, 164, 165
  for crate training, 66
  food-dispensing, 166
  tug, 176
trace elements, 105–106
tracheobronchitis, canine infectious,
  53
tracking, 174, 181
trainability, 19, 22, 29, 29
trainer, finding, 61
training
  adult obedience, 85, 149–155, 150,
    152, 153, 155
  for barking, 163
  basic obedience, 65, 72–77, 73, 75,
    77
  for car travel, 181
  clicker, 205
  collars for, 38
  crate, 63, 65–67, 66
  disease prevention in, 106
  end-of-care, 210
  finding trainer for, 61
  food lures in, 67, 150, 151
  for grooming, 47–48, 95–96, 97, 99
  housetraining, 37, 40, 42, 67–72,
    69, 71
  importance of, 59–60
  lack of, 158
  "leave it" or "drop it," 147
  in multi-dog home, 84, 154, 169
  positive motivation in, 60–62, 75,
    163
  puppy, 31, 59–77
  puppy classes for, 29, 61, 77
  resources for, 215
  senior, 189–190, 192, 205
  socialization, 34, 36, 62–65, 63
  for stacking, 26
  successful, 62, 163
  trick, 175–176
  tug-and-release, 176
transitional period, 63
traveling, 181–185
  by air, 182–183
  by car, 42, 64, 181–182
  crate for, 66
  lodging for, 183
  safety tips for, 182
  without Bulldog, 183–185
Traveling With Your Pet (AAA), 183
treats, 113, 113–114
trick training, 175–176
TTouch (Tellington-Touch), 144
tug-of-war, 176
tug toys, 42, 176
tumors, 140–141

U
UGA (University of Georgia mascot),
  15
United Kennel Club (UKC), 21
uroliths, 107, 130–131

V
vaccinations
  controversy over, 55–56
  infectious diseases and, 51–55, 52
valvular disease, degenerative, 198
verbal cues. *See* commands
Verner, Sir William, 14
vestibular disease, 201
veterinarian
  annual exams by, 117, 118
  dental care by, 97, 98
  emergency care by, 51, 145
  finding, 49–51
  finding breeders through, 34
  first checkup by, 50, 51
  senior checkups by, 196–197, 197
veterinary clinic, 50
veterinary resources, 215
vision loss, 202
vitamins, 106–107
vomiting, 147

W
walking, 176–177
walk nicely on leash, 77, 77, 149–151,
  150, 152
war dogs, 8, 9
water, 107–108
  contaminated, 106
  cooling off in, 166, 173–174
  limiting intake of, 67–68
  for traveling, 182
water bowls, 40
water-soluble vitamins, 107
wax, ear, 93
Websites, 216
weight, 23
Wellingham, George, 11
whining and crying, 42, 43, 67
whipworms, 118, 123
William, Earl Warren, 11
worms. *See* parasites
wrinkle care, 92, 93, 100, 100–101
wrinkles, 27
  dermatitis in, 47, 100, 134, 134–135
  facial, 25

Y
Yale University mascot, 15
yard
  pottying in, 69, 70–71, 71
  puppy-proofing, 37, 37
yeast infections, 94

ABOUT THE AUTHOR

Tracy Libby is an award-winning freelance writer and author of several books, including five breed books and *High-Energy Dogs* for TFH Publications, Inc. Her articles have appeared in numerous dog-related publications. She is a member of the Dog Writers Association of America (DWAA) and a recipient of the Ellsworth S. Howell award for distinguished dog writing. She lives in Oregon and has been involved in the sport of dogs for more than 20 years, exhibiting in conformation, obedience, and agility.

VETERINARY ADVISOR

Wayne Hunthausen, DVM, consulting veterinary editor and pet behavior consultant, is the director of Animal Behavior Consultations in the Kansas City area and currently serves on the Practitioner Board for *Veterinary Medicine* and the Behavior Advisory Board for *Veterinary Forum*.

BREEDER ADVISOR

Jay Serion, Bulldog fancier and breeder, is the owner of Validus Pacific Bulldogs, home of the 2009 National Specialty Best of Breed, in Seattle, Washington. He is also a professional dog handler specializing in Bulldogs dba At Your Dogs' Service, LLC.

PHOTO CREDITS

NATURAL with added VITAMINS

Nutri Dent ®MD

Promotes Optimal Dental Health!

Visit nylabone.com
Join Club NYLA
for coupons &
product
information

360° Design
Cleaning Action!™

Dogs Love 'em!™

AVAILABLE IN MULTIPLE SIZES AND FLAVORS.

Nylabone®

Trusted For Over 40 Years

MADE IN THE USA